Wordsworth's Art of Allusion

Wordsworth's Art of Allusion

Edwin Stein

The Pennsylvania State University Press
University Park and London

Quotations are used with permission of the following:

Columbia University Press, for quotations from Geoffrey H. Hartman, "Evening Star and Evening Land," in *New Perspectives on Coleridge and Wordsworth* (ed. Hartman); John Hollander, "Wordsworth and the Music of Sound," in *New Perspectives on Coleridge and Wordsworth;* W. K. Wimsatt, "Imitation as Freedom," in Reuben Brower, ed., *Forms of Lyric.*

Cornell University Press, for quotations from Leslie Brisman, *Milton's Poetry of Choice and Its Romantic Heirs;* Jared R. Curtis, *Wordsworth's Experiments with Tradition: The Lyric Poems of 1802;* A. Reeve Parker, *Coleridge's Meditative Art.*

Geoffrey Hartman, for quotations from his *Beyond Formalism: Literary Essays 1958–1970* (New Haven: Yale University Press, 1970) © Geoffrey H. Hartman.

New Literary History, for quotations from Geoffrey H. Hartman, "History as Answerable Style."

W. W. Norton & Co., for quotations from Roger Lonsdale, ed., *The Poems of Gray, Collins, and Goldsmith.*

University of California Press, for quotations from John Hollander, *The Figure of Echo: A Mode of Allusion in Milton and After;* Albert O. Wlecke, *Wordsworth and the Sublime.*

Yale University Press, for quotations from Thomas M. Greene, *The Light in Troy: Imitation and Discovery in Renaissance Poetry;* Richard E. Brantley, *Wordsworth's "Natural Methodism";* Jane Worthington Smyser, *Wordsworth's Reading of Roman Prose.*

Library of Congress Cataloging-in-Publication Data

Stein, Edwin.
Wordsworth's art of allusion.

Bibliography: p.
Includes index.
1. Wordsworth, William, 1770–1850—Criticism and interpretation. 2. Allusions in literature.
3. Discourse analysis, Literary. I. Title.
PR5892.A43S78   1987   821'.7   86–43026
ISBN 0-271-00483-5

Contents

PREFACE   vii

INTRODUCTION   1

PART I: The Motives for Borrowing   17

1   A Poet's Remembrance: Using the Tradition   19

2   Echo as Genesis and Mediation in
Wordsworth's Poetic Thought   42

3   Wordsworth and the Renaissance Heritage
of Imitation   83

PART II: The Art of the Borrowings   111

4   The Principles of Wordsworthian
Allusiveness   113

5   Mapping the Intertext I: Comparative
Allusion   122

6   Mapping the Intertext II: Assimilative
Allusion   142

CONCLUSION   211

NOTES   221

WORKS CITED   247

INDEX   254

Preface

Wordsworth's poetry incorporated the English poetic tradition to a greater degree and in more ways than that of any poet before him. This study explores the range and uses of quotations, echoes, and allusions drawn from some 1,300 intertextual instances I have recognized in his work. My goal is to establish the factors which created Wordsworth's allusive habits, to display and theorize about the various forms of his intertextuality, and to provide a taxonomy of the borrowings.

My research into Wordsworth's methods of elaborating text affirmed and led beyond those recent approaches which view him as a self-consciously literary poet, setting aside a long tradition holding him to be a poet of spontaneous habits of composition "without literary intermediary" (Raleigh 44). But because the change in critical position has been expressed mainly in the course of interpretive analyses rather than in theoretical essays, and perhaps because an impulse to naturalize this poet of nature lingered in my mind, I was still surprised to discover how inveterate a borrower Wordsworth is.

The poet's habitual allusiveness (to use an inexact cover term) draws frequently on his post-Augustan predecessors. Not only were they conduits of Miltonic echoes that are common coin in discussions of Wordsworthian textuality, but they transmitted for revisionary deepening the modes, methods, and naturalizing philosophy of echoing which stimulated and guided Wordsworth's growth toward poetic mastery. Elucidation of their role is thus an important part of this study.

Purposive reading of Wordsworth's poems for borrowings led to the discovery of other sources and other kinds of echoing. Though I made finds of my own, "discovery" is a hyperbole, since I relied heavily on the books, articles, and footnotes of scholars who have recorded Wordsworth's literary debts. Nor would I want to pretend to exhaustiveness: The many borrowings on which this study is based represent only a portion of what may ultimately be traced in the Wordsworth canon. The principal interest of the echoes examined here lies in the revaluation of the poet and the theoretical issues his varied use of them suggests.

In attempting to theorize about the poet's manifold allusiveness, I emphasize his practical and metaphorical use of echo—pervasive as image, subject, and rhetorical device in his poetry—to come to terms with his craft and his central concerns. Through echoing, Wordsworth embodies and explicates his assertions of continuity in human development, his vision of interchange between the mind and nature, and his intention to revitalize English poetry by at once mediating and revolutionizing the tradition. Echoic devices also help him accomplish two further poetic goals: the normative one of bringing poetry back in touch with oral discourse and the Miltonic one of giving it a prophetic role. Finally, by finding in echo a metaphor for poetic genesis, he establishes an ontological basis for his literary enterprise.

Wordsworth's modes of echoing are in a formal sense versions of the modes of Renaissance imitation. I discuss this provenance and attempt to show that in the poet's practice they reduce to two: *comparative*, in which Wordsworth develops meaning through an interplay confronting text and subtext, and *assimilative*, in which he sets up a framework of significance by a process of orientation which, without confrontation of text and subtext, contextualizes the authenticating ambiance of a prior poetic realization. The taxonomy shows that, bent on giving voice to "the shadows of moods," Wordsworth's choice of sources in the assimilative process depends on the frame of mind governing him—"moralizing," "anthropologizing," "naturalizing," or "poeticizing."

Both comparative and assimilative modes helped him attain his poetic freedom and distinctive voice. While critics have emphasized his comparative uses of other texts—mainly his allusions to Milton— there has been little effort to generalize or theorize about his allusive practice. In addition, critics have seemed insensitive to the poet's assimilative mode of echoing. It is easier to establish the value of the more familiar comparative mode than that of the assimilative mode; but I believe that study of the assimilative mode will give currency to, and stimulate theorizing about, a neglected mode of intertextuality at once ancient and modern—the felicitous absorption of text within text.

I am myself a borrower. Anyone reading this will see that I owe a substantial intellectual debt to Geoffrey Hartman, and I hope that my use of his thought will in itself sufficiently express my gratitude. Another intellectual debt is owed to Thomas M. Greene for the material in Chapter 3; and my obligations to John Hollander extend beyond the intellectual to practical and personal ones. Without Richard Garcia, this project, in a practical sense but also in the deepest sense, could not have been completed. To Tom Howells I owe the fruit of heroic editorial labors at a late stage, accomplished with remarkable speed. The same debt is owed to Judith Dunford, and if my style lumbers less

than before, it is because of her tooth-grinding patience. The strongest of acknowledgments must go to Patrick Henry, who helped me in
ways too innumerable, too exhaustive, and too self-sacrificing to have
a proper name. Though I acknowledge last my wife Judy's kindness in
bearing so much, she should know it comes first.

Introduction

ALLUSION AND TRADITION

As a critic defending poetic naturalism Wordsworth would have resisted Northrop Frye's antinaturalizing contention that literature is
necessarily allusive, "not externally or incidentally . . . but substantially and integrally so," but as a practicing poet he was deeply committed to using the literature of the past in the making of new poems (46).
He was one of the first major writers in England to think of English
poetry as constituting a long and worthy tradition, more important to
assimilate than the classical tradition, and to make a lifelong practice
of drawing, by way of quotation, echo, or allusion, on a generous
range of its stores. Herbert Lindenberger, noting a parallel between
Wordsworth's use of folk ballads and Spenser's use of Chaucer, points
out a pertinent difference:

> What distinguishes Wordsworth from Spenser is the fact that
> he was able to range so much more widely throughout the
> English literary tradition in search of voices. . . . If his feeling
> that the roll of English poetry was "made up" ever discouraged
> him in his own efforts, it also gave him the opportunity to speak
> through more significant voices than any other major poet be-
> fore him.[1] (282–83)

Wordsworth also evoked those voices in a greater variety of ways than
anyone else had done—something which distinguishes him from that
most compulsive of borrowers, Gray. There were many stops on the
allusive instrument he used, and it produced borrowed tones of different quality and depth: As the thematic voice changed, so did the
undersong. It is my purpose to study this aspect of Wordsworth, not
only to show that echoes abound in his poems much more than has
been recognized, but to display their variety of source and poetic
character, to explore the literary-historical and imaginative factors
which gave him an intense consciousness of poetic parallels and a will

to use them, to analyze the goals and techniques of their use, and to provide a theory of allusion through a taxonomy of the borrowings.

In pursuing these goals, I have tried to avoid dangers inherent in the study of echoes: the overenthusiasm of hearing echoes which are not there or are simply straightforward instances of terms often used in the diction of the poet's era; ascribing an echo to a single illuminating source where a more knowledgeable critic could quickly point out two or three other plausible sources; missing a key echo through concentration on lesser ones; lacking the tact to allow for mere coincidence; shredding a text in examining it closely for borrowings.

I have also deliberately bracketed the issue of influence as much as possible, though by its very nature the study of allusion evokes it and to an appreciable degree treads on the same ground. A profound borrowing, subtle, richly allusive, and radically revisionary, constitutes a passionate and learned confrontation of texts, and it is unimaginable that the plundering poet is not working under the influence of the plundered poetry. But there are less rich borrowings—so many as to require separate consideration—which do not involve the same degree of commitment by the borrowing poet. At the extreme, this is clear to everyone: Simply because he quotes the justly obscure Moses Browne once in *An Evening Walk*,[2] it would be foolish to argue for Browne's spiritual presence in the shaping of the Wordsworthian canon.

By bracketing influence, however, my purpose is not only to silence the thought of it where it is inapt but, more important, to shift the focus from Wordsworth's struggle with certain great precursors to the Wordsworthian text as a kind of linguistic system built up out of previous systems, or subsystems, through the variable process of echoing. In other terms, I set my discussion in the direction of the semiotician's idea of intertextuality. Influence study in the manner of Harold Bloom is rich and convincing at its best, an essential advance in the concept of intertextuality; but I want to try how far another approach may shed light on Wordsworth's art. Furthermore, unique though Wordsworth's art is in its integrity, his modes of borrowing are also representative of processes always functioning at the semantic level in poetry and possibly in all kinds of imaginative literature. Some of these processes, however, have slipped from the field of critical attention.

In more specific terms, I conceive the operation of quotation, echo, and allusion, when approached as a function of poetic language, to be more specialized, often more dependent on specific detail, and generally more limited in scope than influence study. In the main, I have sought to be alert to parallels, whether explicit or disguised by systematic substitutions, whether expressed in the minutest elements or in deep structural equivalents of a deliberate sort. The overall term I favor for the parallelisms is "echoes" (and for the process, "echoing"), despite occasional awkwardness of diction, because connotatively it is broader, more flexible, and, in view of Wordsworth's own attitudes toward poiesis and poetics, more apt than "allusion" or "parallel."

One particular concern of this book is Wordsworth's use of post-Augustan eighteenth-century poets. In his edition of the poems of Gray, Collins, and Goldsmith, Roger Lonsdale remarks on the reorientation of the mid-eighteenth-century poets toward the tradition, the salience of interest in Spenser, Shakespeare, and Milton, and the special influence of Thomson, Akenside, and the melancholy school. This reorientation and the poetic habits it fostered were crucial in Wordsworth's apprenticeship years. All the poets involved—both those looking back at the tradition and those they looked back to—continued to act on his invention. Their poetry surfaced in echoes of the sort Lonsdale frequently detects in Gray and Collins, including some that do not appear to act allusively and some Lonsdale calls "virtual allusion."

In exploring such echoes, I have been ready to make more far-reaching, less easily accommodated assertions than Lonsdale would allow. This is partly because Wordsworth's use of echoes is often more profound than Gray's (though it may be more trivial, too), and his poetic motive for echoing is at once more fundamental and radical. John Hollander's *The Figure of Echo: Echo as a Mode of Allusion in Milton and After* supports in detail the kind of stress I wish to put on echoing, especially his suggestion that echoed terms, even some which are clearly "the common poetic property of the age" and are used with apparent unconsciousness, still may have a fit and noteworthy allusive force.[3]

When I examine examples of nonallusive echoes, the reader will be brought to wonder to what degree Wordsworth was aware of his intertextual referencing. This has been an issue in Wordsworthian criticism, and since I have for the most part passed over it, I ought to make my view clear at the outset. Although in close reading of Wordsworth's poems the question of the poet's self-consciousness was constantly in my mind, I proceeded as if the describable structure of meanings in each poem was intended. Yet I had to recognize a practical value in making up my mind about the degree of his craft-consciousness. It helps to develop a decorum in dealing with any poet's work, a sense of where to draw the line between truth and mere ingenuity in interpretation. In the case of Milton, for instance, allowing him a high degree of poetic self-consciousness and enormous skill at transferring it to verbal artifacts makes a palpable difference: The critic will look more than twice before deciding that there has been an unconscious evasion or a graceless clash of significations. Wordsworth's contrasting reputation as a writer relying on Romantic inspiration, gropings guided by feeling, and unintellectual coherence makes him more vulnerable to accusations of unconscious self-undermining. Yet despite the justness of some of these accusations, I believe he was a highly self-conscious maker of poems, aware of the vast majority of literary echoes in his poems at some stage in their passage from birth to final form.

He was undoubtedly interested in the phenomenon of echoing in nature and ruminated its metaphorical likeness to activities of the mind. Not only do quite a few poems and passages of longer poems take up an aspect of echo as a subject (I have counted thirty-five), but sound, voice, and echo provide thematic substance for a number of his major poetic statements. I want to explore here Wordsworth's interest in the echo and his sensitivity to the mediating powers of the linked connotations of the term as a way of providing a better appreciation of his intense and skillful use of literary echoes in "Remembrance of Collins," an early model of his method that I examine in Chapter 1.

A perception of echo as a responding voice and hence as somehow endowed with a life cognate with the life of the poetic line seems to go back to the origins of recorded poetry. The particularly brilliant handling of echo in Ovid's *Metamorphoses*—in the story of Echo and Narcissus (Book III) and in the creation of the Pan pipe out of Syrinx (Book I)—seems to have set a stamp upon all subsequent conceptions of echo in Western poetry. In the English Renaissance, especially, from about 1580 to 1620, the Ovidian Echo, Pan, and Narcissus provided centrally important mythical or allegorical elements for poets to play with on the conceptual level of mediation (between nature and man, nature and God, God and man, man and his inner self). Thereafter they were a less consuming poetic concern, though they never lapsed entirely from view. In the course of time, echo as a poetic concept was more and more exclusively internalized and naturalized, like the psyche itself.

An example of the distance echo had come by the mid-eighteenth century, several generations before Wordsworth's poetic activity began, can be found in Collins's "Ode to Pity." In the poetry of Collins and other pre-Romantics there is something congenial to Ovidian practice, the peculiar character of its personifications. Though these evolved in part from an Augustan heritage of abstract imaging, they were also strongly influenced by the figures of Milton's minor poems, especially "L'Allegro" and "Il Penseroso," and these in turn owed something to Ovid. They have a contrasting insubstantiality as poetic realizations, but the pre-Romantic personae are like those of Ovid in being part particularizations of the *numinosum* in the natural order and part reflections of human society. In this quasi-Ovidian atmosphere, Collins's Echo appears, half in his mind, half externalized, a potential mediator between the singer and nature:

> Wild Arun too has heard thy [Pity's] strains,
> And Echo, midst my native plains,
> Been soothed by Pity's lute.
> (16–18)

The poet has transplanted Pity, in the manner of the progress poem predominating at the time, to the English countryside and given her an English instrument to play. In the process he has altered her from a classical minor deity with a definite form and secondary attributes to a vaguer presence in the landscape in search of a new temple. As she has been the muse of Otway, so, he pleads, ought she be his muse too. He seems to offer his own mind as a part of the temple she seeks in the hope that he may perfect himself as her poet:

> Come, Pity, come, by Fancy's aid,
> Even now my thoughts, relenting maid,
> Thy temple's pride design.[4]
> (25–27)

Echo is a lesser presence in the countryside, and her localization is more ambiguous—she seems at once a more natural, less immigrant feature and a more mental one. The River Arun, which runs through Sussex, the birthplace of Otway and Collins, stands for Otway's poetic consciousness (he is the revered poet of tragic pity), and by parallelism Echo seems to stand for Collins's poetic consciousness. Reductively paraphrased, Collins is saying, "I too, like the great Otway, have been made sensitive to pity and been inspired poetically by it"; interpretively paraphrased, Collins is locating Echo at once in the landscape (given the necessary substantiality by its wrens and turtles in stanza four) and in his mind. In the landscape, Echo sings back the presence of Pity; in his mind, she is the receiver of his perceptions, and through them she (representing his poetic consciousness) is soothed, informed by the power of pity. But she is apparently an inadequate mediator, since the poet, in search of an unfailing source of inspiration, must still invite Pity to unite directly with his mind—to make it her temple.

Wordsworth assimilates this kind of ambiguous play between inner
and outer attending upon the echo and carries it further. In him, echo
is still more internalized. At the same time it is naturalized and given a
more profound role in poiesis. He comments on the workings of the
creative process in Book I of *The Prelude*, describing his experiences in
beginning that long effort:

> My own voice chear'd me, and, far more, the mind's
> Internal echo of the imperfect sound;
> To both I listen'd, drawing from them both
> A chearful confidence in things to come.
>
> (I.64–67)

Echo is not personified in this passage and hence is not, in the same
sense as Collins's Echo, resident in the countryside. The most externalized element of the passage is the poet's own voice, projected outward
from himself. It goes out toward the landscape, a thing now separated
from him (like an external echo) but, by the very fact of being externalized, enabled to return through his ear. And going on into the silence
of his mind, it creates an "internal echo," which seems to form a more
inspired version of the first attempt at poetic voice realized by his
vocal chords (it cheers him "far more") and to give promise of a
perfect sound to come. That sound, of course, is poetry, perfect in the
sense of "finished" and in the sense of "enduring," like the "immortal
verse" of "L'Allegro."

These lines are unique, staking out a hitherto uncultivated area of
aesthetic psychology, and in a way typical of Wordsworth their originality is partly hidden by the discursive tone and the absence of
striking imagery. The same strong mediating role is even more vividly illustrated in the Intimations Ode. Unresolved obscurities ham-
per the interpreter of its third stanza; however, even the casual
reader can understand that it describes a moment of liberation from
the oppression of inner unresponsiveness and that the liberation is
the result of a "timely utterance." The strength recovered is expressed in a series of images. The first, the cataracts that "blow their
trumpets from the steep," is an image of sound and seems to represent an external response by nature to the utterance, or an aural
perception by the speaker of something that has been there all along,
hidden by the introverted attention of self-concern.[5] The next is also
an image of sound, but it is still more ambiguous: "I hear the Echoes
through the mountains throng." Echoes of what? The cataract trumpets? Of the previously expressed timely utterance? Of random natural sounds, animal or human (the shepherd boy), coming from the

valley or produced in the mountains? Or of his own thoughts, projected outward now that the timely utterance has opened the floodgates? The many possibilities underscore the phantasmal quality of the thronging Echoes, which leaves us uncertain whether they are inner or outer phenomena. As in Collins and in *The Prelude*, they could be both at once; for unless it is the dubiously aural cataracts, no sound answers the timely utterance in this stanza except the echoes (the climactic shouts of the shepherd boy are urged on, urged near, as if only seen and not yet heard: "shout round me, let me hear thy shouts").[6]

If the answering echoes are of uncertain provenance, the following winds are even less easily located. To go from the cataracts to the fields of sleep is to move through poetic lines of increasing ambiguity and, in parallel, increasing interiority. "The Winds come to me from the fields of sleep" takes the last step—it completely blends inner and outer reference. The winds and the fields of sleep cannot be localized because they are in two places at once, in nature and in the mind.[7] We may picture the winds moving in both together without a sense of strain, since we recognize the image as an analogue of the process of inspiration. We see the analogy just *because* of the ambiguity: inspiration, too, is at once internal and external. It comes to consciousness "from above" and "from within"; it is often stimulated by an external object, but the writer recognizes the object as a vehicle for a complex of internal impulses—a complex that begins as a pass from a subconscious "nowhere" and ends by blowing with gale force upon the conscious mind. The fit of Wordsworth's images to the subjective experience of creative imagination is exact.

From vocal impulse through natural cataracts and echoes àt once internal and external to inspiriting winds—again, the echo is seen as mediating. It links the original vocal impulse and the inspiration as the energy that fashions the final form, providing movement, direction, and refinement in a process that leads from sound to voice. It can mediate because it is internal and external, self and other, human and nonhuman. The rocky cave that echoes the human voice absorbs something of the human as it reflects the sound, and the reflected sound carries something of the dark rock in it. The echo, being thus both natural and human, is a vital part of the process of naturalizing and humanizing which Wordsworth understands as true poiesis. It catches something moving outward from man to give it a separate existence enriched by otherness and then carries it back for refashioning. Without it, or something like it, poetic voice would not emerge from its chrysalis. Absolutely idiosyncratic, it would be the murmur of a solipsism which in the end distorts, denaturalizes, and dehumanizes man; completely conformist, it would be the stillborn cry of an inane, impersonal conventionality (such as Wordsworth thought one found too often in Augustan and post-Augustan literature), or of creeping custom, which is singled out in the Intimations Ode as a dehumanizing agency.

The inhuman aspects of the two extremes, solipsism and impersonal convention, are easily grasped, but the inclusion of custom here does not explain itself so easily. It seems paradoxical that custom, a thing of man's devising, should be dehumanizing. The reason is not that custom has no human features, but that—"Heavy as frost, and deep almost as life"—it substitutes itself for or covers over what is most human: the energy needed to go out of the self toward otherness, the will to offer oneself. The "Boy of Winander" episode in Book V of *The Prelude* (lines 389–413) dramatizes Wordsworth's belief that the impulse to awaken an echo-like response in the not-human is elementary, archetypally human. The episode also shows that the isolated impulse is not a complete expression of the human: An act of self-forgetting attention must allow the response to come back into the impulsive heart where, the external response creating an internal echo, a humanizing of the enlarged self takes place. The details suggest further a naturalizing of the self: "a gentle shock of mild surprise / Has carried far into his heart the voice / Of mountain torrents." But the focus of these lines is on the youth's surprise. What is surprising to the boy is the independent life of otherness entering him. For Wordsworth, the central act of living (often beset with hesitations and dangers) is offering oneself to not-self and, by a quasi-religious attention to it, evoking and accepting its response. This response best defines the character of the Wordsworthian echo.

The offering of self is not, cannot be, habitual. It is normally of the moment, always tending toward epiphany. But often repeated it leaves traces:

> Look where we will, some human heart has been
> Before us with its offering.
> (*Home at Grasmere*, PW5.328, lines 440–41)

In their context, these lines refer to the visible, and invisible but felt, traces of man's intercourse with nature. For Wordsworth, intercourse with nature leads to poetry, and the poem is one more trace or inscription of an offered heart. Even Collins wanted his natural relation to Pity to assume a religious form, so that, his thoughts becoming part of her temple,

> Its southern site, its truth complete,
> Shall raise a wild enthusiast heat
> In all who view the shrine.
>
> (28–30)

In *Home at Grasmere* Wordsworth is celebrating the establishment of his own more natural temple, the possession of the home where his poetic career will begin in earnest. He seeks to tap "a stream, / Pure and unsullied, flowing from the heart / With motions of true dignity and grace" (409–11) in order to develop

> An art, a music, and a strain of words
> That shall be life, the acknowledged voice of life,
> Shall speak of what is done among the fields,
> Done truly there, or felt, of solid good
> And real evil, yet be sweet withal,
> More grateful, more harmonious than the breath,
> The idle breath of softest pipe attuned
> To pastoral fancies . . .
>
> (402–9)

A revolutionary art—yet in his desire to impart his "inward lustre," to "chant, in lonely peace, the spousal verse" of man's intellect "wedded to this goodly universe," and to "express the image of a better time," he will not obliterate the poetic traces of the past (*Home at Grasmere* 677; "Prospectus" 57, 103). On the contrary, he sees these too as echoes, echoes needed for the mediation of his self-offerings. They will help objectify his outgoing poetic impulses, catching them up, carrying them back inward, refining and perfecting the words. There is really no gap between the conceptions of echo as a natural phenomenon, as a midwife in poiesis, and as a reflection of past literary voices. The same principle of resonance is at work in the making of poetry, from Wordsworth's viewpoint, whether the poem responds to nature or the poetic tradition.

THE RANGE OF WORDSWORTH'S SOURCES

A great many sources are echoed in the 280 pieces which form the corpus of this study. In these pieces, representing almost two-thirds of the 60,000-plus lines in the complete poetical works, Wordsworth has borrowed from, paralleled, reflected, or alluded to roughly 150 writers. The most echoed writer is Milton, as any more-than-casual reader of Wordsworth knows without having to count specific instances; but if they are counted, Milton's works will be found the source of about 550 echoes out of a grand total of some 1,300.[8] The next most echoed writer is Shakespeare, represented by nearly 100 instances. Following these giants come (with the number of echoes, rounded off to the nearest multiple of five, given in parentheses) Gray (50), Spenser (40), the Bible (40), Thomson (35), Coleridge (35), and the ballads found in Percy's and other collections (25). Other authors overheard more than five times may be divided into two groups (the order is that of decreasing frequency): (a) *from 10 to 20 times*—Collins, Pope, Virgil, Burns, Beattie, Cowper, John Dyer, Akenside, Bowles, Drayton, and Daniel; (b) *from 6 to 9 times*—Chaucer, Young, Johnson, Dryden, Michael Bruce, and Ann of Winchilsea.

The variety and periodization of the sources is a matter of interest. Michael Bruce, a minor Scottish poet, is echoed some seven times, a relatively large number; but though a few lines from the melancholy, pre-Romantically picturesque and naturalizing *Lochleven* may have provided a passing means of focusing Wordsworth's voice, it seems certain to me that there has been no detectable influence of Bruce on Wordsworth's poetic development or habits of invention. On the other hand, some clearly important influences are but slightly represented in the list of echoic sources, or not at all: Winchilsea, of greater early influence, is represented by the same number of echoes as Bruce; Daniel, of still greater and more enduring influence, by only a few more; Shenstone, whose "School-Mistress" was cited by Wordsworth himself as of historical importance and instrumental in his learning how to treat rural life in verse, and Swift and Bunyan, both important in Wordsworth's literary education, are not represented by echoes at all, as far as I can discover in the verse I have studied. The same is true of the Italian poet Chiabrera, who clearly had an important influence on Wordsworth's understanding of the poetic inscription (see Hartman, *Beyond Formalism* 206–30). Ovid, whom he declared to have been the great love of his school years, is echoed only five times according to my count, and three of these occasions belong to late poems written when the poet was turning increasingly to classical literary material for inspiration.

Of the 130 remaining authors who are echoed, the majority are eighteenth- and early nineteenth-century poets, some famous, some quite obscure. Many are contemporary with Wordsworth, or nearly so (George Bell, Blake, Campbell, Cottle, Crabbe, Crowe, Cunningham, Erasmus Darwin, Robert Greenwood, James Hogg, James Hurdis,

Keats, Landor, James Montgomery, Rogers, Walter Scott, Shelley, Southey, and Helen Maria Williams; Lamb's "Sonnet to Himself" is also echoed). Pre-Romantic and related poets form another sizable list (Blair, John Brown, Moses Browne, Elizabeth Carter, Chatterton, John Home, John Logan, Macpherson, John Scott, Smart, Joseph Warton), as do Restoration and Augustan poets (Addison, Vincent Bourne, Butler, Churchill, Garth, Gay, William Gilbert, Goldsmith, William Hamilton of Bangour, Langhorne, Oldham, Parnell, and Prior). Together with those first cited, the period from the Restoration to Wordsworth's day includes, then, about sixty poets among the echoed voices.

It also includes at least twenty-eight prose writers. Three of these, Addison, Gray (Wordsworth read and echoed his *Guide to the Lakes*), and Lamb, have been mentioned among the poets, where Gray, of course, properly belongs; on the other hand, I have not found any traces of Landor's or Sir Walter Scott's prose, though Wordsworth particularly admired Landor's *Imaginary Conversations* and read Scott's novels.[9] The remainder may be divided for convenience into three groups: (1) writers of novels, belles-lettres, and treatises (Fielding, Godwin, Johnson, Smollett, Mandeville, and Adam Smith);[10] (2) writers of personal and travel narratives (John Barrow, William Bartram, James Bruce, Peter Henry Bruce, Jonathan Carver, William Dampier, Samuel Hearne, Robert Heron, John Newton, Mungo Park, Thomas Pennant, George Shelvock, and Henry Wilson as recorded or represented by George Keats); (3) writers on antiquities and the aesthetics of nature (Joseph Forsyth, William Gilpin, William Hutchinson, Uvedale Price, Johannes Scheffer [a seventeenth-century Scandinavian writer in a Restoration translation], Thomas D. Whitaker, and Thomas Wilkinson).

Wordsworth also took from the ballad and song collections made in the eighteenth century. These included poems written or "improved" by the collectors and also modern imitations of ballads written by other hands, so that among the ballads Wordsworth echoed were four or five eighteenth-century poems. The list of compilers and composers includes Burns, William Hamilton, David Herd (editor of *Ancient Scottish Ballads*), James Johnson (editor of *The Scots Musical Museum*), Logan, Percy, Allan Ramsay, and Walter Scott. Two of the ballad-like poems Wordsworth recalls were by the German poet Gottfried August Bürger; and he echoes also Bürger's compatriots, Schiller and Frederika Brun. In his early poetry, mainly in *Descriptive Sketches*, he echoed a number of French eighteenth-century writers as well: Delille, Montesquieu, Ramond de Carbonnières, Rousseau, Voltaire.

When these continental authors are summed with the English authors already cited—some are late seventeenth-century, some early nineteenth, but nearly all may be considered as working within the orbit of the eighteenth century—it can be seen that the clear majority of the authors Wordsworth echoes belongs to the century he was born in, broadly conceived. It is true that the majority of *echoes,* if each poetic instance is enumerated separately, is accounted for not by these ninety authors but by Milton and Shakespeare alone; and yet, these twin geniuses being the great inspiriting literary figures for almost every eighteenth-century writer, their large presence in Wordsworth's work represents at the surface level no sharp disparity of models: Wordsworth's tastes in literary echoes were overwhelmingly eighteenth-century tastes and not decisively different from those of most pre-Romantic poets.

Like most later eighteenth-century poets, and unlike the Augustans, Wordsworth was more attached to British literary traditions, including the ballads, than to the classical tradition (still the standard in his education and in poetry contemporary with his youth). Among the many ways he tried to distance himself from neoclassicism was that of consciously avoiding casual allusions to classical mythology. Of course, his distaste for idle classicizing was shared by many post-Augustan figures, including Dr. Johnson, but in completely shedding antique lumber during the years of the *Lyrical Ballads* he went far enough to differentiate his poetry from that of the pre-Romantics as well. Later on, however, and increasingly after the great decade, he indulged in classical reference (as well as what he would earlier have considered "poetic diction").[11] Thus we find scattered echoes of or references to Homer, Sophocles, Theocritus, Moschus, Herodotus, Plato, Aristotle, Archimedes, Polybius, and Plutarch among the Greeks, and to Virgil, Horace, Seneca, Livy, Cicero, Pliny, Curtius, and Eusebius, as well as to Ovid, among the Romans and church fathers.

The roster of postclassical continental authors writing before the eighteenth century whom Wordsworth evokes in one way or another is as short as the number of evocations is small—one dubious evocation of Dante's *Paradiso,* a quotation from Petrarch in *Descriptive Sketches* (written just after the Cambridge years, when Wordsworth had been reading Italian with Isola, the Tasso scholar and friend of Gray), a passage reworking a description in Ferdinand Columbus's *Life and Actions of Christopher Columbus,* one or perhaps two echoes of Michelangelo's sonnets (which Wordsworth had worked at translating), several echoes of Tasso, and a curious use of Cervantes and Descartes in Book V of *The Prelude.*

Most of the remaining echoes and allusions draw on the English poets of the era between Elizabeth and Charles II. The only large group of echoes which might be classed apart contains about forty-five evocations of Scripture; but since Wordsworth's Bible was the King James version, and since the language of this version is a development of and strong influence on the same era, there is propriety in associating Wordsworth's biblical echoes with his seventeenth-century sources. With the exception of Chaucer, the presence of writers earlier than Spenser is slight—Bede, Skelton, Wyatt, Golding, and Churchyard are each represented by a single borrowing or animadverting phrase. Of the twenty-five or so times Wordsworth has paralleled a ballad or folk song, I have found none with a pedigree that reaches back earlier than the Elizabethan period. Most of Wordsworth's balladic sources, like "Balowe," "Dulcina," "The Rising of the North," and "The Children of the Wood," are late sixteenth- and early seventeenth-century pieces and may, in accord with Percy's principles of selection in his *Reliques of Ancient English Poetry*, be traditional folk ballads, broadside ballads, or popular songs.

Thus the other period of great importance to Wordsworth in the act of composition stretches from the end of the sixteenth century to the Restoration. In the pieces I have studied, the sum of evocations of Milton, Shakespeare, and Spenser is, in round numbers, 700 out of a total of 1,300 quotations, echoes, and allusions; Daniel and Drayton account for another 20; John Beaumont, Sir John Davies, Jonson, and Sidney among the Elizabethans, and Francis Beaumont, Butler, Cotton, Richard Corbet, Marvell, Vaughan, Waller, Webster, John Weever, and Wither among the succeeding generations, add 35 more. (There are scattered evocations of prose writers—Bacon, Burnet, Greville, Edward Haie [a writer in Hakluyt's *Voyages*], Walton, and Jeremy Taylor, in addition to Milton—but for the most part these are no more than allusions to the persons themselves.) About three-fifths of all instances of echoing refer to this period.

In sum, the majority of authors Wordsworth drew on belonged to the orbit of neoclassicism, and the majority of his echoes belonged to the orbit of the English Renaissance. Yet one must avoid drawing conclusions from this that merely confirm the artifice of chronological lumping. Wordsworth's cultivation of Milton and Shakespeare was steady, but his interest in other poets or periods varied with the direction of his work. To take just one instance, Jared Curtis has shown in more detail than others before him the indebtedness of Wordsworth's lyrics of 1802 to the poets of the sixteenth and seventeenth centuries whom he was reading in 1801–2.[12] This interest, an inner response to stresses of the period, was supplanted by others after 1802. The lumping of echoes fails to take into account the transitory nature of a portion of Wordsworth's Renaissance indebtedness.

There is another sense in which this lumping is less an artifice than an inevitability. For to note a rough equality between the two literary orbits and Wordsworth's significant involvement in them may say no more than that his sources were coterminous with the English literary tradition as then conceived. A look at Anderson's *Works of the British Poets* or any other of the comprehensive anthologies in his library will show a similar picture: a select group of pre-Restoration worthies, containing few or no poets between Chaucer and Wyatt, and a veritable host of poets from the Restoration on.[13] Yet the numbers I have adduced do point beyond the mere fact that Wordsworth's tastes are those of his time. When Milton, Shakespeare, and Spenser are subtracted from the earlier period, relatively little is left—about 60 echoes (excluding the ballads, which have an ambiguous status because they belong to both periods). On the other hand, when Thomson, Gray, and Coleridge are subtracted from the later period, nearly 340 echoes remain, close to twenty-five percent of the total of 1300. This indicates that Restoration and eighteenth-century literature was a diffuse source, whereas the Renaissance provided a narrow source, concentrated mainly in its greatest poets—which suggests in turn that Wordsworth's echoic use of the two periods was different.

The earlier period was the locus of geniuses, the main pillars of the English tradition. It is thus not hard to understand why Spenser, Shakespeare, and Milton are special cases whose relationship to Wordsworth is particularized and dialectical, richly allusive in the primary sense of invoking an interplay of contexts. To a degree, Thomson, Gray, Collins, and Coleridge share the same role, but they too are often subsumed in the glancingly reminiscent, collegial, yet self-distancing and evolutionary relationship that Wordsworth had with the eighteenth century. The remaining Elizabethan and seventeenth-century authors have a relationship to Wordsworth analogous to the one he had with the pre-Romantics. Together, the poets excluded from the quaternity Wordsworth had set up as his grand models (Chaucer, Spenser, Shakespeare, and Milton) force the reader to recognize new facets of the idea of "allusion"—or, rather, as I shall attempt to show, reworkings of certain Renaissance ideas of imitation.[14]

Indeed, an understanding of all aspects of Wordsworth's allusive practice depends on seeing how he assimilated and transformed habits of imitation developed in the Renaissance and revamped in Augustan and post-Augustan practice. I try to establish the imaginative basis for his interest in these modes of imitation in Chapter 2, and then to articulate his reappropriations of them in Chapter 3 with the aim of showing how they function in his poetry. This demonstration provides the basis for the classification of the broad and confusing range of his borrowings I have given in chapters 4 to 6. Before setting about these tasks, however, I propose to look at Wordsworth's beginnings and to show by analyzing a single early poem how his habit of borrowing begins in tandem with his forming poetic conceptions.

"Remembrance of Collins" was probably composed during his university years, when he was first coming to a mature understanding of himself, the natural world, and the craft of poetry. This was before the crisis of self-loss and self-recovery documented in *The Prelude* brought about the full development of his mythic conceptions of the alliance between the mind and nature. Yet his ideas about how the mind is fitted to the world by literary, physical, and unmediated spiritual encounters were not then merely inchoate, either. They provided a thematic basis on which to experiment with voices from the tradition as a means of enriching the *donnée* of the poem beyond a pensive prettiness. We know from *An Evening Walk* that literary borrowings characterized his early style; yet it is still surprising to see, in the years before he was irrevocably determined to be a poet and began to educate himself systematically in the literary tradition, how intensely he was bent over the poetic past, striving to assure his continuity with it by drawing off strong drafts.

Part I

The Motives for Borrowing

1

A Poet's Remembrance: Using the Tradition

Remembrance of Collins

Composed upon the Thames near Richmond

Glide gently, thus for ever glide,
O Thames! that other bards may see
As lovely visions by thy side
As now, fair river! come to me:
O glide, fair stream! for ever so,
Thy quiet soul on all bestowing,
Till all our minds for ever flow
As thy deep waters now are flowing.

Vain thought!—Yet be as now thou art,
That in thy waters may be seen
The image of a poet's heart,
How bright, how solemn, how serene!
Such as did once the Poet bless,
Who, murmuring here a later ditty,
Could find no refuge from distress
But in the milder grief of pity.

Now let us, as we float along,
For *him* suspend the dashing oar;
And pray that never child of song
May know that Poet's sorrows more.
How calm! how still! the only sound,
The dripping of the oar suspended!
—The evening darkness gathers round
By virtue's holiest Powers attended.

In the third stanza of this poem, echoing a line of Collins, Wordsworth evokes the earlier poet's "Ode Occasioned by the Death of Mr. Thomson," particularly the following stanza:

> Remembrance oft shall haunt the shore
>   When Thames in summer wreaths is dressed,
> And oft suspend the dashing oar
>   To bid his gentle spirit rest!
>
> (13–16)

This stanza seems to have suggested the first word of Wordsworth's last stanza in its first published form ("Remembrance! as we glide along," *Lyrical Ballads*, 1798), a word that was transferred to the title, as we now have it, in 1805. The subtitle recalls an advertisement inscribed by Collins above his poem to inform the reader that his scene was on the river near Thomson's burial place (Lonsdale 488). And if one joined Collins's quatrains into stanzas of eight lines, it would be seen that Wordsworth's metrical and rhyme schemes are practically the same, the only difference being his patterned use of feminine rhyme in lines 6 and 8 of each stanza.

These echoes are "remembrances," memories prompted—as if on the occasion of the poet's visit to the same spot Collins had honored—by a pious impulse to celebrate a cherished predecessor and rescue something from his death. But the poem is hardly an occasional one. A later note by Wordsworth informs us that the poem was not originally connected with the Thames, or a boat, or any external occasion of social moment. Five stanzas long in 1798 and entitled "Lines Written near Richmond, upon the Thames, at Evening," it had arisen, he says, from a private observation of the different intensities of light reflected by upstream and downstream waters at sunset:

> It was during a solitary walk on the banks of the Cam that I was first struck with this appearance, and applied it to my own feelings in the manner here expressed, changing the scene to the Thames, near Windsor.[1]

The isolation of the last three stanzas was carried out at Coleridge's suggestion in the second edition of the *Lyrical Ballads* (1800), creating two poems from one. Coleridge's reasons for suggesting the alteration are not known. Perhaps he recognized the rather intricate involvement of the later stanzas with the poetry of Collins (the allusion to Collins's ode on Thomson had already been made overt in 1798 by Wordsworth's note identifying the "later ditty"). The severance of "Remembrance of Collins" from the whole, in which its stanzas had been integral parts of a meditation on "death and the poet," seems a conscious attempt to heighten their allusiveness. Isolation makes the first stanza of the new poem less particular and less comprehensible, but the added abruptness and the concentration fostered by the double title create a more subtle poem. The small but palpable manipulations which over a period of years brought the poem to its final state are evidently those of a mind experimenting with the resources of literary echoes.

All the echoes were already present in the original. That the poet was at this early point oriented toward allusive methods should not be surprising. Wordsworth's literary apprenticeship was served according to the usual model, learning by singing in borrowed robes. Among his juvenilia are imitations or reflections of Augustan forms and diction, gothic motifs, ballads, Gray, the post-Augustan schools of melancholy and the graveyard (along with gloomier Restoration poetry, like certain pieces of Parnell and Ann of Winchilsea), contemporary ad hoc forms of the numerous types described by Robert Mayo, and contemporary poets like Helen Maria Williams, Elizabeth Carter, and the English "della Cruscans." In addition, there are classical imitations and translations (of Homer, Anacreon, a Greek drinking song, Moschus, Virgil, Horace, Catullus, Juvenal). Frequently bits of Milton are found, almost always borrowed from "L'Allegro" and "Il Penseroso."

If, then, the presence of allusions and echoes in "Remembrance of Collins" is neither surprising nor inappropriate, nevertheless the earnest preoccupation with allusiveness displayed in the poem is not a poetic orientation admirers of Wordsworth have generally been comfortable with.[2] Apprenticeship is one thing; but, in 1805, after the experiments of 1798, 1800, and 1802, after the spontaneous upwellings which led to *The Prelude*, still to be tinkering with the allusive elements of a poem that is essentially the elaboration of a sunset view does not present the image of the artistically evolved Wordsworth readers have prized. And yet a will to echo is not a temporary aberrancy in this poet. It is not to be dismissed as simply early Wordsworth, with sporadic appearances in his later verse, nor is it to be sequestered with Miltonic influences which have been increasingly recognized, and which have been discussed in terms of the poet's complex echoes of Milton in his weightier pieces. The drive to use textual reference was an important part of Wordsworth's art. "Remembrance of Collins" is an instructive paradigm because, brief and simple as it is, it forecasts many of his allusive techniques.

Even in the evocation of Collins, the motive of which is pious and plain, there is more sophistication than is readily apparent. Wordsworth was aware that the echoed Collins himself echoed, in his poem,

the poet he was praising—Thomson; and Thomson was in his way a
determined echoer of Milton, whose "Penseroso" Wordsworth seems
to echo in his last lines, as if completing a circle:

> —The evening darkness gathers round
> By virtue's holiest Powers attended.

These lines recall the evening appearance of Melancholy, the "pensive
Nun, devout and pure" (accompanied by various companions, including two—"calm Peace and Quiet"—evoked by Wordsworth's "How
calm! how still!"), who will bestow a prophetic strain on the man who
chooses her. This evocation is appropriate because the poem's central
concern is to assure poetic speech: Its poet-speaker prays that the
future "child of song" may know the inner quiet that will allow his
mind to "flow," thus assuring his continued poetic output.

But the evocation is scarcely specific, and on further inspection it
becomes clear that the allusive link is more indirect than I have made
it seem. It is mediated by something more powerful in Collins's poem,
the penseroso mode developed out of readings of Milton by the
Wartons and those who paralleled or learned from them, including
Collins. To the reader for whom it was a still-living tradition, this
mode conveyed a sense of participation in a particular kind of natural
scene, one characterized by softly contrasting sensuous qualities, muf-
fled numinosity, and Virgilian pastoral features (such as the gathering
darkness here). It is a reshuffling of the very elements—Milton, Virgil, enthusiastic nature description—from which Thomson developed
the English georgic (though his Miltonic text was *Paradise Lost* and his
mediating mode the Miltonic parodies of John Philips). When Collins
praises Thomson in his ode, he reenacts the paradigm of literary
evolution from georgic to penseroso mode and in the process develops the central theme of poetic voice—the very theme which Wordsworth, in his turn, reworks by a further conversion of Collins's
penseroso mode.

Wordsworth's use of Collins to rework the theme of poetic voice,
and the built-in justification of allusiveness as a means of doing so, are
both illuminated by a careful reading of the movement in Collins's
ode on Thomson. It is Thomson's georgic voice chanting the seasons
which Collins honors when he invokes "the year's best sweets . . . / To
deck its poet's sylvan grave" (3–4). But by lamenting the father of
eighteenth-century nature poetry in the penseroso mode, Collins
transforms Thomson into something like a *genius loci*—a lapsed genius, to be sure, since he rests in earth untranslated: "In yonder grave
your Druid lies" (the final line; the poem opens with almost the identi-

cal line: "In yonder grave a Druid lies"). It is an incomplete Lycidan maneuver: Collins is trying "to interpose a little ease," and though he admits the vanity of the endeavor ("Ah! what will every dirge avail?" [22]), he persists. Amid a growing sense of absence, darkness, and death—the nymphs departed, night falling, the boat carrying the poet off downstream, the dominant image of the "pale shrine glimmering near" now fading—he indulges in the "false surmise" of allowing a redeeming piety to the act of dressing "with simple hands thy rural tomb" (40). He blesses with imagined flowers in death the man whom the real "genial meads" blessed in life.

This abruption of the final movement of "Lycidas" is the point of Collins's poem. The poet refuses to seek a vertical resolution he cannot believe in—that turning from the world toward the divine order which he found in "Il Penseroso" and "Lycidas." He remains in the position of the speaker of "L'Allegro," though with the mood and conditions reversed: For him the natural order is sad and self-emptying. The shift in the otherwise identical first and last lines from "a" to "your" encapsulates the movement of the ode, for, starting and ending with the grave, we are united with the dead man by a reverence born of no more than a heightened sense of common mortality.

In the face of the vertical orientation, the strong redemptive tenor of seventeenth-century and Augustan attitudes, and especially of the poetic spirits who reigned over the post-Augustan period—Milton and Thomson—Collins's stance seems movingly honest. This honesty is the driving force behind his boldest stroke, "naturalizing" Thomson, the poet of nature. Collins's ambiguous and at the time controversial epithet for Thomson, "druid," reflects this naturalizing drive and focuses the issue of poetic voice.[3] To call Thomson a druid is of course a way of recognizing his reputation as a nature poet. But *The Seasons* shows that Thomson understood the nature he celebrated in the traditional religious way as the Book of God: The sun that rules his world (as described in the hymn that follows *The Seasons*) is Christ, not Phoebus or a merely natural force. Thus to see Thomson as a druid is also to take a disturbing position on the poet's role, even though the primary meaning may be "a poet-priest of nature, . . . a devout enthusiast of a benevolent creative Spirit, a hymn-maker," because in the context of Collins's poem less idealized implications of the epithet are brought to the surface.[4] A druid is also a pagan prophet of a primitive natural religion, whose divinities and office are now irredeemably dead. The voice of failed gods and buried prophets sounded in "Lycidas" hovers here—the Muse ineffectual against death, the nymphs absent from the River Dee and the Isle of Anglesy, on whose eastern steep the "old *Bards*, the famous *Druids*, lie" ("Lycidas" 53).

Thus in a tone which combines his own Shakespearean dirges and the penseroso mode (but with a harder edge), Collins elegizes his friend as a patron saint of a new poetic vision that sings, like the Aeolian harp (6), with the voice of nature. He captures him as the tutelary spirit of his, Collins's, own kind of verse, giving him this unforeseen honor but no other solace beyond remembrance—the remembrance of the living who bless him with imagined flowers and with prayers for his rest as they pass, halting momentarily to do so:

> Remembrance oft shall haunt the shore
>   When Thames in summer wreaths is dressed,
> And oft suspend the dashing oar
>   To bid his gentle spirit rest.
>
>   (13–16)

Collins is being true to death and the grave, refusing transcendence. What he is exalting is a literary movement, a style and attitude of which, by subtle maneuvers, he makes Thomson the prophet. He gives it an authority in this way, while expressing a heartfelt lament for his friend. And he gives it density through the use of literary echoes. With the help of Lonsdale's edition, the modern reader can appreciate this:

> But thou, lorn stream, whose sullen tide
>   No sedge-crowned Sisters now attend,
> Now waft me from the green hill's side,
>   Whose cold turf hides the buried friend!
>   (29–32)

The poet is echoing Pope's *Windsor Forest* ("The gulphy *Lee* his sedgy Tresses rears: / And sullen *Mole*, that hides his diving Flood" [346–47]), and Pope is echoing Milton ("Or sullen *Mole* that runneth underneath, / or *Severn* swift, guilty of maiden's death, / Or Rocky *Avon*, or of Sedgy *Lee*" ("At a Vacation Exercise" 95–97), who is echoing Spenser's *Faerie Queene* 4.11.29–32 (in manner) and 2.10.18–19 (in theme). Collins is also echoing himself:[5]

> And many a nymph who wreathes her brows with sedge,
> And sheds the freshening dew, and, lovelier still,
>   The Pensive Pleasures sweet,
>   Prepare thy shadowy car.
>   ("Ode to Evening" 25–28)

These and still other borrowed elements have a collective effect: They form a literary warp which substantiates the woof of poetic discourse, seeming at once to organize its colors and to authenticate. The poetic discourse has been loosened from the guiding terms of the Chain of Being, which had supported Thomson's poetic flights, and is in danger of floating free, of losing its power of reference to the grand natural themes Collins still felt, despite his gloomy vision, to be the matter of poetry. The warping reattaches the discourse to these themes in a more subtle, less ideologically committed way and hence allows it seemingly to encode a more natural language. In moving from Spenser through Milton to Thomson, and then concluding with pictures of rural figures and a solitary muser who stands in for himself, Collins embeds a vision of the continuity of literary tradition in such a way that it becomes the guarantor of his naturalistic theme, the voice that partly resolves his fear of loss of voice.

This sense of continuity is also reflected—and qualified—in the seasonal element, ostensibly a mere imitative bow to Thomson but given fresh force by the circularity of the verbal structure. Unidirectional drift into darkness and death is balanced by the suggestion of recurrence—the yearly renewal of the meads, the repeated visits of the hinds and shepherd girls to the tomb, the reiterated recognition by the vales and woods, through the mediation of the future poet, that their genius dwells among them. It is not a transcendent but a limited "redemption," a rescue from oblivion by a continuing poetic tradition which honors its dead founder as a living voice.

Wordsworth seems to have understood thoroughly the fusion of theme and technique in Collins's ode. His own allusiveness, combined with similar concerns, enables him to field the poem's nuances and give them a further turn. While his capture of Collins's maneuvers may have been partly intuitive and unconscious, it cannot have been entirely so. His original insight was spontaneous and seems not to have been established in reference to Collins, but in the final acts of composition (if not earlier) the insight was amalgamated with thoughts about Collins and his poetry. And the process of composition includes an active will to master that art of echoing which gives Collins, and Gray, a measure of power. This art is related to but not the same as Augustan allusion and imitation, because it is not witty or pointed or interested in rich contextual interplay between poems or genres, nor does it necessarily begin in a conscious intention to allude.[6] Insofar as it is distinctive, it seeks the authority-lending support given by general thematic, tonal, and musical consonances with the original texts—not contrapuntal but chordal harmonies that seem to call up for the reader "the full voic'd Choir" which "through [the inner] ear," and often with only slight specificity, frame and weight the secondary text ("Il Penseroso" 162, 164).

It is an art Milton seems to propound by his wonderful handling of atmosphere in "L'Allegro" and "Il Penseroso" and to practice in his Italian sonnets in the effort to assimilate a foreign tradition. But he far overshadows it with his brilliantly learned baroque contrapuntal allusions—overshadows it to the point that the assimilative style of echoing has always been viewed as an inferior display put on by those who lack true poetic imagination. Though I shall try to show that this is not necessarily so, there is no doubt that in the Age of Sensibility it often was.[7] Such, it seems, is Wordsworth's judgment of Gray's eclectic echoing:

> He wrote English Verses, as he and other Eton school-Boys wrote Latin; filching a phrase now from one author, and now from another. . . . if I were to pluck out of Gray's tail all the feathers which, I know, belong to other Birds he would be left very bare indeed.[8]

But Wordsworth did not practice what he preached here. He had filched phrases patently in *An Evening Walk* and *Descriptive Sketches*. This sort of borrowing seems inseparable from the echoic mode he grew up with and as a young poet felt compelled to master. Even looking back in 1816, when the remarks just quoted were written, he justifies poetry that is "very highly and artificially laboured" (the phrase is that of Sir Edgerton Bridges, whom Wordsworth is contradicting), where "artificially" can be understood as "artfully":

> The word "artificially" begs the question, because that word is always employed in an unfavourable sense. Gray failed as a Poet not because he took too much pains, and so extinguished his animation; but because he had little of that fiery quality to begin with; his pains were of the wrong sort. . . . Do not let any Body persuade you that any quantity of good verses can ever be produced by mere felicity; or that an immortal *style* can be the growth of mere Genius—*Multa tulit fecitque*, must be the motto of all those who are to last. (*MY*2 301)

Fully evolved, his practice shows that he resists phrase-filching, not because the filched phrase itself corrupts but because its unprincipled use is motivated by a lack of imagination in the whole, and this leads to a saltatory, dissociated ingenuity applied to mere parts, as is the case with clever school-boy translations. Clearly, Wordsworth did not feel repelled by Gray's poetry. Not only was the "Elegy" one of his great favorites, but he echoed Gray more, and more widely, than he echoed any other poet except Milton, Spenser, and Shakespeare.

Collins, to whom he was also a substantial debtor, borrowed in the manner of Gray but more selectively, and to more brilliant effect. For this reason, I believe Wordsworth learned more from him about this kind of echoing than from Gray. Collins's use of echoes in the ode on Thomson is organically functional and imaginative, releasing rather than suppressing "animation." Whatever the stages in the history of its composition, "Remembrance of Collins" uses the same art of allusion to carry Collins's meditative theme further and achieve a revision of it. Its speaker shows explicitly that he is a young poet concerned, like Collins's speaker, about the life and death of poetry as well as poets; and he evokes the "Ode Occasioned by the Death of Mr. Thomson" because he interprets it as a statement about the continuity of poetic voice that implicitly provides a basis for it.

Insofar as Collins has preempted Thomson as the prophet of his own mode of poetic discourse and pictured a future musing Briton, a figure of the Poet, whose words of pity make his meditations a pious rite for the founder of a vital tradition, there is no distortion in Wordsworth's interpretation. But this interpretation does not seem to come to grips with the predominantly negative element of time in Collins's poem (the downstream drifting, the gathering dark, the formal and thematic enclosure of the whole by the grave, the possibility that the musing man's pity is a cry of deepened despair); and so the last two lines ("—The evening darkness gathers round / By virtue's holiest Powers attended") may seem an unwarranted reversal of Collins's unconsoled elegiac mood. The impression of failure to confront Collins's negative view of time is, however, an illusion created by the partitioning of the original poem. In its first stanzas (which in 1800 became "Lines Written While Sailing in a Boat at Evening," PW 1.40), drift, darkness, and death were the central elements of Wordsworth's primary insight. The driving force of these stanzas was "the following gloom," which made the youthful bard's exclusive attention to the glowing west a "fond deceit." But the poet's confrontation of the youth with the gloom produced a rather shallow defiance:

> And what if he must die in sorrow!
> Who would not cherish dreams so sweet,
> Though grief and pain may come to-morrow?
> (14–16)

The order of poetic ideas was fatally anticlimactic (from death to pain), and the insight remained hackneyed ("unanimated" Gray used a similar insight with far greater power in his Eton Ode). Something more was needed.

It was provided by the last three stanzas, subsequently renamed "Remembrance of Collins." They were at once a correction and a completion of the shallowly defiant attitude of the second stanza. Their severance from the first two stanzas was advantageous, because the interposition of white space and a title allowed greater emphasis on the idea of reconsideration. The tenor and the form of "Remembrance of Collins" are themselves both metaphorically reconsiderations: The phrasings in their progression ("Oh glide," "Vain thought," "Yet be as now thou art," "Now let us") enunciate wishes, bow to reality, look again, salvage a significance which was not originally seen.

The progression is already typically Wordsworthian. It has the outline of the situation so often seen in the lyrical Wordsworth and described by Geoffrey Hartman as archetypal for the self-conscious mind—that of "the halted traveler confronting an inscription, confronting the knowledge of death and startled by it into feeling 'the burden of the mystery' " (*Wordsworth's Poetry* 13). The halted traveler here is the rowing speaker who suspends his oars; the inscription (the actual one on Thomson, if it existed then, being out of sight in Richmond Church) is his "image of a poet's heart" in the glowing Thames; and the knowledge is of the familiar Wordsworthian pair: of death (the death of Collins and Thomson, of the "bright visions," and proleptically of the speaker's poetic voice) and of peculiar calm (the calm of "How bright, how solemn, how serene!" and of the suspended oar that provides a "stillness at the heart of endless agitation"). The image of the poet's heart is a still point—a focused spot in the diffuse light of sunset, a mental place of rest, and a point of view from which the speaker can look into both the future and the past and see a tortured but finally blessed persistence of the poetic spirit.

For the drive of this poem, generated reactively by the pause in the mindless rush of circumstance, is to bless. The desire to bless is an impulsive orientation that became typical of Wordsworth after 1797. He seems to strike this note most often when he has worked through baffling thoughts or thoughts that fail at first to affirm the movement of his heart.[9] The word "bless" is also used in Collins's poem, but without large connotations. It means no more than "give joy to" or "make fruitful": "The genial meads, assigned to bless / Thy life, shall mourn thy early doom" (37–38). In Wordsworth the blessing is part of a deeper consolation, one as fragile as Collins's solace but implicitly more redemptive. He aims to counteract, without contradicting it, the wasteful hithering-and-thithering of life by voicing "the burden of the mystery" in an appropriate way and, building on Collins's own insight, to assert a continuity of poetic voices that reaches behind and ahead of this poised moment and will not let its inner blessedness fade like the bright visions on the surface.

Wordsworth asserts the continuity explicitly by his argument but implicitly, and more effectively, by his use of literary echoes. Though in typical Enlightenment fashion the poem is addressed to a general readership, it is explicitly the meditation of a young poet looking at the life of poets, and by "all our minds" he means "the minds of all us poets." Thus some of the same considerations set forth in the opening lines of "Resolution and Independence" are entered on here. The speaker really has three concerns, all of which rise up to challenge the shallow resolution of "Lines Written While Sailing in a Boat at Evening": (1) poets cannot keep their minds flowing steadily in deep channels, and thus their visions and powers come and go; (2) poets die, like anyone else; (3) though the poet's art gives access to high mysteries and lovely visions, it does not necessarily give peace or happiness to its servitor. These concerns may all be understood metaphorically to describe painful discontinuities naturally experienced in life—discontinuities between the mind and its powers, between one voice and its successor, between ideal vision and existing reality.

This subjective experience of discontinuity forms the explicit theme of the poem. Wordsworth tries to universalize and objectify it by linking it to the concerns of past poets. We have already seen how he joins his original insight to that of Collins's ode on Thomson's death. Quite on the surface of Wordsworth's poem is another echo of Collins which speaks of the discontinuity in Collins's own poetic life—his loss of poetic intimacy with that serene image of a heart,

> Such as did once the Poet bless,
> Who, murmuring here a later ditty,
> Could find no refuge from distress
> But in the milder grief of pity.
> (13–16)

These lines lead us to compare the ode on Thomson with Collins's earlier ditty, "Ode to Evening" (especially lines 5–32). There, the poet's mind flows in images of calm, afloat in the wake of Evening—the "maid composed" who at her "genial loved return" draws her veil over the setting sun and invites the poet to suit his "softened strain" to her rich stillness. In this magical moment the mind is fitted to nature

and nature to the mind, forming an alliance by means of which the
attention of the poet is repaid twofold, by inner peace and by the
exaltation of vision, or the sense of possibility, that comes when the
offering of self is fully accepted:

> So long, sure-found beneath the sylvan shed,
> Shall Fancy, Friendship, Science, rose-lipped Health,
>   Thy gentlest influence own,
>   And hymn thy favourite name!
>
> (49–52)

It is a moment of reciprocity that awakens untrammeled poetic voice,
a moment, Wordsworthian in its promise though not in manner,
when what is found is a reflection of the human in nature and the
natural in man. Wordsworth's evocation of the "Ode to Evening"
accomplishes four things in parallel: It lends reason to his finding the
image of a heart in the sunset-lit river, it gives appropriateness to his
attitude of prayer in lines 19–20 (for we are in the presence of Collins's "calm vot'ress"), it adds poignance to the moment of calm, and it
sets up perfectly the benign transformation of the gathering darkness
into something vaguely suggestive of a priest or priestess carrying out
a rite, "By virtue's holiest Powers attended."

It is only suggestive, because Wordsworth does not personify. A
major difference between him and Collins is his more overt naturalizing of the scene. The evening darkness resists anthropomorphosis,
and though both "virtue" and "Powers" are typical eighteenth-century
abstractions in sound and sense, they are given no emblematic shape.
Wordsworth's echoing of Collins is not radical allusion in the manner
of Milton echoing the classics. It is not even as bold as Collins's use of
Thomson. It seems, rather, to be a means for completing the naturalizing begun in earnest by Thomson and John Philips and pursued by
Akenside, Gray, Collins, and the Wartons, among others. These poets
were often sidetracked by feckless Miltonizing, compulsive personification, limiting Augustan diction, and a too-self-conscious harking after
sublimity through manipulation of psychic or natural descriptive
elements. Wordsworth, though still obviously imbued with "pre-
Romantic" poeticizing impulses, generally steers clear of such eddies.
He attempts to set his course in the poetic mainstream with a more
assertive movement toward naturalism while further developing the
ideas of his immediate predecessors.

This urge toward a more "manly" and natural manner accounts for
the echoes of Bowles which seem to be present in the poem. Whether
Wordsworth read Bowles's *Fourteen Sonnets* before he brought the

five-stanza poem to its primitive form is a matter of dating which cannot be resolved.[10] But since a reasonable case that he had may be built on external possibilities and internal grounds, I feel free to argue that Bowles's voice was present at a crucial stage in the poem's formation. Both the first stanza of "Lines Written While Sailing in a Boat" and the first stanza of "Remembrance of Collins" seem to me Bowlesian in character:

> And see how dark the backward stream!
> A little moment past so smiling!
> And still, perhaps, with faithless gleam,
> Some other loiterers beguiling.
>
> Such views the youthful Bard allure;
> But, heedless of the following gloom,
> He deems their colours shall endure
> Till peace go with him to the tomb.
>   ("Lines," 5–12)

These lines recall the sighing nostalgia and intimate melancholy that breathe through the whole canon of Bowles's sonnets, as when the "friendless" (taking their cue from Collins's Evening veiling "with gentlest hush the landscape still") watch the sunset tints

> Hang lovely, oft to musing fancy's eye
>   Presenting fairy vales, where the tir'd mind
>   Might rest, beyond the murmurs of mankind,
> Nor hear the hourly moans of misery.
> Ah! beauteous views, that hope's fair gleams the while
> Should smile like you, and perish as they smile!
>   (*Fourteen Sonnets* VI.9–14)

The sentimentalism is grosser, the melancholy heavier and more self-pitying; the language is less concrete, more hackneyed; the tendency to personify is greater; and the embodiment of insight or situation is much less imaginative than in "Remembrance of Collins." Yet Wordsworth picks up the tone and some of the manner, and possibly even some of the phrasing: The "beauteous views" of VI.13 become the "lovely visions" of Wordsworth's "Remembrance"; "Hope's fair gleams" of the same line the "faithless gleam" of "Lines"; "smile like you, and perish as they smile!" of line 14 the "little moment past so smiling" of "Lines."

Wordsworth's use of these now bathetic-sounding Bowlesian tones

might be explained as the atmospheric seduction of the young Wordsworth into a popular vein. Bowles represented a final resurgence of
the penserosan manner, which never never quite lost its grip on Milton's coattails or became wholly incapable of expressing the *Leiden* and
Schmerzen of the eternal adolescent in man:

> Languid, and sad, and slow, from day to day,
>   I journey on, yet pensive turn to view
>   (Where the rich landscape gleams with softer hue)
> The streams, and vales, and hills, that steal away.
> So fares it with the children of the earth . . .
>   (Bowles, *Sonnets,* 2d ed. [1789], II.1–5)

Echoes of the end of *Paradise Lost,* a picturesque taste in scenery, a
stylized melancholy mood, moralizing, heightened historicism (expressed here as nostalgia)—these notes were in the air the youthful
Wordsworth breathed.

But seen from the perspective of his era, Bowles did offer a new
departure, something of his own worthy of imitation—or so it seemed
to Coleridge. It was a special kind of fluency, as Coleridge explains in
Biographia Literaria,

> a style of poetry so tender and yet so manly, so natural and real,
> and yet so dignified and harmonious. . . . in the more sustained
> and elevated style . . . Bowles and Cowper were, to the best of
> my knowledge, the first who combined natural thoughts with
> natural diction; the first who reconciled the heart with the
> head. (1: 10, 16)

He sees the natural style as the forerunner of Wordsworth's "uniform
adherence to genuine, logical English" (*Biographia* 2: 77), though elsewhere he expresses his disillusioning discovery of Bowles's poverty of
thought. It seems probable, though there is no recorded comment to
prove it, that Wordsworth also initially recognized in Bowles's early
style a personal, relatively conversational and unadorned discourse
that was able to sustain a sensitive, but manly and natural-seeming,
meditative note. In my view it was this supple meditative voicing,
rather than the sympathetic ring of melancholy insights he was already beginning to reject, which led Wordsworth to experiment with
the Bowlesian manner in "Remembrance of Collins." He sought, like
Bowles and the more sinewy Cowper, to achieve a discursive flowing-
ness that overcomes the system of end-stopping and gemlike insetting
of images inherited from the witty Augustan style.

A new poetic mode stirring in esthetic trends and in his private "fields of sleep" may account for Wordsworth's desire to pick up on the flowing style, but in "Remembrance of Collins" he also had a vital thematic reason: His central though unsustainable wish for present and future poets is that "all our minds for ever flow." This wish becomes vain as reality confronts him with the discontinuities of human experience, the inability of consciousness to flow steadily. He then substitutes for the first a second wish more consonant with the desultory operation of inspiration, a wish that at each critical juncture between consciousness and the world every "child of song" find it possible to develop an imaginative response which calls up "virtue's holiest Powers" against the dark. The wish is plausible, because poetic responses through history have formed a chain of poetic voices. He can thus rescue the hoary topos of the flowing stream of rhetoric as the "under-image" of his poem by translating it into a river of serial songs, an uninterrupted channel for the linked succession of poetic voices—in a word, by making it represent the tradition.

To the speaker's eye, this river holds in its depths the image of a poet's heart caught at an ideal moment. The primary function of the image is to represent the poised emotional center, which as visionary source allows insight and poetic speech. An exemplary product of this heart is Collins's "Ode to Evening." But if the human heart is the source of poetry, utterance is its lifeblood. The most unendurable poetic sorrow is being blocked, not being able to sing; and the next-to-most unendurable sorrow is not being able to sing *to* anyone. Finding and giving voice is the poet's blessing.

Finding and giving voice was the locus of Collins's difficulties as a poet. In Wordsworth's poem, the failure of his "later ditty" truly to resolve his "distress" is dramatically reinforced by his "murmuring" his song: His voice has been reduced. The fear of extinction of voice through distress and alienation moves Wordsworth not only to imagine the true source of voice but to pray that there will be no divorce between that source and future poets. This prayer for continuity of voice is more reasonable than the "vain thought" with which he began (the wish for an uninterrupted sublimity of consciousness), and less callow than the fashionable fin-de-siècle sentimentalism of "Lines Written While Sailing in a Boat." The prayer is supported by the relatively naturalistic handling of the scene and manner, which makes the union of poet and source seem easier to attain, more "natural."

This union is further supported by the temporal train of echoes representing the poetic tradition. Bowles's voice is preceded in time by Collins's, and Collins's evokes Thomson's; together these poets help the poem breathe the atmosphere of the meditative nature poets of the eighteenth century. Milton's anterior voice, filtered through them, is also evoked, especially in the last two lines. And Wordsworth has implanted in this temporal train a still-older echo. The first line and a half of "Remembrance of Collins" ("Glide gently, thus for ever glide, / O Thames!") cannot fail to suggest the famous refrain of Spenser's "Prothalamion": "Sweete Themmes, runne softly, till I end my song." But there are as well more subtle links between the poems. Spenser too gives voice to the personal distress of a poet, himself in this case, telling us that he has "walkt forth to ease my payne" brought on by the "sullein care" which "did aflict my brayne" because of disappointed ambitions at court. If something of this distress is reflected in Words-worth's image of Collins, Spenser's situation is reflected also in the implied depression—the sense of "following gloom"—settling on Wordsworth's youthful poetic ambition as he suddenly becomes con-scious of the illusoriness of fancy, the griefs and discontinuities of imaginative life, and the fact of death. Both poets request the river to sustain their song, and both are relieved by visions the river supports.

These resonances, though tenuous, show how Wordsworth's imagi-nation could be quietly responsive to a strong literary work of the past even when engaged in meditation on a spontaneous insight into na-ture. But the echoic process here does not engage fully with its source: Many aspects of "Prothalamion" are not picked up in Wordsworth's echo and in fact must remain muted if the effect of the echo is not to be thwarted. For instance, "Prothalamion" takes place on a hot sum-mer morning, while "Remembrance of Collins" has neither season nor temperature; the first is masquelike, with the form of a dream-vision, the second inward and meditative, with the tonality of pastoral elegy. It is important to note this, because a peculiar selectiveness character-izes a large class of Wordsworth's allusive references and is at times awkward enough to trouble critics.[11]

The Spenserian echo in "Remembrance of Collins," though selec-tive, is nonetheless not a simplistic manipulation. If there are enough consonances between the poems to sustain the echo, it is also true that an aspect of the differences between them—the technique—functions in support of Wordsworth's theme. Both he and Spenser turn a moment of care into a celebration. Spenser, with his emblem-atic technique, spends much energy on mythological artifices; yet at the end, though the concluding celebratory imagery has flattering deific and cosmic elements (the noble lord issuing "Like radiant Hesper," the two bridegrooms-to-be "like the twins of Jove" [164, 173]), the fictions of nymphs, strewn flowers, Swans—emblematic, not naturalistic figures—are suddenly dropped in favor of the sim-plest, most natural completing statement. The two gentlemen

Received those two faire brides, their loves delight,
Which, at th' appointed tyde,
Each one did make his bryde.[12]

(176–78)

The court, so miserly toward Spenser, is dutifully glorified, the aristo-
cratic parties to the marriage are praised, as from the overt *raison d'être*
of the poem they must be, but what is valued most is the plighting of
ordinary human bonds. The poet, meanwhile, is left alone, looking on
from a distance, just as he started out, in possession of "idle hopes,
which still doe fly away" (8) as the river flows on. This allows us to
understand that the central action of the poem, what happens to the
poet, is both less and more than the change of situation he sought: It is
a readjustment and assertion of values, accompanied by a change of
mood.

The movement in Wordsworth's poem is similar, but the technique
contrasts. Wordsworth eschews emblematic figuration. The image of
the poet's heart in the water is superficially emblemlike, but Wordsworth does not want the reader to visualize a literal heart-image in the
river. He wants us to imagine something vaguer, closer to "inner
condition, like that of a poet's heart in ideal circumstances, suggested
by the physical state of the waters." And the quasi-mythic element
which would identify river and mind is dismissed as vain. No true
deity or transparent personification of numen is invoked, though in
the prayer, the calm, the Miltonic echoes, and the final suggestion of
an evening service, there is an informing religious spirit.

But a humanizing movement is set up, as in "Prothalamion," and
here, too, this movement brings about a readjustment of values and a
change of mood. Like Spenser, Wordsworth looks forward to an
alliance—not a marriage made in heaven, however, but an earthly
alliance between the poet and nature. Through this alliance the river
can reflect the poet's heart and the poet's voice the river, the evening
stillness contain a prayer and prayer convey the relief of stillness, the
gathering darkness embody the death of the poet being remembered
and yet be filled with a vaguely numinous blessing conveyed through
a living poet who links his consciousness to it. In contrast to Spenser,
Wordsworth conducts his humanizing movement entirely by means of
naturalistic images, and external nature provides the poem with more
than emblematic conventions.

The reader sensitive to the echoes can thus look back from Wordsworth through Bowles, Collins, Thomson, and Milton to Spenser and
feel stirring in the poem an evocation of a whole tradition and its
changes. As one reflectively traverses the historical layers of echoes

one gains a heightened sense of the power of the naturalistic mode. Wordsworth thus makes it seem as though the history of his art were a progression toward the birth of naturalism. He does, however, build a limitation into his argument for allying poet and scene. He expresses the longing of the mind to have a power like that of nature—to flow like the Thames—but in the service of the imagination; he rejects the *identification* of man with nature:

> O glide, fair stream! for ever so,
> Thy quiet soul on all bestowing,
> Till all our minds for ever flow
> As thy deep waters now are flowing.
>
> Vain thought! . . .
>
> (5–9)

This imagined (and then demystified) consonance between the poetic mind and the Thames contains yet another echo. It recalls a poem which fathered the dominant type of English topographical poem, and particularly certain lines of it so often imitated that they became commonplaces of Restoration and Augustan poetry:

> O could I flow like thee, and make thy stream
> My great example, as it is my theme!
> Though deep, yet clear, though gentle, yet not dull,
> Strong without rage, without ore-flowing full.
>   (John Denham, *Cooper's Hill* 189–92)

Denham's poem, published in an abbreviated form in 1642 (a mere decade after Donne's death) and in its full form in 1655, established the device of incidental meditation, which created the possibility of a dialogue between the poet and external nature.[13] The meditation was incidental to a review of history, and the new combination made the didacticism inherent in the topographical poem (because it was bound to tell facts about a place) more functional. It was altered from a mere aria—a moral excursus not dramatically motivated—to organic moralizing prompted by the natural features, cultural objects, and human associations of the landscape. The new mode invoked a sense of alliance between man and place, and this in turn suggested to a degree an alliance between man and nature.

Wordsworth's poetry of the great decade would seem to be a culmination of this dialogic potentiality. And yet in 1789 he belittles Denham's plea as vanity. The paradox is only apparent, however, for

Wordsworth's poetic instincts are accurately focused, and they make his use of Denham an allusion of the richer sort that holds the original up for ironic exploration and radical revision. Denham's poem, with its discursive manner, rationalizing imagery, submerged wit, and ability to marshal the antithetical structure of the heroic couplet, is a determining forerunner of English neoclassicism. The success of this new mode results from Denham's having discovered how to deploy these techniques to dramatize his argument. His aim is to reconcile his reader to the fact that a new order cannot be created without the energetic breaking up of the old. Like Virgil, he wants us to accept history as a particular kind of process: a cyclic self-renewal of the social order that is almost never rational, evolutionary progress. This is not simply because events depend on the arbitrary will of rulers, but because the social order expresses more fundamental forces. A high culture has no vitality if it is not built on the active contention of primal opposites. As Nature "wisely . . . knew, the harmony of things / . . . from discord springs":

> Such was the discord, which did first disperse
> Form, order, beauty through the Universe;
> While driness moysture, coldness heat resists,
> All that we have, and that we are, subsists. . . .
> Such huge extreams when Nature doth unite,
> Wonder from thence results, from thence delight.
>   (203–8, 211–12)

The weight of Denham's *discordia concors* argument falls on the side of *concors*. Even in the passage on discord, the coloring descriptive element is drawn from conceptions of the Italian picturesque style of painting, where, for all the heightening of contrasts, the ultimate emphasis is on harmony of composition: "While the steep horrid roughness of the Wood / Strives with the gentle calmness of the flood," an agreement comes about between these opposed elements, and together they form a remarkable but unthreatening whole.

The opposed elements are not fused but made to occupy middle ground. Thus, while Virgil turns at last to myth to locate his principle of redeeming vitality, Denham comes to rest on the golden mean for his: a firm standoff between opposites, a calm and fluent common sense that keeps extremes in tow. *His* youth peering in the stream of Thames is not the "youthful Bard" of Wordsworth's vision, who sees the universal poet's heart in its inspiriting calm, but Narcissus cured of his extreme passion by the clarity and restraint that reign in a rational nature based on an order of balanced opposites:

> The stream is so transparent, pure, and clear,
> That had the self-enamour'd youth gaz'd here,
> So fatally deceiv'd he had not been,
> While he the bottom, not his face had seen.
>
> (213–16)

Not only Denham's discursive manner but his metaphorical plan turns sharply away from those of his metaphysical contemporaries who used their violent yoking together of opposites to insist on the gap between compositional elements while they explored the hidden threads uniting them. Instead, he sees the opposites as the sustaining pillars of reasoned argument, supporting a universal framework and not gossamer webbing between fine local points. Thus the self-exhortation of "O could I flow like thee" is not a prayer for poetic inventiveness like that of external nature but a prayer for the plenitude of classical balance: opposites reconciled without fusion but also without jarring; Apollonian order. The novelty is that Denham's balance is depicted as a moving one, dynamic but steady through time.

The celebrated lines which embody this dynamic balance are a revamping of an old image, the river topos for classical eloquence—compelling fluency of speech properly regulated. Thus the Thames is taken at this point less as an external presence than as a "shadowy type" of the ideal mental, or expressive, activity of the poet and becomes a means of envisaging a forceful, energetic classicism. This classicism is aimed in part at explicating the cosmos and its relation to man, but not dramatically by generating meaning through the interaction of poetic consciousness and external nature. Rather, nature for the neoclassical poet is an amphitheater laid out by the same architect who designed the central stage where men play out their roles, and the main function of poetry is to depict and explore the human comedy. While this poetry is not disdainful of the natural world—indeed may view it with delight (especially through Claude glasses)—its metaphors cannot encompass the idea that a value inheres in an active *exchange* between the human mind and nature.

Wordsworth, whose metaphors come to support the idea of such an exchange and make it the ground of his poetic revolution, is certainly not rejecting it when he dismisses the Denhamian image of flow as vain. He is, rather, using allusion to contest neoclassical assumptions. Evoking the most famous couplet of a crucial document in the poetic development of the neoclassical attitude, he allusively construes the lines to represent a false attitude toward nature, which he seeks expressly to overcome in what follows. Simply put, this revision says that the classical attitude is too superficial. In seeming to offer the poet a plenitude of inspiration ("Wonder from thence results, from thence delight") by placing him on a line moving between opposites, it really keeps him sequestered from reality, whether psychic or external. He moves not between fundamentals but between surfaces, where alone things may seem to flow smoothly. The truth for Wordsworth is that the movement of the mind is saltatory, and also that nature cannot be a source of imaginative energy for the poet without his active participation in it, his offering of himself. Denham's poet is not a rational but a rationalistic spectator, one who sees through to the plain bottom because he cannot see deeply within or offer himself, while Wordsworth's can look into the murky layer of self and achieve fullness of inspiration by pursuing an exchange between his consciousness and nature.

At this stage of Wordsworth's career, the pursuit is only implicit. But it is unmistakably there because the intertextual references to support it are there, and they constitute a technique. Through its uncontentious echoes and for the most part mildly revisionary allusions, "Remembrance of Collins" demonstrates the middle range of uses to which Wordsworth put his literary borrowings. It does not display those outer ranges which offer either trivial echoes and inert quotations, puzzling when not downright embarrassing, or preemptive allusions of a power approaching the Miltonic. The failure of the first sort and the force of the second are clear to every sensitive reader, but the literary values of echoes that fall between these extremes have not always been appreciated. Casual readers of "Remembrance of Collins" are not likely to be conscious of the wealth of things echoed in it; even Wordsworth was not thinking at every moment in composition of all the relevant possibilities in the tradition. Yet I believe that the words which sprang to his mind as he walked out of doors composing aloud or sat indoors revising were often resonant with echoes of the tone or phrases (or images, syntax, concepts, structuring forms) of other poetic works or genres, and that at some point he recognized them for what they were and treated them purposively—altering, strengthening, canceling, or subtly contextualizing them.

"Remembrance of Collins," less burdened with merely specious borrowings and better shaped than many other early pieces, aptly shows that Wordsworth's echoic techniques, while akin to those of Gray and Collins, were not used as an inert Gravian heritage or in a fumbling attempt to match Milton, but as an intensive experiment with tradition in which he sought the means to express a new vision of things. He developed the means and the vision more or less, though not wholly, in tandem; and since his aim was to revolutionize and yet renew the tradition, echoing was an inherently sympathetic means. It enabled him to diminish the violence of those discontinuities he seemed always to dread and to have to confront, whether in a movement of consciousness or in a revision of the tradition.

Certainly he was ready to challenge the tradition directly in his prefatory prose, in the tenor and form of his poems, and in the revisionary allusions to Milton and other poets. But side by side with these aggressive techniques, he developed his eighteenth-century heritage of fragmentary quotation, atmospheric echo, slight allusion. If his revisionary methods, true to his vision of things, enabled him to slip free of confining conceptions of order—the leaden Chain of Being and the golden noose of neoclassical poetic diction—his echoic techniques allowed him to lean without ideological or stylistic commitment on poets who were fettered in these ways. He drew on these poets because they harbored the germs of his own naturalizing insights and had nurtured them in meditative structures which still, though he saw their weaknesses, could support his developing vision. He could garner their insights, the gestalt of their poetic worlds, their poetic authority—numen, notion, and nomos—by allowing them to function echoically in his poetry.

Wordsworth is thus like other figures who profoundly affected the course of English literature, at once radical and traditional. He carried the gradually changing significance of the poetic concept of nature to a revolutionary conclusion, and he did so vigorously enough in the *Lyrical Ballads* to provoke violent opposition. It is significant from the point of view of my argument that of all Wordsworth's poems the ballads have the fewest echoes or obvious traditional elements, so that the Advertisement of 1798 has to warn the reader overtly to approach the pieces as experiments. Clearly, the poet knew what to expect and to a degree relished provoking it, as all deliberate reformers must. Looking at the events of his early life, one can see that he had the capacity for making and even celebrating abrupt shifts of course—for instance, his initial welcome of the revolution in France, his abandonment of Annette Vallon, his ecstatic reaction to the death of Robespierre. Nonetheless, he soon felt compelled to make amends for such rents in the fabric of consciousness.[14] Already in 1800 we find him arguing in defense of his lyrical experiments that he had introduced no discontinuity into the poetic main line. And by 1807 a certain number of echoes and quotations and backward-glancing phrases had crept even into the poems of *Lyrical Ballads*.

One need only compare Wordsworth to Blake at the same stages of their careers to see the difference between a poet whose primary orientation was toward continuity, or naturalizing revision, and one whose primary orientation was toward discontinuity, or apocalyptic revision. Blake's early pieces show him to be a natural genius at imitation, but he used the tradition only to intensify his break with it. Wordsworth instinctively as well as deliberately moderated his revolutionary impulse by elaborating a pre-Romantic mode of literary borrowing that subtly proclaimed unbroken allegiance to a grand tradition. His vision deepened, and his style changed several times, but although he wrote some poems untrammeled by quotations, echoes, or allusions, he never abandoned echoic techniques or his conception of echoing as a fundamental principle of poiesis.

2

Echo as Genesis and Mediation in Wordsworth's Poetic Thought

THE PERVASIVENESS OF ECHO AS IMAGE

Wordsworth's standard biographer has noticed that there are "four faithful images that haunt his poetry to the end, each of which, . . . 'When it hath pass'd away, returns again / In later days.'" These images are the "rainbow or the Cuckoo's shout, / An echo, or the glow-worm's faery lamp" (Moorman 1: 21).[1] Not only the echo but the other three images as well participate in several dimensions of the idea of iteration. In Wordsworth all are revenants, perceptions which return after a time, though changed, from a mental hiding place to confront again an active consciousness. In this sense, they are all echoes, echoes of earlier experience. But each image also has something echolike in its very nature. The cuckoo has a peculiar "twofold shout," as Wordsworth tells us in another place, "At once far off, and near." This "wandering Voice" seems to be an image of echo itself, among other things, for its repetitiveness is emphasized in the numerous doubled assertions of the poem Wordsworth devotes to it, and the dominant metaphorical impulse is auditory.[2] As the bird of "To the Cuckoo" is more firmly established through the imagery of sound, it gains in power over time, until at last it seems to restore the past, "That golden time," whole. Yet through deliberately restraining terms—"appears," "unsubstantial," "faery"—we experience this redemption of time as the perception of a song that will soon fade away. In hearing through the tension of opposite attitudes the music of the restorative echo, and in being made to feel the iterative relation of past to present, we know nonetheless that we have not toyed with a mere fancy but have confronted "A voice, a mystery." We are left with a weight of experience, the "burden of the mystery," rendered by an avian *imago vocis*.

The firefly, particularly in its glowworm stage, is the repetition in small of a star, of a flower that peeps in the grass, of the fire or light man kindles at night. This iterative relation is just barely presented by implication in "The Glow Worm" (*PW* 2.466), which begins:

> Among all lovely things my Love had been;
> Had noted well the stars, all flowers that grew
> About her home; but she had never seen
> A Glow-worm, never one, and this I knew.
>
>   (1–4)

Moorman informs us that the poem "was written in the spring of 1802, when William was riding back to Dorothy after a visit to Mary Hutchinson, with whom he had just completed the arrangements for their wedding." She thinks Wordsworth wrote it "to reassure [Dorothy] that the communion between them could never be changed." It has this power because it embodies and affirms an "incident" that "took place about seven years ago between Dorothy and me," as the poet wrote to Coleridge shortly after composing the poem.[3] The glowworm symbolized the fervent companionship of William and Dorothy at Racedown in 1795 and therefore, also, the spiritual regeneration of the poet. It was at Racedown—the place for Dorothy "dearest to my recollections upon the whole surface of the island"—that the sister "had watched and fostered her brother's slow recovery; had 'preserved him still a poet,' by turning his eyes back to the things that had given him his primitive and most profound delight" (Moorman 1: 318).[4] The poem echoes both the healing process worked by Dorothy and the spiritual spousal of the siblings by telling the story of a gap in knowledge filled in. Finding, preserving, and blessing the glowworm, which suggests the light of consciousness maintained against the "stormy night" of time by being set down in the orchard of love beneath the cosmic "Tree," the poet is able to show it to his sister intact and arouse the double response of joy which unites them and ends the poem.

Mention of the glowworm, then, repeats this "spot of time" and so overcomes a threatened gap in experience. That was the function of the cuckoo, and it is also the function of the rainbow. The rainbow is at once a natural event and a supernatural sign, and looked at either way its significance for human life is essentially the same. As a natural sign, it means the return of the sun and a restoration of equilibrium among the elements after a rainstorm; as a supernatural sign, it is a pledge by God not to interrupt again until the end of time the natural history of the earth and the development of the human culture the earth supports. It is this doubly affirmative, natural-supernatural strength of the rainbow as a sign of renewal which makes the poet's heart leap up and wish his days might be bound together by natural piety.

These poems and fragments are typical of Wordsworth's whole oeuvre not simply in being structured by echoic techniques but in making echo an implied or overt part of their subject matter. For the echo is an emblem of a central Wordsworthian concern, the continuity of consciousness; and, broadly conceived, it embodies the givens of his psychological makeup, his ideas of the function of creativity, and the prime issue of poetic voice which he inherited.

THE PRE-ROMANTIC STRUGGLE: CALLING A VOICE OUT OF NATURE

The use in Wordsworth of the echo as a metaphor for various continuities—the sense of temporal and spatial relatedness in human experience of subjective and objective realities, especially the related- ness of past and present or mind and nature—was a deep develop- ment of poetic attitudes he found in the eighteenth-century poets who stood to one side of the central Augustan canon or succeeded it. In these poets a primary concern was finding a strong poetic voice. Ambi- tious of achievement yet aware of the relative inferiority of their tal- ents, sometimes mentally disturbed and almost always depressed by the pressured give-and-take of polite society, led on by the *ignis fatuus* of the sublime and the popular muse of the picturesque, they self- consciously sought out inspiration that would lead not only to the inditing of particular poems but to the voice that could sing poem after poem in "Such strains as would have won the ear / Of *Pluto*" to set free the Orphic anima (Milton, "L'Allegro" 148–49).

One important way in which they sought voice was to image it overtly, and this often meant placing or evoking it in the landscape that was a regular feature of their verse. As one image of voice in later-eighteenth-century poetry, echo, more or less personified, is at once a device retrieved from the lumber rooms of classical and Renais- sance poetry and a hesitant, incomplete embodiment of a new poetic idea. In prefiguring the Romantic conception of interchange between individual consciousness and nature, it shows us an empty convention beginning to be filled with a new meaning. Overtly or in disguise, echo is the voice of the *genius loci* and therefore both a literary and a natural voice. For embedded in the general eighteenth-century view asserting the historical "westering" of culture from Greece through Rome and Italy to France and England is the English sense that the spirit of poetry can be wooed to inhabit permanently the landscape of Albion. As Geoffrey Hartman puts it:

> The thought that a new poetry might be founded, peculiarly English, both great and enlightened, enchanting and rational, inspire[d] the hope that culminate[d] in Romanticism.... It suggested that the demonic, or more than rational, energy of imagination might be tempered by its settlement in Britain—its naturalization, as it were, on British soil. This conversion of the demon meant that the poetical genius would coincide with the genius loci of England; and this meant, in practice, a medita-tion on English landscape as alma mater—where landscape is storied England, its legends, history, and rural-reflective spirit. The poem becomes, in a sense, a seduction of the poetical genius by the genius loci: the latter invites—subtly compels— the former to live within via media charms.
>
> (*Beyond Formalism* 319)

To this new life the westward-traveled poetic genius brings its hand-maid, Echo. She has the classical-pastoral function of expressing na-ture's sympathy for man's experience of loss—of being (in Hartman's phrase) the voice of *natura plangens*—and also the Renaissance func-tion of affirming the direct link between poiesis and that natural music which images the divine harmony established by the Creator. The latter function, first imaged by Macrobius in the marriage of Pan and Echo, was later turned into an image validating the method of natural science by Bacon. Asserting that the self-enjoying creative world has no need except of discourse which Echo supplies, he takes the marriage to be "of nature to the true poetry of natural philosophy, the marriage for which he himself claims, in the *Novum Organum*, to be writing the spousal verse or epithalamium" (Hollander, *Figure of Echo* 10).

The function of echo as a link between poiesis and divine harmony was vestigial by the eighteenth century, and the once-popular Ovidian image of Echo as Narcissus's deprived natural counterpart had faded away almost completely; but echo as the voice of sympathetic lamenting

in nature had grown stronger. The typical pre-Romantic poet expresses a peculiarly uncomfortable awareness of social tensions, the
most evident basis of the "white" melancholy or anxious boredom that
signals a threatened self—a self felt to be insufficiently strong to main-
tain itself against the energies of those competing with apparent success
for a place in the sun. "The imaginative literature of the years 1740–
1760 was largely the literature of low spirits," Henry A. Beers wrote at
the turn of the twentieth century (162–63), and recently Thomas
Weiskel discussed "the languid melancholy, the vague boredom that
increased so astonishingly during the eighteenth century" (97). Weiskel
tells us that the sublime was the main remedy for such "leuchocholy": If
it did not cure, it "transformed this state into the firmer, morally sanc-
tioned melancholy of the gloomy egoist" (97).

Though Weiskel is surely right in this, there was something short of
(though not precluding) an encounter with the sublime which might
also help. The excursion, or walk into nature, could momentarily allevi-
ate depression and restore a sense of power to the ailing ego. The
growing fashion of taking a rural walk—a psycho-literary exercise devoted to peasant-watching, flora-observing, hilltop-climbing, chasm-
perusing, panorama-meditating—was embodied in the neogeorgic, topographical, and pastoral works by such poets as the two Philipses,
Thomson, and Dyer. It was also incorporated in the meditative-
rhetorical vein of Gray, Collins, and Akenside, and generally in the new
verbal impulses of an evolving post-neoclassical consciousness, which
put theatrical semidivine presences back into nature.

All this—the new poetic modes and the new attitudes—helped
make the natural scene an anodyne to troubled poetic hearts. And of
course it ultimately became, after Thomson's example, *the* locus of the
sublime. But in its typical eighteenth-century realization by such poets
as John Dyer, the Wartons, William Crowe, Michael Bruce, and John
Logan, the poetic experience of the natural scene could only soothe. It
could not heal, until Coleridge and Wordsworth further transformed
it, because it was not a place of confrontation or (even if it led to an
encounter with the sublime) of working through and deepening one's
understanding of the self. There were no terms for such an understanding beyond vague didactic generalizations and self-exhortations,
in a dead moralizing vein, against giving value to worldly ambition or
social scrambling. The natural spot provided an escape, and hence
was a place of evanescent charm.[5] To leave it was to lose it, or at least
to lose all its efficaciousness, except for the bare recollection of it
memorialized in verse. Typically, the ending of William Crowe's
Lewesdon Hill (1788) is reminiscent of the turn to "pastures new" by
the speaker in Milton's "Lycidas," while its thrust is opposite:

> Now I descend
> To join the worldly croud; perchance to talk,
> To think, to act as they: then all these thoughts,
> That lift th' expanded heart above this spot
> To heavenly musing, these shall pass away
> (Even as this goodly prospect from my view)
> Hidden by near and earthy-rooted cares.
> So passeth human life; our better mind
> Is as a Sunday's garment, then put on
> When we have nought to do; but at our work
> We wear a worse for thrift. Of this enough:
> To-morrow for severer thought; but now
> To breakfast, and keep festival to-day.

In Coleridge and Wordsworth it is a confrontation, whether sublime or not, whether in the mode of ethos or pathos, which requires a working through—in the memory, in meditation, in the act of writing the poem—and must bring about a deepened understanding and a changed heart (see Lindenberger 23–26). In Wordsworth, particularly, the working through is sustained by a slow process of internalizing which readies a complex of thought and feeling for a sudden leap back to consciousness out of its mental hiding place. Hence the nature–experience is not evanescent but originating, not an escape but a passage across a threshold—the ramble become excursion become inner journey.

Both poets, and especially Wordsworth, were nourished by post-Augustan poetry because they found in it imperfect explorations of the relation between the mind and nature that suggested a dialectical process in consciousness. Wordsworth drew from this body of work, even from poems of insignificant poets, terminology for subject-object relationships. It is remarkable (even keeping in mind Wordsworth's beginnings as a loco-descriptive poet) how often key words or familiar images leap to the eye when we read Crowe or Bruce or Logan or Beattie. In *Lewesdon Hill,* for instance, the closing sequence pictures oblivion "following dark behind" as it devours the prey of time (lines 435–37). The conventional personification is not Wordsworthian, but the image of an eastern darkness pursuing at the poet's back as he gazes on the bright west is frequent in the later poet. A few lines later in Crowe we read about the "wondrous Power of modulated sound" and cannot help thinking of Wordsworth's title "On the Power of Sound" (*PW*2. 323); further down, the phrase "blended power" (line 452) recalls a central Wordsworthian term from the "Prospectus," "blended might" (70). There is a host of examples, some more

striking—even to groups of lines, like the following from Akenside's
The Pleasures of Imagination (1744), which Wordsworth might almost
have written if they were not quite so programmatic:

> Hence the breath
> Of life informing each organic frame,
> Hence the green earth, and wild resounding waves;
> Hence light and shade alternate, warmth and cold;
> And clear autumnal skies and vernal showers,
> And all the fair variety of things.
>
> (I.73–78)

Both poets have drawn, especially in the more trivial examples, on
stock diction or inevitable spirit-of-the-age terms; but the point is that
Wordsworth found these terms embodied in such forbears as Akenside and Crowe, and their embodiments, telling something of what he
was seeking, stocked his prodigious memory.

The contexts of the embodiments which provided him with the
material for his transmutings to some degree determined their shape.
Thus, in *Lewesdon Hill* black thoughts of time are followed by an
alleviating experience provided, in a sense, by time itself. The clock
strikes nine, and its chimes start ringing, to the poet's delight:

> O wondrous Power of modulated sound!
> Which like the air (whose all-obedient shape
> Thou makest thy slave) canst subtilly pervade
> The yielded avenues of sense, unlock
> The close affections, by some fairy path
> Winning an easy way through every ear,
> And with thine unsubstantial quality
> Holding in mighty chains the hearts of all;
> All, but some cold and sullen-temper'd spirits,
> Who feel no touch of sympathy or love.
>
> (442–51)

Though the thought is commonplace, the passage is a model, for a
poet in search of one, of a redemptive movement born out of a perception of what is there in the scene and internalized by meditation.
Crowe's "False-measured melody on crazy bells" (441) may have only
a coincidental relation to the "crazy old church-clock, / And the bewildered chimes" that bring about the resolution of Wordsworth's "The
Fountain" (*PW*4.71; composed 1799), but it is close enough to make
one wonder whether Wordsworth had stored Crowe's words away for

future use. On the other hand, Crowe's overly neat antithetically structured paradox of music's "unsubstantial quality / Holding in mighty chains the hearts of all" has nothing to do with Wordsworth's image in "The Power of Music" (*PW*2.217) of the giant who can't stand still because "The music stirs in him like wind through a tree"; for in that passage the later poet has broken through to a fresh vision of things consistent with his revisionary sense of nature, while Crowe is just lashing about with clichés. But the blind musician in "The Power of Music" spreading blessings with his "harmony merry and loud" is an assertion of a natural principle of compensation which Wordsworth could see at work in Crowe's crazily chiming bells, their delightful sound springing from the wounding strokes of iron time.

The fact that Crowe immediately rejects the blessing of music as "an empty pageant of sweet noise" which, once past, leaves "but an echo dwelling in the ear / Of the toy-taken fancy" (454, 456–57) does not affect Wordsworth's ability to read the bells as emblematic of a compensatory principle. The transformation or reverse valuation of such turns in his eighteenth-century predecessors is precisely what the Romantic poet's creative insights are constantly effecting in the great decade. The "echo dwelling in the ear" becomes a key to poiesis in *The Prelude*, as these previously quoted lines show:

> My own voice chear'd me, and, far more, the mind's
> Internal echo of the imperfect sound;
> To both I listen'd, drawing from them both
> A chearful confidence in things to come.
> (I.64–67)

That which is externalized—caught or produced by nature—and its internalized *semblable* together drive the poet's invention. Throughout, poiesis is a process of perceiving and creating, and these two functions, not to be disentangled, have an echoic relationship.

In this passage from the opening of *The Prelude* the focus is on the poet and his sense of renewed dedication to poetry, his "vernal promises" (I.50). The internal echo is the vision of perfection which gives purpose to the stammerings of actual performance in its first effort. The poet must listen to both, because the inner voice will remain forever insubstantial without the outer voice, which has the power of natural or real vibratory existence, and the finished poem must be both visionary and real, the product of a dialogue between what is actually uttered in the process of composition and its imaginative echo. Yet it is not finally clear which, inner or outer voice, is primary, more real in a subtler sense. Wordsworth keeps to the border territory

between inner and outer through strategies of vagueness in defining
forces which, he believes, seek balance by acting in reciprocal ways:

> I felt that the array
> Of outward circumstance and visible form
> Is to the pleasure of the human mind
> What passion makes it, that meanwhile the forms
> Of Nature have a passion in themselves
> That intermingles with those works of man
> To which she summons him. . . .
> (*Prelude* XII.286–92)

Thus the poet, standing "by Nature's side," can substantiate in his
poems a world that is

> fit
> To be transmitted and made visible
> To other eyes, as having for its base
> That whence our dignity originates,
> That which both gives it being and maintains
> A balance, an ennobling interchange
> Of action from within and from without,
> The excellence, pure spirit, and best power
> Both of the object seen, and eye that sees.
> (XII.371–79)

Because the ennobling interchange is ultimately vocal, the process
can be understood as one of echoing. The human voice travels from
its silent birth in the brain to its second birth in the vocal chords and
out into the natural world, to which it is now fitted. Rebounding, it
returns via the ear, altered by its union with nature's substance and
carrying intermixed in its changed but still similar vibrations a message from the natural world. Or the voice of nature passes first
through the ear into the brain, where it becomes fitted to human
mental process, and now travels back into nature, bringing the mind
to perceive natural presences hitherto ignored or barely sensed. And
then the presences into which the altered voice passes respond to the
perception: They are, or seem to be, humanized, associated effica-
ciously with human life.

This implicit echo structure, evolved from the methods of his
eighteenth-century predecessors, allows the poet to hold that the
mind is fitted to nature and nature to the mind, as he does explicitly in
the "Prospectus." It enables him to recognize the power of time, alter-

ations of psychological conditions, and other discontinuities of human experience—"fallings from us, vanishings"—and still assert in poem after poem an ultimate continuity. It is a troubled faith, certainly, asserted despite doubts, qualified in expression, and often in need of special attempts at poetic substantiation. These include the explicit use of echo as an image, or of its cohorts, reflection and afterimage, and frequently of its linear representation in repeated words, phrases, and syntax. These sorts of explicit and implicit doubling were something Wordsworth was endowed by his temperament and his psychological history to exploit, but he learned how to pursue them in part also through his encounters with the embodied concerns of his predecessors in the Age of Sensibility.

One of the most important of these concerns, often overlooked in the "poets of vision," as Patricia Meyer Spacks has called them, was the representation of auditory elements. Spacks has shown that the poetry of Thomson, Akenside, Collins, Gray, and Cowper brings into play all the senses of seeing, from the physical to the visionary, and that visual imagery held a central place in their ideas of poiesis, which foreran the general theoretical shift from an imitative to an expressive theory of poetry. But it is significant that she finds Thomson, early on, seeking to develop through visual imagery a statable meaning (a normative Augustan endeavor), and Cowper, in the later years, engaged in attempting to express feeling more directly (Spacks, chap. 1). The attainment of a strong voice under the aegis of expressive poetic practice is highly dependent on the embodiment of strong feeling; and one of the main routes to its embodiment is the exploitation of the auditory elements available to poets, both in verbal arrangement and in imagery. The search for voice in the poets of vision and other later eighteenth-century poets was tied to the expressive use of auditory perceptions.

They encountered the expressive use of auditory perceptions in their primary model of poetic power, Milton. "L'Allegro," "Il Penseroso," *Comus*, "At a Solemn Music," "Lycidas," and other central texts of the poets of vision are permeated with aural as well as visual effects; but it is important to understand that these purveyors of Miltonic devices approached sound in a spirit that reflected literary-historical changes in perception and favored the sort of rapprochement of mind and external nature so congenial to Wordsworth's ideas.

John Hollander has discussed the shift of attention in English poetry from the sound of music to the natural music of sound—outdoor sound.[6] The two Renaissance themes of music as a representation of universal order and music as a means of manipulating human passions were still alive and balanced in Milton. The blending of lore, intellect, and passion in the Jubal passage of *Paradise Lost* (XI.556–64) was made possible by a period which saw indoor music to be as much a part of Nature as what sounded in the fields and woods, its harmonies expressive of the soul, the voices of earthly creation, and the song of the spheres all at once; and it could represent this in convincing tropes. But music and verse began to split apart in the Baroque age, through ornamental practices in opera and song, and also through the increasing Baroque emphasis on the other power of music, its ability to manipulate the passions. This emphasis tended to relegate words to poetic argument; thus in the new conception, words addressed the intellect while music addressed the feelings. The relation of music to the Newtonian cosmos became unconvincing, and among the Augustans music began to be seen as mere embroidery of language, verbal argument and not verbal song now being more explicitly the poet's primary discipline. While the echo song of *Comus* implied in a vigorous turn that the corded shell, the ur-trope for the lurking place of music, was to be identified with the whole cope of the sky, the Augustans uninventively shrank the trope of the shell to a stock metaphor and often used it without allowing it an essential thematic function.

At the same time, however, music in the eighteenth century began to move out of doors to inhabit the pastoral surfaces of the earth. It became metaphorically identified with the sounds of nature, suggesting a new way to heal the split between music and verse. One grand symbol of this shift of locus from indoor culture to the outdoor border where it blends into the natural world is, as Hollander points out, the Aeolian harp: Blowing across its strings, the wind converts its rude untutored sound into music voiced on a human scale. Hollander shows a confusion to have arisen at this time between Hermes' corded tortoise shell and Triton's trumpeting spiral shell. The first was a natural object converted by divine power to cultural use as a harp or lyre; the second, in a fancy of relatively recent origin based on the similarity of its insides to the ear's helical sound tube, was imagined to contain and translate the sea roar for the human ear. This confusion is the perfect emblem of the movement of music into nature. The movement culminates in the English Romantic poets, who show no poetic interest in formal music of the indoor sort despite the contemporary flowering of German music and, in Coleridge's case at least, a genuine liking for it.

Blake, it is true, rejected the seashell as a reciprocal ear, asserting that it was attuned, by being fallen into the abyss of reasoning, only to rationalistic effects of discord and harmony and closed—unlike Milton's "evening ear"—to heaven. But the seashell was a positive image for Wordsworth, because it spoke of and through its element. As the dream passage on the shell and the stone in Book V of *The Prelude* so dramatically presents it, the seashell is the speaking-singing instrument which transposes the language of nature into meaningful song—"A loud prophetic blast of harmony, / An Ode, in passion utter'd" (V.96–97). Here it puts forth the ultimate message, apocalypse, with the sublime sound of the last trumpet, and so represents the complete fusion of verse and music—sound become the singing voice of prophecy. Human culture, the natural world, and a shadowy spiritual reality are united in a "scale of moral music" ("On the Power of Sound," *PW*2.323, line 170). Thus, in the vision of Book V of *The Prelude,* Wordsworth has achieved a harmonizing of realms equivalent to Milton's in that poet's use of music.

Wordsworth has done so, to state it in its simplest terms, by calling a voice out of nature, by converting—in a subtle and spiritual, rather than a crude and obvious, sense—outdoor sound to voice. Voice in the Renaissance was already music, because either song or human speech was representative of divine creation; mere noise represented chaos. The poetic sublime of the eighteenth century converted some noise into "good" sound:

> The sublime incorporates what had been previously considered the noises of chaos into the rural orchestra; torrents, the sounds of landslides, cataracts, thunder, and the sounds of storm all come to signal the authenticity of the *locus terribilis* even as the choir of birds and water and wind accompanies the lovely one, and the mingling of piping or song and waterfall . . . identifies a world in which poetry is creative and evocative force. (Hollander, "Music of Sound" 48–49)

But, although Wordsworth certainly read the eighteenth-century poetry of nature as a carrier of both the sublime and the picturesque, what most attracted him to it, when after his sublime and picturesque loco-descriptive beginnings he had begun to find his own way, was its power to imagine the brooding mind in the act of hearing a scene-haunting voice and making it into poetry. This representation of scenic voice might be mingled with exclamatory sublimity or picturesque description, but it could not be strictly identified with either. It was peculiarly attuned to presences that were hard to articulate, and it was more indirect and tenuous.

Hollander notes that in most Romantic attempts to transcendentalize the perceptual functions, sound had to take second place to sight because there was no term turning hearing into a transcendent activity in the same way as visionary vision could replace physical vision (45–46). Hearing is thus given the different, and ultimately deeper, role of mediating the mysterious energies, never to be manifested in clear and distinct form, that flow back and forth between the mind and nature as initially inarticulate feelings. Yet hearing has one power that vision does not: In the process of perceiving and articulating voice, it can evoke a direct response in the vocal chords and issue in poetry. The metaphorical chain of listening, ruminating the internal echo of sounds, re-sounding them mentally in words and phrases, and vocalizing them is as close as the poet can come to an experience of *natural making*. For the Romantic poet, and especially Wordsworth, to indite out of the mind's direct contact with nature was to find authentic voice.

There is a seeming paradox in this idea, since to become a medium for the voice of the other would seem to suppress the voice of the self. But Wordsworth always took it for granted that "unmediated" experience involved perceiving *and* creating. He could thus feel that the eighteenth-century poets he cared about were, in their search for voice, attempting unmediated expressions of the imagination in their nature poetry. And he could see that their journey led, as he knew his own must, through Milton. They not only looked for Miltonic personifications in the landscape but were listening to the presences his personifications constellated in it. The voices of these presences could articulate, or at least give a sort of substance to, *numina*, powers that were the correlatives of obscure feelings of the observer in flight from the pressures of daily life. These feelings, whether personal, social, or religious, were rendered homeless and vague by the loss of belief in the metaphor of a divine order which could name and accommodate—or exorcise—them. To give them a communicable shape was to rescue the prophetic function of poetry from the abyss of silence into which it had fallen under the hounding of Enlightenment attempts to eliminate superstition and to reform institutionalized magical views of the cosmos. In the eyes of post-Augustan poets, poetry had been restricted to witty argument playfully embroidered, and in the hands of lesser geniuses than Pope had become too discursive, too unimaginative. They turned back to Milton because he was the great example of an enlightened mind which could somehow preserve the energy of numinous presences, holding them in tension with the Christian symbols that shaped his view of things and thus enlarging that view into a richer representation of Nature.

Milton's poetry is resonant in every way: through its literary allusions and associations, through the sonority of its syllables, through the range of a diction which represents the central texts of Renaissance education, through its links with biblical rhetoric, imagery, and ideas, through its visionary suggestiveness, and—most important to the argument here—through its powerful metaphors of sound. Music for Milton is a central image of "good" sound, and the process mediating the role of divinely originated music on earth is echo.

In *Comus* the metaphor is explicit:

> Sweet Echo, sweetest Nymph that liv'st unseen
> Within thy airy shell
> By slow *Meander's* margent green,
> And in the violet-embroider'd vale
> Where the love-lorn Nightingale
> Nightly to thee her sad Song mourneth well.
>
> Canst thou not tell me of a gentle Pair
> That likest thy *Narcissus* are?
> O if thou have
> Hid them in some flow'ry Cave,
> Tell me but where,
> Sweet Queen of Parley, Daughter of the Sphere,
> So mayst thou be translated to the skies,
> And give resounding grace to all Heav'n's Harmonies.
>   (230–43)

The translation of Echo to the skies is here only a promise, since it is proleptic of the not-yet-fully expounded redemptive theme of *Comus:* the transformation of the pagan-divine to the Christian-heavenly by the power of Chastity. But its function is implicit in its characteristics—it inhabits the whole corded shell of the sky, being the "Daughter of the Sphere" which God created *ab origine,* and the "resounding grace" it is to give to all the harmonies of heaven is merely an extension of the grace (a technical term of music as well as a religious one) it gives to the nightingale. It is, in effect, the voice of the divine order on earth.

At the same time, it is the amplification of sound generated on earth: It vocalizes from the Book of God, the songbook of natural creation. Thus Milton, grounding himself in a sense of the primal unity of human speech, human music, the pure sounds of physical nature, and the music of the spheres, is able to experiment with the representation of sound in his companion poems, which explore the earthly potentialities of life before we come "To live with [God], and sing in endless morn of light" ("At a Solemn Music" 28). These poems are filled with sound imagery. Among the "horrid shapes" that create "L'Allegro"'s setting for Melancholy are "shrieks" and a singing

"night-Raven," and the Mirth that opposes Melancholy is accompanied by a "Wind that breathes the Spring" and "Quips," among other
more visual figures. As the allegrian poet begins his imagined life with
Mirth "in unreproved pleasures free," he hears the lark sing at dawn
to "startle the dull night" and then "bid good-morrow" at his window
as day comes on. The cock responds "with lively din" as the "Hounds
and horn" echo shrilly through the wood; and these are followed by
the whistling plowman, the singing milkmaid, the mower whetting his
scythe, and the shepherd telling his tale (whether it is story or sheep
he is telling, he does it aloud). "Merry Bells" and "jocund rebecs"
accompany the dancing youth, and story-telling time follows their
holiday in the sun (concluded by the image of the goblin flinging out
of doors "Ere the first Cock his Matin rings"). As "whispering Winds"
lull these rural figures to sleep, the speaker goes to the city to join "the
busy hum of men" and hear learned Jonsonian actors declaim or
Shakespeare "Warble his native Wood-notes wild."

These twenty auditory representations are climaxed by the long,
brilliant imaging of the "*Lydian* Airs"—at once melodies and southern
breezes—"married to immortal verse." Their "untwisting all the
chains that tie / The hidden soul of harmony," an aural-visual image
that suggests both fulfillment in the overwhelming freedom of ecstasy
and dissolution into a chaos of pleasure, completes the poet's Or-
phean quest and closes the poem on an apparently triumphant note.
But this note is morally ambiguous. The ambiguity is brought to focus
in the phrase which, following the packing off of the attendants on
Melancholy, inaugurates the contrasting adventure with familiar,
everyday "unreproved pleasures free." There is in the human psyche
a genuine desire for freedom which opens the way to inner development when it is translated into action, and there is the infantile lust for
freedom to indulge in regressive gratifications. It is often difficult to
tell them apart when the urge is still wholly mental and there has been
no commitment to action. "Unreproved pleasures free" could describe either an autoerotic urge or a genuine desire to enlarge the self.

This ambiguity cannot be fully resolved, since what Milton has created in "L'Allegro" is a mixture of both sorts of longing, indistinguish-
able except in relation to the contrasting "Il Penseroso," where a morally finer mixture is shown. Through the experience of the second
poem we can reflect on the fatally earthbound, self-mazing quality of
the choice of life in "L'Allegro." And we can see, among other things,
that the sounds of "L'Allegro"—the sounds, whether human or nonhuman, of rural or urban life—are echoes of its central music. They
speak of the natural order with a freshness still potent today, but they
are the slanted perceptions of an observer listening for Lydian airs. As

convincing voices of this world, they are exhilarating; as exclusively voices of this world, they are tainted.

In "Il Penseroso" there are far fewer aural images, and many of these describe unearthly, distant, or absent sounds. Such subtle reductions of sound in "Il Penseroso" are no doubt related to Milton's Baroque conviction that sound as music or speech was the great manipulator of human passions, and that hearing, as the sense-conduit more liable to invite self-gratifying indulgence, was lower on the moral-religious scale than sight. To return again to the point raised by Hollander, there is no auditory term parallel to "vision": We can have "insight" but not "inhearing"; and though we can "listen in," a thoroughly extroverted process, we cannot "en-listen," an introverted action by which we might perform the auditory counterpart of "envisioning."

But of course there are ways of suggesting by periphrasis and context a spiritual application of hearing equivalent to that of sight, and Milton has elaborated them in "Il Penseroso." Indeed, the work of this poem being aimed at the redemption of the earthbound, Milton expressly makes the transformation of the cruder sense one of its major movements. He gives hearing the power to perceive more than meets the ear and thus to manipulate upward the most stubborn of resisters to accord with the divine, the self-gratifying, pleasure-seeking impulse; and he links it to the principle of divine harmony, which can be expressed in music, so that it is the ultimate instrument of rescue—of bringing "*through mine ear . . .* all Heav'n before mine *eyes*" (164, 166; italics added). By the end of the poem, listening has become a primary way of "seeing" the invisible.

Even more obviously than in "L'Allegro," then, the sounds of "Il Penseroso" are keyed observations of a poetic observer able to perceive, under the aegis of Melancholy, the divine order. They are echoes, with earthly tonalities, of music from the cope of heaven. I have ignored the parallel movement of the poem's visual turns (many sight images are in fact unseen, for example) in order to emphasize that, along with the effects on the poets of vision of the visual-visionary elements in Milton's minor poems, the aural-transcendental elements had an equally potent influence on their practice. In their desire to find a realm of expansive poetic freedom and power, they let the moral ambiguities of "L'Allegro" slide from view and fused the two companion poems into a single resonant source of nature consciousness. Allegrian sensuality, license, and plenitude were joined with penserosan insight and "inhearing," and the hybrid, playfully or seriously conjuring sublime, semidivine presences in nature, vigorously celebrated this world. Along with visualized elements of sensuous arcana, there are voices. These make themselves heard through the

sounds of nature, and at their most "visionary" often speak through
the persona of Echo:

> Can gilt alcoves, can marble-mimic gods,
> Parterres embroider'd, obelisks, and urns,
> Of high relief; can the long, spreading lake,
> Or vista lessening to the sight; can Stow,
> With all her Attic fanes, such raptures raise,
> As the thrush-haunted copse, where lightly leaps
> The fearful fawn the rustling leaves along,
> And the brisk squirrel sports from bough to bough,
> While from an hollow oak, whose naked roots
> O'erhang a pensive rill, the busy bees
> Hum drowsy lullabies? The bards of old,
> Fair Nature's friends, sought such retreats, to charm
> Sweet Echo with their songs; oft too they met,
> In summer evenings, near sequester'd bowers,
> Or mountain-nymph, or Muse, and eager learnt
> The moral strains she taught to mend mankind.
>   (Joseph Warton, "The Enthusiast" 5–20)

In Warton's demotion of the tailored garden landscapes created by
eighteenth-century taste in favor of the wilder natural scene, he has
given a visual emphasis to his image of the former and an aural emphasis to his images of the latter. Indeed, in this characteristic passage, the
nature spot, in its sequestration, has almost become the cavern of Echo,
of whom mountain-nymph and muse are counterparts—Echo being
the voice the poet wakes out of nature, the mountain-nymph or muse
the wisdom that speaks through the wakened Echo. Mindful of his
source in "Il Penseroso" and emphasizing hearing (note the "rustling
leaves," the "pensive rill," the bees with their "drowsy lullabies," the
singing bards, and so on), Warton tells us he will invoke Contemplation
to lift him above the earth and "purge my ears, / That I may hear the
rolling planets' song, / And tuneful turning spheres" (208–10). He
immediately adds a more earthly alternative drawn from the more
earthy Shakespeare, but still ear-oriented:

> if this be barr'd,
> The little Fays that dance in neighbouring dales,
> Sipping the night-dew, while they laugh and love,
> Shall charm me with aerial notes.
>   (210–13)

And he ends with a Hesperidean vision of himself transported to "western climes," where he can celebrate the natural world in recovered innocence. He compares his sequestration to the "Serenely gay" court of Thetis beneath the turbulent sea, and ends with an image that marries divine music, verse, and natural sound, as "according lutes / Grace the soft warbles of her honied voice" (251–52).

The marriage of divine music, verse, and natural sound is celebrated more profoundly by Collins. In many ways, Collins represents for Wordsworth the model example of the poet struggling to win a voice out of nature, for he is successful, when he is successful, because he is able to naturalize his vision by establishing a genuine echoic relation between his poetic consciousness and the external scene. That this is a central concern of Collins is emphasized by his evoking external nature in a poem in which it need not appear at all—"The Passions. An Ode for Music." Here Collins is writing in a traditional form—the musical ode—which suits his semi-allegorical style. This subgenre of the ode had become a bearer of Baroque ideas about the psychological relationship between music and the human passions, whose nosological spectrum was determined by Renaissance psychology. These are seen in the grand models of the subgenre, Dryden's "A Song for St. Cecilia's Day" and "Alexander's Feast." Collins differentiates his procedure from Dryden's by his special treatment of personification. As in other poems of his, the emotions acting in his argument are more than abstract titles; they are personae. But as personae they are only dimly realized, concrete in faint touches. They are detached from the psyche, objectified by being brought on stage to act; yet rather than figures in the full sense, they are psychological templates in motion. And Collins gives the Baroque tradition a further twist by having the passions seize the appropriate instruments and express *themselves*, instead of having them conjured into life by the hand of a musical artist.

This original twist led the poet to set his characters in an outdoor scene, an imaginative device which in turn brought about a confrontation of three ideas of music previously discussed—the old one of music as a man-created, indoor-concerted analogy of the structural harmony of the universe, the Baroque one of music as expressing and manipulating the emotions, and the new one of music as the sounds of God-created things in the out-of-doors. In all three cases music is "the sound of nature," but in the first instance it is the echo of *natura naturans*, the voice of the cosmic principle of order, and in the other two it is the echo of *natura naturata*. All, for the religious mind, speak of God, but in practical ways these ideas of music are quite different from one another. The shift between the high Renaissance and the

Romantic period, from the cosmic to the earthly and from the music of praise to the praise of verbal music, is what John Hollander has called "the untuning of the sky" in his book of that name. And in "Wordsworth and the Music of Sound" Hollander notes that Collins's ode on the passions forms "the most important stage in the untuning of the musical ode." Collins's primary aim is not the representation of sound but the presentation of the emotions as an orchestra. This entails a break with the cosmic analogy and a peculiar concentration on metaphorical images of the human psyche. Further, by making musicians of the passions, Collins has transformed his poem from a *laus musicae* into one "about language and feeling, and hence, about poetic tradition" ("Music of Sound" 71).

And finally, to elaborate on Hollander's ideas, in placing this orchestra scenically out of doors, Collins has explicitly linked the mind and nature, giving a naturalized meaning to the psycho-musical effect of outdoor sounds. By embodying the newer idea of music while holding on to Baroque musical psychology, he has given nature a role in the economy of the passions and given the mind a role in the ordering or interpreting of natural life. In other words, he has set up an echoic relationship between man and nature.

This relationship is overt in the passage on Hope:

> But thou, O Hope, with eyes so fair,
>   What was thy delightful measure?
> Still it whispered promised pleasure,
>   And bade the lovely scenes at distance hail!
> Still would her touch the strain prolong,
>   And from the rocks, the woods, the vale,
> She called on Echo still through all the song;
>   And, where her sweetest theme she chose,
>   A soft responsive voice was heard at every close,
> And Hope enchanted smiled, and waved her golden hair.
>   ("The Passions" 29–38)

The echo trope is an old pastoral motif, but in the context of this poem it argues the reciprocal dependence of psyche and Gea, adding a note of healing. The destructive passions—Fear, Anger, Despair, Revenge, Jealousy—can scarcely order themselves sufficiently to play music on their instruments, and hence evoke no response from nature.[7] The healing ones, however—Hope, Miltonic Melancholy, Cheerfulness, Joy, Love, Mirth—not only evoke a response but are imagined as part of the natural scene, blending into it. Hope's golden hair, tossing about the smile raised by Echo's reply, suggests wheat or grasses in the vale.

Melancholy, retired in "her wild sequestered seat," permeates "In notes
by distance made more sweet" the whole of the scene about her and gets
it to join in, to echo back in "hollow murmurs" or otherwise express her
sound, which is a form of her being (lines 59, 60, 68).

Hollander has perceived in the passage on Melancholy "an almost
canonical instance of the expressive tone-sound *blending*":

> it is Melancholy's aria with obbligato of *cor anglais* which gives
> its modality to the moving water resounding in the sublime
> landscape. The mingling is total and reciprocal, for the tradi-
> tional authenticating force of the outdoor sound-scene is a nec-
> essary part of the personification itself. ("Music of Sound" 73)

I would add that though the landscape is sublime in the penserosan
sense, it is nonetheless expressively natural and dimly humanized;
and though the outdoor sound-scene is traditional, its having been cut
loose from the music of the spheres and the concert chamber, and
approximated to the human psyche, forms the prime stuff of the new
poetry Wordsworth is to dream into form. The leading thread is the
implied blending of mind and nature.

This blending achieves its finest expression in Collins's finest poem,
"Ode to Evening." Like so many other odes of Collins, this one embodies the search for poetic voice, incorporating once more the conventions of the progress theme and the prayer for poetic inspiration.
The difference is that, as in the strong Romantic odes and crisis lyrics,
it succeeds in its invocation of poetic powers by the very act of invoking them, the poet finding voice in the process of calling it out of the
scene.

One reason for this novelty is that what Collins personifies cannot
be dissociated from external nature, and he sees to it that Evening's
ties to rural landscape are firmly stated. They are stated by Collins's
use of description, of pastoral diction, and of literary echo—for example, his borrowing from Virgil's first eclogue, Spenser's *Faerie Queene*
and *Hymne to Heavenly Love*, Milton's Nativity Ode, "Il Penseroso,"
Comus, and description of Eden in *Paradise Lost*, Pope's *Windsor Forest*.
At the same time, the associations of Evening with deep thought are
emphasized: her solemnity, her calm and gentle pensiveness, her religious melancholy, her shadowiness (half presence of dusky substance,
half absence of busy, distracting light)—all aspects of the interior landscape of meditation. Then again she is the westering muse and a local
Hesperidean semidivinity—a characteristic fusion seen in the personifications of numinosity in poets like the Wartons, or Akenside when
he represents "sylvan powers."

Geoffrey Hartman, discussing the forces at play in the figure of Evening, shows not only that the *genius loci* is central but that it is used in a fresh way. Noting W. K. Wimsatt's observation that Romantic poems represent landscape as pregnant at once with its own and a transcendent spirit, and Martin Price's equivalent observation of Evening's dual role as a divine person and the energy immanent in the scene, Hartman says the fusion is possible because

> Evening has a double nature modeled on that of the genius loci. As spirit of place, she is both spirit and place. She is also, as the poem makes clear, a divine guide ("Now teach me," "Then lead me") and a wisdom figure who outlives temporal change (lines 41 ff). Collins's Evening is virtually the guide, guardian, and nurse of the poet's moral being. These functions belonged preeminently to the genius loci. (*Beyond Formalism* 321)

While in Milton, Pope, and Gray personifications are distant figures, in Collins the web

> weaving together person and element is complete. . . . If Collins is inspired by the ancient concept of the genius loci, he is differently inspired. . . .
> The new poetry projects a sacred marriage: that of the poet's genius with the genius loci. To invoke the ghost in the landscape is only preparatory to a deeper, ceremonial merging of the poet's spirit and the spirit of place—hence the new structure of fusion. (ibid. 322)

The lines which most forcefully present this fusion as the achievement of poetic voice are those expressing the speaker's direct plea to Evening:

> Now teach me, maid composed,
>   To breathe some softened strain,
> Whose numbers stealing through thy darkening vale
> May not unseemly with its stillness suit;
>   As musing slow, I hail
>   Thy genial loved return!
>
> (15–20)

The "softened strain" the poet seeks is in fact the hailing he engages in while "musing slow." His mind and Evening's presence become one in this deep, dusk-calmed thought, which is reflection in the sense of mirroring or identifying, as well as in the sense of meditating—"contemplating," exchanging nuclear poetic RNA to form coordinate templates of presence. And with their presences coordinated, their songs becoming one, the poet has been taught to sing to Evening with her own music. This is authentic poetic voice.

In Hartman's words, Evening is a spirit of place because she is "a regent ('Thy Springs,' 'Thy darkening Vale'), and the region governed is less a specific country than the West, the *Abendland*," so that it is "the Westering of the Spirit which is hailed" (*Beyond Formalism* 323). If we accept this, we can see the poem as fusing classical, Enlightenment, and proto-Romantic motifs. Its voice attains the numinosity and authenticity of classical naturalism without the artificiality of dead classicizing convention; its truth reflects the humanistic, demythologizing Enlightenment spirit, conscious of assuming the mantle of superior refinement in knowledge, without the worn-out didactic and glossy verbal programming of late neoclassical poetry; and it opens the way to participation in the Romantic "sense of Being" without either killing dogma or mystical pantheism. It may be true that "an alliance of the poetical genius with a Western or English climate remains doubtful" (*Beyond Formalism* 323). Yet such a model attracted the emerging Wordsworth seeking his own voice—seeking it in a mental landscape embodying a unique experience of nature, an altered idea of the Enlightenment, and a new sense of literary tradition.

ECHO AS ONTOLOGY

Granting that Collins's triumphant blending of mind and scene in the "Ode to Evening" was irresistible to a poet seeking to express a unique sense of the natural world, we may also see that the concept of echoing embodied in it prompted Wordsworth to go beyond merely refining the traditional schemas of nature poetry. He was not standing at the same point of vantage as his eighteenth-century predecessors. Like them, he had to struggle to find his voice, but unlike them he had no crippling sense of inferiority and because of his mystical experiences no need to work at calling a voice out of nature. This relative freedom was also a freedom from confining conventions with which the eighteenth-century poets had to contend. Thus he could afford to indulge an impulse to demythologize the modes of nature poetry he adopted in order to enhance (so he imagined) the direct mediation of nature itself.

Yet this process of demythologizing in the interests of naturalizing led to remythologizing as well. I think Wordsworth's imagination entertained an idea of utterance as an originating power. This idea was an element of a personal ontology which aimed to undo the deistic idea of God as maker he so abhorred, substituting speech for the deist's absconded artificer as the agent of genesis. Utterance poetically viewed becomes the source of being and consciousness, and thus supports the role of the poet as renewer of human life.

In an early fragment embodying a rudimentary form of this myth of utterance, written at Alfoxden, the speaker attempts not to call a voice out of nature but to explain the voice he heard spontaneously, a voice that gave him a paradoxical "eternity feeling." He is standing before three knots of fir trees "too formally arranged," his "favourite station when the winds were up":

> Right opposite
> The central clump I loved to stand and hear
> The wind come on and touch the several groves
> Each after each, and thence in the dark night
> Elicit all proportions of sweet sounds
> As from an instrument. "The strains are passed,"
> Thus often to myself I said, "the sounds
> Even while they are approaching are gone by,
> And now they are more distant, more and more.
> O listen, listen how they wind away
> Still heard they wind away, heard yet and yet,
> While the last touch they leave upon the sense
> Is sweeter than whate'er was heard before,
> And seems to say that they can never die."
>
> (PW5.342)

The fragment, as Hollander has shown, exemplifies the way Wordsworth naturalizes a conventional figure for representing the blending of human consciousness and the landscape (the aeolian harp, imaged here by the trees) through a revitalized use of aural tropes, images, and syntactical or sonantal devices. Particularly prominent is the verbal doubling, which, "ranging from the idiomatic 'more and more' echoing and reechoing the 'more distant,' through the 'listen, listen' and the repeated 'wind away' with the echoing senses of 'blow,' 'twist,' and almost 'wend' (as of 'way'), culminates in the last 'yet and yet' of lingering audibility" ("Music of Sound" 66). The effect of this doubling is to support the final assertion that what is at first imaged as passing has enduring life. Thus, although the "doublings and amplifi-

cations are finally echoed in the literal sense of 'die,' which outlasts . . .
the figurative one" of musical cadence, the term "die" is negated—not
simply by the syntax but by the vitality of the poetic utterance. As
Hollander notes, it is the moment of experience itself, the transformed act of hearing, which seems to become immortal (ibid. 67).

Utterance here has the power to transform the act of hearing, in
part because it evokes and expresses immortal longings, in part because it is associated with what in Wordsworth's poetic orientation is
primal or ultimate. Sound for him, more directly than sight, can beat a
sensory path through the faded bracken of conventions (intellectual
wit, picturesque or mock-sublime detail, physicotheological rhetor-
icism), and put him in touch with the origin or end of the earth, or of
his own life on it. He tells us that in his solitary childhood night
rambles he

> felt whate'er there is of power in sound
> To breathe an elevated mood, by form
> Or image unprofaned; and I would stand,
> Beneath some rock, listening to sounds that are
> The ghostly language of the ancient earth,
> Or make their dim abode in distant winds.
> Thence did I drink the visionary power.
> (*Prelude* II.324–30)

A famous episode of guilt is expressed in visual terms—the mountain
striding after him in the boat-stealing scene—but, strikingly, in the
deeper reaches of this guilt the eye is baffled:

> and after I had seen
> That spectacle, for many days my brain
> Work'd with a dim and undetermin'd sense
> Of unknown modes of being; in my thoughts
> There was a darkness—call it solitude,
> Or blank desertion—no familiar shapes
> Of hourly objects, images of trees,
> Of sea or sky, no colours of green fields,
> But huge and mighty Forms that do not live
> Like living men mov'd slowly through my mind
> By day, and were the trouble of my dreams.
> (*Prelude* I.417–27)

The sense of hearing more easily conveys radical otherness than the
sense of sight, as when in another guilty episode he hears

> Low breathings coming after me, and sounds
> Of undistinguishable motion, steps
> Almost as silent as the turf they trod.
>   (*Prelude* I.330–32)

Or sound may lend this power to the visual, as in "Tintern Abbey": "with an *eye made quiet* by the *power* / *Of harmony*, and the deep power of joy, / We *see into* the life of things" (47–49; italics mine), or in the following:

>   Oh! when I have hung
> Above the raven's nest, by knots of grass
> And half-inch fissures in the slippery rock
> But ill sustain'd, and almost, as it seem'd,
> Suspended by the blast which blew amain,
> Shouldering the naked crag; Oh! at that time,
> While on the perilous ridge I hung alone,
> With what strange utterance did the loud dry wind
> Blow through my ears! the sky seem'd not a sky
> Of earth, and with what motion mov'd the clouds!
>   (*Prelude* I.341–50)

What Wordsworth called "audible seclusions" (*Prelude* VIII.794)—sounds contained within visually sequestered scenes (really versions of the classical locus of Echo, the cavern)—reach the feelings by a straighter path, often with intimations of being that are harder to articulate rationally, and always with a phenomenal otherness that in being perceived enlarges simultaneously the consciousness and love of the listening subject:

>   in all things
> I saw one life, and felt that it was joy.
> One song they sang, and it was audible,
> Most audible then when the fleshly ear,
> O'ercome by grosser prelude of that strain,
> Forgot its functions, and slept undisturb'd.
>   (*Prelude* II.429–34)

The inner ear experiences the full power of the "vision," transmuted as we read from a visual to an aural intimation.

Another passage of *The Prelude* subtly posits a link between voice and life.

Wisdom and Spirit of the universe!
Thou Soul that art the Eternity of Thought!
That giv'st to forms and images a breath
And everlasting motion! not in vain,
By day or star-light thus from my first dawn
Of Childhood didst Thou intertwine for me
The passions that build up our human Soul,
Not with the mean and vulgar works of Man,
But with high objects, with enduring things,
With life and nature, purifying thus
The elements of feeling and of thought,
And sanctifying, by such discipline,
Both pain and fear, until we recognize
A grandeur in the beatings of the heart.

(I.428–41)

This meditation on the early education of the poet by nature flows out of a celebratory invocation to an *anima mundi* which, by giving the natural world breath and motion, endows it with a speaking life. "Motion" metonymically defines an active universe; "breath" metaphorically defines the universal quality of life and speech (as in biblical, folk, and Greek traditions). Wordsworth uses both together in a totalizing hendiadys ("breath / And everlasting motion") which constitutes an image of originary voice—divine breath expelled into the void, where it establishes external nature as its echo.

Indeed voice would appear to reach even further, dominating the visual while subsuming conceptions of both genesis and apocalypse:

A Voice to Light gave Being;
To Time, and Man his earth-born chronicler;
A Voice shall finish doubt and dim foreseeing,
And sweep away life's visionary stir.

("On the Power of Sound," *PW*2.330)

But it functions most importantly in Wordsworth's poetic conceptions of genesis, which are elaborated in the first three stanzas of the Intimations Ode. These stanzas present a revision of the biblical account— "And God said, Let there be light. And there was light"—since the light, a "glorious birth," fades and cannot endure. By implication, the original fiat is altered to "Let there be voice," which brings into existence a power that continually generates more life. Voice gives being to light, though in progressively more inward ways, over and over; as breath and motion, it becomes the timely utterance which deals with loss and sorrow, bringing relief and strength to the mind. It blows through the trumpets of the cataracts (25), throngs the mountain with echoes (27), draws winds from the stasis of death or the sleep before rebirth (28), reconnects the "now" (19) of mental grief with a relational "Thou" (34, 109, 111)—nature's representative child of joy—by means of those feelings that awaken through passion to the shout of being, "the fullness of . . . bliss" (41). The reborn poet can thus say, toward the end of stanza IV, "I hear, I hear, with joy I hear!" (50).

The rebirth only prepares the way to deal more fully with the problem of vision, as the question of the fled visionary gleam returns and new anxieties present themselves. Yet there is already a difference: those things the eye sees—the "Tree, of many, one" (51), the field (52), and the "Pansy at my feet" (54)—now *speak*, albeit of something that is gone. The glorious light fades, nothing can prevent the "Fallings from us, vanishings" (144); but "The song of thanks and praise," celebrating "obstinate questionings" (141–42), transmutes them into an inward vision of the "immortal sea / Which brought us hither" (164–65)—a vision inclusive of sight and hearing, in which we can

> see the Children sport upon the shore,
> And hear the mighty waters rolling evermore.
>
> (167–68)

This vision suggests that poetic utterance is the externalizing of what has first been deeply internalized, made the "internal echo" of what was initially perceived, whether within or without. The various perceptions are united as they are converted into thought. The heart is brought into the equation by this internalizing process, seemingly elevated to be the seat of deepest thought—of "primal sympathy," of "soothing thoughts that spring / Out of human suffering," of "faith that looks through death," and even of "the philosophic mind"—for the ability to live under the "habitual sway" of nature depends on the observer's feeling its might in his "heart of hearts" (stanzas X–XI).

Historically, it is music, whether perfectly wedded to verse in the ancient Greek fashion or, in the Baroque fashion, felt to be a sphere-born sister art that transforms the feelings into inward mediators of reality; but in the poet for whom pure song or instrumental music has lost its conjugal and cosmic functions, it is the music of poetic utterance that makes the heart fully conscious and the images of nature vocal. As in a responsory, nature becomes (in the words of *The Prelude*) "the speaking face of earth and heaven" (V.12) in answer to the heart and to the mind of man, which "is fram'd even like the breath / And harmony of music" (I.351–52). The power of utterance therefore is the vehicle of life in this poet's vision of things, and the act of uttering, though it may take years to complete itself, is the constituting act, the Wordsworthian genesis.

The conception of utterance as genesis is not something that Wordsworth worked out metaphysically or theologically. Not only was he uninterested in, and maybe incapable of, philosophical speculation of that sort, he did not even feel compelled to deal radically with the theism to which he clung, like so many Enlightenment figures. Instead, he elaborated it into an unsystematic outlook that Lamb called "natural methodism" and that Richard Brantley thinks suffused his thought in all periods.[8] Yet even granting that Wordsworth's way of reading nature and using it in his poems has important links with the Methodism of his day, his religious views were not fully coherent and included, despite disavowals, heterodoxies. Thus the universe constituted by his poetry in the great decade seems to declare the independence of nature, making the traditional Artificer-Creator (as opposed to nature's animating spirit) so vague and poetically ineffectual as to be frequently elided:

> Should earth by inward throes be wrench'd throughout,
> Or fire be sent from far to wither all
> Her pleasant habitations, and dry up
> Old Ocean in his bed left sing'd and bare,
> Yet would the living Presence still subsist
> Victorious; and composure would ensue,
> And kindlings like the morning; presage sure,
> Though slow, perhaps, of a returning day.[9]
>
> (*Prelude* V.29–36)

Nature in Wordsworth seems more a force than a product of creation, fundamentally enduring rather than mutable. In this implicit sense, nature is a given, and thus genesis is not the beginning of everything. If it were, the fiat, "Let there be voice," would be a self-defeating paradox, since there would be a preexistent entity giving existence to another that is in fact itself—a voice creating voice. This paradox is resolved if we allow that Wordsworth's genesis does not *produce* nature, or the bodily image of nature, but *reproduces* the animating principle that permits us to participate in nature and hence achieve fullness of being. This animating principle is most fundamentally metaphorized as utterance: breath and motion combined as speech. Milton speaks of "the mysterious power and efficacy of that divine voice which went forth in the beginning, and to which, as to a perpetual command, all things have since paid obedience" (*The Christian Doctrine*, Hughes 989). What the fiat creates in Wordsworth's view, however, is not something out of nothing, but a power of duplication of itself: not "Let there be sound" in an absolute sense, but "Let there be a power of voice in nature like mine"; that is, "Let there be echo."

That voice in nature and man is echoic, mirroring the speech of the "sovereign Intellect," in no way devalues it. The duplicating action has biblical precedent in another divine fiat: "Let us make man in our image, after our likeness" (Genesis 1.6). And remaking man, remaking the heart of man through fostering his concourse with nature, is Wordsworth's main poetic purpose. In his revaluative way, the poet is reversing the classical myth of Echo, who through confrontation with the destructive self-love of Narcissus was drained of her humanity, bereft of original speech. In Wordsworth, narcissistic man, awakened to otherness by attending to the alien yet conformable face of nature, is rehumanized by hearing it speak—that is, brought to love of otherness by realizing that its speech echoes original life or being, of which there is already an echo in himself. The internal and external echoes allow a common language, stimulating man to a dialogue with nature which brings about an internalizing process leading to the fullest participation in being. All aspects of being, from the sovereign Intellect to the inmost recesses of the heart, are mediated by voice. Voice, that most human of powers, ties all of existence together, as all parts echo each other in the expression of their original life.

This mediating power of voice also helps us to see why echoing is involved in another concern of the poet's—the articulation of insights into the origin, development, flowering, and continuation of consciousness. His vision here is proto-tragic. Coming to consciousness—the dramatic action of so many of his stronger lyrics—is his primary model for the remaking of alienated man, and yet it is the source of the problematic issues of existence with which as a true humanist he must struggle. Thus, each stage brings forward at once something essential to spiritual maturation and something that appears to negate it. The origin of consciousness engenders what is most human but also involves the incorporation of otherness which threatens the self; the development of consciousness brings spiritual growth but also inescapably entails loss; the flowering of consciousness opens us to participation in being but also makes us painfully aware of nonbeing or death; the continuation of consciousness through stubborn obstacles images redemption but is shadowed by all the discontinuities which day-to-day living forces on us.

This vision of consciousness often produces an echo structure in the poetry. For instance, a link between the origination of consciousness and the spiritual importance of recalling earlier stages of the self is forged in the Intimations Ode. Here the idea of the "spot of time" is altered to refer to Platonic images of preexistence, and recollection becomes an imaginative instrument of redemption, made all the stronger by being set against opposed perspectives: the demythologized view of human life as creeping habit—steadily increasing, even compulsively courted—and as descent through continual losses into the darkness of the grave. What gives vitality to Wordsworth's mythologem of recollection is its closeness to the power center of his imagination: It is another form of echo—the echoing of the past in the present.

The literary process so central to Wordsworth's method of composition, comprising quotation, imitation, nonconfrontational reference, and strong allusion, is also a form of echoing. It is thus consonant with the Wordsworthian vision to make echoing, which implies the sister-term "voice," a master metaphor. The poet who begins as a descriptive writer with an eye which "Could find no surface where its power might sleep" (*Prelude* III.164), ruling his consciousness with a tyranny he was determined to escape from (XI.171–84), and ends by finding his true voice in a new naturalism that blends aural and visual perception, puts echoic process at the center of his poetry.

In the Intimations Ode, sound counteracts sight to the point of redeeming it, or redeeming the human condition of loss which sight reveals. As the birds sing and the lambs bound to the tabor, and the celebrants pipe and play—all aural affirmations of feeling at heart "the gladness of the May" (175)—the poet will join them in thought. His thought is the internal echo, sound amplified by structured feeling, that allows him to accept the fading away of radiance and declare his unsevered love of nature.

In relation to voice, the famous final image of thoughts that lie too deep for tears appears paradoxical. It seems to reduce the poet to silence. But it is only a deeper internalizing of speech, for these thoughts are verbal or proto-verbal, not a train of formed images, and the tears they do not provoke would have provided a relatively shallow and incoherent translation. "To me the meanest flower that blows can give / Thoughts that do often lie too deep for tears": the verb "blow," then still a standard term for "bloom," overtly creates a visual image of process, but the aural sense of "blow" is also at work here. The character of the image is twofold, as it is earlier, when the ambiguously aural and visual cataracts "blow their trumpets from the steep," and through a "timely utterance" the poet comes to a first stage of renewal. The hiddenness of the vocal element in the poem's final image is matched by the inwardness of speech in the poet's last thoughts, and both together dramatize the internalizing process that permits the restoration of the poet to the fullness of visionary life. For Wordsworthian life is originated by and finally identified with utterance, "the breath of God" (*Prelude* V.222), and it is given human direction and application by echoic response.

THE ROLE OF ECHO IN WORDSWORTH'S
REVISIONARY POETICS

Another obvious path led Wordsworth toward a highly conscious concern with poetic voice: his desire to remake the language of poetry. This desire was closely associated with his desire to remake the heart of man; thus his early conception of poetic reform involved making poetry the language of "a man speaking to men" in urgent tones and directly communicating diction (1802 Preface to *Lyrical Ballads*, PW2.393). His uncertainty about his audience and about the model speaker he was imitating has been amply documented by critics from Coleridge forward; but despite this uncertainty, the spirit of his reform managed to assert itself through the shifting poetic languages he fashioned in the great decade. An important aspect of that reform has been stated in general terms by Geoffrey Hartman:

> [Literature] becomes an institution easily infected by *ratio* and must be led back to its source in *oratio*. This surely is what the great work of fiction (or criticism) achieves: it recalls the origin of civilization in dialogic acts of naming, cursing, blessing, consoling, laughing, lamenting, and beseeching. These speak to us more openly than myth or archetype because they are the first-born children of the human voice. Myth and metaphor are endued with the acts, the gesta, of speech; and if there is a mediator for our experience of literature, it is something as simply with us as the human body, namely the human voice. (*Beyond Formalism* 39)

However inadequate his attempts at theoretical justification in the Preface to the *Lyrical Ballads*, Wordsworth's radical simplicity of diction and syntax, his self-conscious addressing of his reader, his selective, revisionary use of folk- and street-ballad techniques, his modelings of and borrowings from contemporary popular forms of literature, his depiction of familiar rural life, and his prosaicisms—along with frequent willful violations of the particular properties each of these conceptions demanded—all tended to give his poetry the quality of being spoken.

By the time of Pope's death, *ratio* had begun to seem too dominant, but in their pressured search for voice the poets who succeeded him generally did not think of bringing their verbal texture closer to ordinary speech. Their poetic discourse, though in some ways less lacquered and impersonal than that of the typical Augustan piece, was still didactic, still better suited to the rostrum than the marketplace. As noted already, Wordsworth's capture of a nature-inspired voice was not a matter primarily of inner poetic reorientation but of technical development. Since nature spoke so strongly to him, his problem was how to externalize the voice that was already in him in such a way that it would at once teach in the Enlightenment sense and join *ratio* to the discourse of a speaker engaged in brotherly dialogue. In other words, he had to find a way to lead *ratio* back to *oratio*.

It is an irony of literary history that a poet so bent on remaking the language of verse should have chosen to live in retirement, far from the center of bourgeois life and literature in London and thus far from his audience. He had to imagine this audience, and though it could not be radically different from the cultivated urban readership supposed by Augustan and mid-eighteenth-century writers, it could not be wholly the same—not only because literacy was rapidly increasing, but because Wordsworth had to see it as sympathetic with his visions of nature, rural life, and the inward concerns of "Man" as he conceived him. In the prefaces he felt compelled to write, and in telling his readers "that every author, as far as he is great and at the same time *original*, has had the task of *creating* the taste by which he is to be enjoyed" ("Essay Supplementary," *PW*2.426), the poet is coming to grips with this problem of imagining his audience. At the same time he is developing an apologetic for what he has already written. The fuzziness of his original aim of using "the real language of men" is due to his difficulty in conceiving an audience which, he knows, is not likely to contain many rural speakers like those he imitates. The situation is further complicated by his noble but also vague Enlightenment view of the poet as "a man speaking to men." It seems clear, therefore, that part of his deep concern with voice was forced on him by a need to establish vocal community with his distant readership while being compelled to speak to it in an impassioned imitation of its own language. His borrowing of method, manner, and phrase from poetry based on oral tradition was part of his struggle to meet this need. The ballad seemed to him the model of a poetic form addressed to a universal audience that lacks sharp definition.

Succoring this need to establish community with an ill-defined universal audience is Wordsworth's emphasis on his prophetic role. The idea of the poet as *vates,* proximally descended from Milton and cultivated by the poets of vision, enabled him to believe in the authority of his private and heterodox insights and reach his audience as a strong voice—unsupported by the dogmas that were no longer living truths to him, but granted the power to compel, to regenerate thought. The vatic act of communion with a universal audience was peculiar in Wordsworth's case, however, in that it was an act of self-exposure. It involved laying bare his singularities, his doubts, the very awkwardness of his iterated comings-to-consciousness, as well as his visionary convictions and prescriptions. In part, the actions traditionally associated with prophecy figured forth the process of poetic creation as he experienced it: the spontaneous overflow of "poetic numbers"; the feeling of being "singled out . . . For holy services"; "The mind's internal echo of the imperfect sound" of the first vocalizings, which initiates the process of revision and perfection of insight.[10]

The process of perfecting vision involves correction on a number of levels—correction of phrasing, meter, and sound, of poetic tradition, of one's fellow men, and of self. In *Milton's Poetry of Choice and Its Romantic Heirs,* Leslie Brisman has examined the way in which Wordsworth's concern with voice was tied to correction of self. Wordsworth re-creates his voice as he tries to embody it, and he does so not only because he is forced to by formal necessities that engage every poet but also because he writes in the spirit of his desire to renew the hearts of men. At the center of this desire is the wish to re-create himself, so that even when he grows less certain of the capacity of poetry to redeem man, he remains sure that poetic voice has the power to renew the uttering poet. In Brisman's terms, he can never divorce the growth of consciousness in himself from the act of correcting voice. Discussing what Wordsworth calls the "trick of memory" that presses upon him two lines from *Samson Agonistes* and leads him to use them as the opening verses of an untitled poem written in 1816—" 'A *little onward lend thy guiding hand* / *To these dark steps, a little further on!*' "—Brisman suggests that

> the poem has naturalized and humanized the satanic temptation to rest at ease in the moment of choice. But it retains from Wordsworth's initial reaction to the quotation from *Samson Agonistes* the sense of awe before visitation of higher voice, and the expectation that, for all the discontinuities such interven-

tion may imply, the "trick of memory" that finds Milton's voice now will prove redemptive of the intervening time. (217–18)

Milton's power to confront and heal discontinuities (including his own blindness) is one of the things that made him such a strong model for Wordsworth. It led the Romantic to discover his own poetic method of healing discontinuities: elaborating the "trick of memory" into a myth of psychosocial development and informing this myth with a new view of subject-object relations.

Voice is thus centrally linked to the spiritual concerns of Wordsworth's poetry in an overdetermined way: through his view of the genesis of being; of the origin of consciousness; of the experience of the fullness of the moment; of the renewal or redemption of the self through the visitation of remembered spots of time or the intervention of a higher will; of the correction or diminishment of self by social experience; and of apocalyptic vision or infinity experiences (when silence itself may become a voice, "the stillness at the heart / Of endless agitation"). And echo is one of Wordsworth's most important metaphors for voice, because it expresses voice as something at once naturalized, humanized, and poeticized—three conditions that, in Wordsworth's mind, are brought about simultaneously by the right exercise of the poet's art.

This threefold function of echo becomes clearer when one puts together the many passages in which Wordsworth uses the term echo explicitly or implicitly. The spiritual concerns of his poetry cover the gamut of existential possibilities, from the genesis of being to eternal life. He seeks a guarantee that these possibilities will remain alive through affirming the continuity of consciousness against the threat of all sorts of discontinuities. This search for a guarantee is the structural dynamic of the poet's echo passages, since the echo is a model of continuity-in-change—a strong model precisely because it recognizes discontinuity, indeed incorporates it into its structure. Hartman has stated essentially this in a discussion of the second verse paragraph of the Boy of Winander episode in *The Prelude* (V.389–422). This passage expresses "how broken or devious the path is that leads from the 'marvelous Boy,' whose portrait has been drawn [in the lines on his hooting and subsequent silence], to the mature person, the fully 'cultivated' poet" standing before the grave of the dead boy:

> We are presented at once with the image of a split self and with that of a split sound, in the form of a curiously awkward syntax [the "break" after "There was a boy"]. . . . There is a special sort of split or broken sound which is Wordsworth's "natural"

model for the way experience elaborates itself by growing into
thought or fading into redundance. . . . I mean the sound we
call an *echo*. . . . The one act characterizing the Boy of Winander is that he makes nature—its hidden life—echo respon-
sively. The reflective man standing over the boy's grave does a
similar thing, for the logic of the episode as a whole imposes the
thought that he, just like the boy, is calling a voice out of silence. We find ourselves before a tragic ode to Echo. There is
no *imago* here (to borrow the psychoanalytic term), only an
imago vocis . . . (*Fate of Reading* 288–89)

But if the echo structure recognizes how a vital part of the self,
through loss or repression, has become other, it also marks the fact that
in Wordsworth this alien self is not wholly inaccessible in the typical
moment of insight. Nature, rather than encouraging a process of internalizing which buries "the possibility of response . . . on the bourne
from which no traveller returns," usually stimulates the lost self to
reappear to the mind or else affirms in some way the continuity of
human experience. It affirms, as Hartman puts it, "the idea of a ground
out of which things [grow] slowly, precariously; where accident [is]
important, some [grow] and some [don't], but where there [are], for
humanity generically considered, infinite chances of birth and rebirth." Even the Boy of Winander episode reveals the "winding or
'eccentric path' (Hölderlin) of individuation, leading from nature to
death, or through the consciousness of death to the counterbalancing
vision of a self uninjured by time" (*Fate of Reading* 290, 292).

Continuity of consciousness, with its promise of the possibility of
healing or restoration, asserted against a heightened sense of discontinuity or death, is the most salient element in the passages that levy
more or less explicitly on the idea of echo. In the manuscript fragment discussed in the preceding section, Wordsworth asserts a natural
continuity of experience:

> "O listen, listen how they wind away,
> Still heard they wind away, heard yet and yet,
> While the last touch they leave upon the sense
> Is sweeter than whate'er was heard before,
> And seems to say that they can never die."
> (*PW*5.342, lines 15–19)

The piece has emotional force because we understand the poet's response as an inward-looking, paradoxical defiance of a reality we all
must recognize. In the physical description and its rhetorical manipu-

lation, we experience a dramatic tension between passage and gradually extended lingering; but the tension is not realized richly enough for us to take at full value the surprising assertion of eternity in the last line. The line is strong in the shock of its insight but weak in not having a preparatory image to fall back on. The iterative rhetoric of "still" and "yet and yet" is not sufficient, nor is the figure of the windharp. We need an eternizing image, a Wordsworthian equivalent of what a poet writing in the Metaphysical style could have supplied with punning grace.

We know that bold play with words could never have been Wordsworth's way of strengthening his insights. This device, along with Augustan stock diction, generality, and wit, is precisely what the poet is trying to replace in his experimental attempts to develop a Romantic form of imagination. Yet he does after all strengthen his assertions of continuity by resorting to a sort of grand pun when he comes to base his contextual strategy on the metaphor and rhetoric of echoing. Such a pun can be seen in "Stepping Westward" (*PW*3.76), which supplies the explicitly eternizing echo metaphor which the tree-harp image of the Alfoxden fragment cannot.

The headnote to this poem and its first stanza together establish the inward and outward setting: the westward journey in solitude, accompanied by a fear of meaninglessness and death and a countervailing awareness of a compellingly grand sky. The actions described are commonplace, but the scale of meaning is large, indeed allegorical, as the end makes clear. What the poem must do is justify the poet's sense of elated affirmation as he pursues life's journey toward personal extinction. At first he adduces an allegorizing metaphor in support, the movement out of gloom into light. This, he says, converts a possible "*wildish*" destiny into a "*heavenly*" one (the italics are Wordsworth's). Then he describes an infinity feeling, created in him directly by the sound of the Scottish woman's greeting (" '*What, are you stepping westward?*' "):

> 'twas a sound
> Of something without place or bound;
> And seemed to give me spiritual right
> To travel through that region bright.
> (13–16)

The scene is typical of Wordsworthian places of insight during the great decade, a solitary spot that enhances the numinousness of a single figure (the headnote tells us there were two figures, but the companion does not appear in the poem). It is not, however, the numinousness, compounded of fear and elation, which is principally celebrated here or brings about the resolution. The poet's triumphant good feeling is created by a humanizing force, which alone gives meaning to it. And that humanizing force is an echo:

> and while my eye
> Was fixed upon the glowing Sky,
> The echo of the voice enwrought
> A human sweetness with the thought
> Of travelling through the world that lay
> Before me in my endless way.
>
> (21–26)

The "endless way," like the "heard yet and yet" of the Alfoxden fragment, leads to a denial of the finality of death. The implicitness of the denial, as compared to "seems to say that they can never die," is no doubt one reason for the dramatic superiority of this ending, but a companion reason is the power of the echo metaphor to dramatize (rather than merely assert) the psychological process taking place in the speaker. In "The Solitary Reaper" (*PW*3.77), the echo metaphor is more implicit, but again the continued reverberation of the woman's song in the speaker's heart "long after it was heard no more" effects the humanizing of an ambiguous solitude in which a lone figure raises to acuteness the issues of loss and death. The reaper's voice is compared to the cuckoo's, which we have already seen is an emblem of iteration; the girl's singing is itself a present mood-matching echo of matter enacted in the distant or near past—of "old, unhappy, far-off things" or "Familiar matter of to-day . . . / Some natural sorrow, loss, or pain, / That has been, and may be again."

The poem suggests further kinds of doubleness: The Highland fieldworker is alone, but she is doing the work of a community—reaping—and representing that community in both the feeling and the matter of her songs; her reaping is associated with the fullness of life (the harvest) and its end (winter coming on); she sounds melancholy, but her voice is a carrier of joy—of "welcome notes" that are "thrilling" and in their energy overflow the valley in which she seems enclosed; her tongue is alien, but she speaks directly to her listener's feelings. This last element, a fresh reworking of the poetic cliché introduced into the English tradition by Sidney at the start of *Astrophel and Stella*—"look in thy heart and write"—is the clue to the humanizing of the "eternity structure" elaborated in the poem's final movement. "The Solitary Reaper" develops out of the same tension as "Stepping Westward," out of a moment of uncertainty whose *numen* opens up feelings of doubt and loss and feelings of affirmative power, and the conversion of this doubleness to an incorporative unity is brought about by an echoic process in the heart.

In almost every passage or poem by Wordsworth that features the idea of echo or some equivalent element of iteration, the assertion of continuity against disruptive facts or forces is achieved by an internalizing of the echo until it becomes a kind of soul music, a mediator of endless life experienced as a change of attitude. In *The Prelude* (V.470–81), the drowned man Wordsworth watches being brought up from the bottom of the lake (a revenant, his living person echoed, so to speak, by his corpse being hauled to the surface "bolt upright") is not terrifying to the nine-year-old boy because the return becomes an internalized reflection of what he has seen before in books of romance. Out of this echoic experience comes "a spirit hallowing what I saw / With decoration and ideal grace" (478–79). And, following hard upon the Boy of Winander scene, a tale in disguise of his own growth to maturity through apparently irreparable loss, there is redeeming repetition in a different form of that scene in which the poet "oftentimes" stands "A full half-hour together . . . / Mute—looking at the Grave in which he lies" (V.420–22). Here he is learning to internalize by repeated meditative steps the fact of death and so to assert against the inevitable discontinuities of growth the continuity of a deeper consciousness.

The power of echo to achieve such deepenings results from its being re-creation rather than slavish repetition. We are always more or less aware of the poet's self-consciousness limiting his stronger statements, characterizing them as the insights of a particular mind in particular circumstances of observation. Whether it is the character of the description, the intrusive use of first-person pronouns, the stance of the speaker, the use of "seems" or its verbal analogues, or the dramatic structure, we are always made to feel that the speaker is describing his own consciousness, not making an absolute, independent truth-statement—that he is, at least in part, constructing a reality rather than passively relaying it:

> And I can listen to thee yet;
> Can lie upon the plain
> And listen, till I do beget
> That golden time again.
> ("To the Cuckoo," *PW*2.207, 25–28)

The final "again" is significant: The experience is a rebegetting, the poem a re-creation. Composition is a process of echoing, of inward re-creation of what is perceived, followed by external re-creation of that re-creation, refashioning "the mind's / Internal echo of the imperfect sound." Even the external sound or voice that impinges on the human ear is an echo, a representation of Being offered in nature; and the poem is the re-representation of Being registered first as the internal echo of that voice in the heart, and then as its externalized echo in verse.

Both echoing processes in the poet—the perceiving-internalizing and the re-externalizing one—are creative repetitions and stand as Wordsworthian parallels for Coleridge's primary and secondary imagination, the "repetition in the finite mind of the eternal act of creation in the infinite I AM," and "an echo of the former, co-existing with the conscious will, yet still as identical with the primary in the *kind* of its agency" (*Biographia* 1: 202). But Wordsworth differs from Coleridge in a way that allows him actively to join the poetic echo and consciousness. Unlike Coleridge, he assigns an apparent spiritual life to nature that goes on independently of man and can be voiced without the participation of human mentation (though he never shows this incontrovertibly, always limiting it to implication or the speaker's supposition). In "Yes, it was the mountain echo" (*PW*2.265), we hear "voices of two different natures" that parallel the cuckoo's shout and the cragborn "unsolicited reply, / . . . Like—but oh, how different!" The one voice is our everyday voice, the other is a giver of "Answers . . . / Echoes from beyond the grave, / Recognized intelligence!" It is clear that these echoes are at once altered representations of ourselves and the voice of another life which we recognize, but which has not emanated from us.

In this poem, Wordsworth for once labels that life explicitly (if still vaguely) divine, saying of the echoes, "For of God,—of God they are." As mediators of divine reality, the echoes make clear the poetic link between genesis and continuity. Wordsworth's rejection of the deistic world-maker from his religious conception meant that, for him, living reality had to be understood as the result of a process of creation—not continuous in the simple sense, but repeatedly and frequently renewed; and his rejection of original sin brought the problem of the inward losses accompanying natural and spiritual growth into first place as the grand obstacle to be overcome in human life.[11] Loss was overcome by assurances of a deeper continuity, and this was ultimately guaranteed by the regenerative power of concentrated spirit, which overflows into poetic utterance. Utterance is genesis, and repeatedly renewed genesis assures continuity.

There is no conflict with Wordsworth's view that the soul's activity,

Not only general habits and desires,
But each most obvious and particular thought,
Not in a mystical and idle sense,
But in the words of reason deeply weigh'd,
Hath no beginning.

                    (*Prelude* II.232–37)

For nature and soul are not seen as crafted *ex nihilo* but given—given
with the necessity of being continually rejuvenated. The generative
power is regenerative power, the begettings of memory are rebeget-
tings, utterance is reiteration of the one life. Wordsworth's view is thus
related yet opposed to the Miltonic view, which as we have seen declares in *The Christian Doctrine* that "nature cannot possibly mean anything but the mysterious power and efficacy of that divine voice which
went forth in the beginning, and to which, as to a perpetual command, all things have since paid obedience." Nature yields a voice for
Wordsworth, and it is the expression of a spirit which, as Milton says,
"upholds and preserves." But it is not experienced as the proclama-
tion of "the immutable order of causes appointed by [God] in the
beginning"; rather, it is the model of continual re-creation, of the
"ground out of which things [grow] slowly, precariously; where accident [is] important . . . but where there [are] . . . infinite chances of
birth and rebirth."[12]

If Wordsworth's view of nature goes beyond both Milton's and Coleridge's, his view of the soul coincides with Coleridge's in one crucial
respect: For both, the soul is endowed with a reflex consciousness of
its own continuousness, and the great end of all its energies and
sufferings is the growth of that reflex consciousness. In Wordsworth
reflex consciousness is affirmed by perceptions of a generative voice
in nature, in memory, and in literature. Natural echoes, echoes of
buried consciousness, echoes of the literary past, and echoes of original responses recollected in tranquillity all go into and guide his process of composition. The echo is thus a central feature of his technique, as well as a master metaphor in his oeuvre.

Wordsworth images his own origin, growth to maturity, and end in
terms of echo. There is not only the metempsychotic myth of the
Intimations Ode but the picture of the River Derwent presiding over
his early years:

                    —Was it for this
That one, the fairest of all Rivers, lov'd
To blend his murmurs with my Nurse's song,

And from his alder shades and rocky falls,
And from his fords and shallows, sent a voice
That flow'd along my dreams? For this didst Thou,
O Derwent! travelling over the green Plains
Near my "sweet Birthplace," didst thou, beauteous Stream,
Make ceaseless music through the night and day
Which with its steady cadence, tempering
Our human waywardness, compos'd my thoughts
To more than infant softness, giving me,
Among the fretful dwellings of mankind,
A knowledge, a dim earnest, of the calm
That Nature breathes among the hills and groves[?]

(*Prelude* I.271–85)

Reflector of nature as a whole, repetitive in its winding course and in the uninterrupted action of its "steady cadence" on the poet-to-be, internal voice that "flow'd along my dreams," old topos of eloquence and image of modern balladeer blending with the nurse's song, objective correlative of childhood memories, the Derwent is a multiply determined echoic image. And there is also the poet's four-times-penned vision of his last days, structured as a visual "echo" that brings his beginning into his end:

Dear native Regions, whereso'er shall close
My mortal course, there will I think on you;
Dying, will cast on you a backward look;
Even as this setting sun (albeit the Vale
Is no where touched by one memorial gleam)
Doth with the fond remains of his last power
Still linger, and a farewell lustre sheds
On the dear mountain-tops where first he rose.

(*Prelude* [1850] VIII.468–75)[13]

The idea of echoing permeated so many aspects of Wordsworth's thinking, including his conception of poiesis, that when he began to school himself in the literary tradition he sought models that would help him embody the echoic modes of expression he found natural, an inalienable part of the act of inditing.

3

Wordsworth and the Renaissance Heritage of Imitation

One major Renaissance rediscovery, which came with the accession of classical texts, was historicity. The literary men who had a consuming passion for the classics found that they were separated from them by an unbridgeable gap: They could read Latin and Greek works with complete devotion, but being born in fourteenth- or fifteenth-century Italy they could never fully enter the Latin or Greek mind. The very attempt to do so forced them either into self-loss or self-projection upon the originals. Petrarch, the grand type of the classics enthusiast, could no more carry on a direct dialogue with his beloved Homer than he could directly woo Laura, though in both cases he created fictions that attempted to cross over the real boundaries that stood in his way.[1] That Petrarch's sense of historical difference was painful is made clear in his "Letter to Posterity," where he expresses the unworthiness of his own age and a yearning to live intellectually among the ancients alone. This feeling of diminishment and loss was widespread at the start of the Renaissance, when literary cultural life was experienced as a fall into time more than as a journey into a golden land, a movement not toward a final home where one could rest at ease but toward "a past that is slipping into indistinctness" (Greene 10).

Petrarch and others used a number of literary strategies to deal with the pain of historicity, none really new (one can find them in the ancients) but all developed with a persistence and an intensity born of frustrated love. They were embodied forcefully enough to last into the eighteenth century and become part of Wordsworth's heritage. All are based on the fertile idea of textual imitation—making one's work like, or able to manipulate, or permeated by the spirit of some original.

The idea of "taking over" in all its senses is present in imitation,

though in practice not all of these senses are fulfilled. Following
Thomas Greene, one can list four fundamental strategies (see Greene,
chap. 3). The first unconsciously suppresses historicity, since its aim is
to celebrate an enshrined text by rehearsing it, so to speak, liturgically,
as if it were not inscribed in a temporal succession but were always
fully accessible without translation. One may thus call it sacramental
imitation. In this kind of imitation, whole quotations and close echoes
that do not set up an interplay of contexts dominate the imitating text.
Greene cites as an example Petrarch's close imitation of Cicero's *De re
publica* in Books I and II of *Africa,* where the dream of Scipio is given
(38). Juvenilia aside, Wordsworth has no example of a poem written
in this spirit. Among his near predecessors, the Wartons often come
close to the sacramental method, enshrining "L'Allegro" and "Il
Penseroso" over and over in their ambulatory nature poems:

> Oft near some crowded city would I walk,
> Listening the far-off noises, rattling cars,
> Loud shouts of joy, sad shrieks of sorrow, knells
> Full slowly tolling, instruments of trade,
> Striking mine ears with one deep-swelling hum.
> Or wand'ring near the sea, attend the sounds
> Of hollow winds, and ever-beating waves.
> Ev'n when wild tempests swallow up the plains,
> And Boreas' blasts, big hail, and rains combine
> To shake the groves and mountains, would I sit,
> Pensively musing on the outrageous crimes
> That wake Heaven's vengeance: at such solemn hours,
> Demons and goblins through the dark air shriek,
> While Hecat, with her black-brow'd sisters nine,
> Rides o'er the Earth, and scatters woes and death.
> (Joseph Warton, "The Enthusiast" 180–94)

Of course, the matter is complicated by the appeal to other enshrined texts of Milton and of earlier eighteenth-century pastoral,
georgic, and graveyard kinds. (We recognize bits from Book II of
Paradise Lost—the hollow winds, the far wanderings, the appearance
of Hecate—and bits from Thomson's *Winter* and Blair's *Grave.*) The
enterprise is further complicated by the built-in contradictions of the
technique: The only pure liturgical rehearsal would be just that, a
repetition of the original text; but once one begins to restate and
reorder, modifying diction and syntactical connections, the later piece
becomes a version. Thus, what is a denial of historicity in spirit becomes a demonstration of historicity in effect.

A piece may be categorized as sacramental if it combines an apparent intention to rehearse and a notable closeness of echoes. The intolerably banal James Hurdis comes as near to purity as one can in his *Village Curate*—the stupid purity of mere repetition:

> Of Man's first disobedience, and the fruit
> Of that forbidden tree, whose mortal taste
> Brought death into the world, and all our woe,
> With loss of Eden—of the glorious year,
> In all her changes fair; of gentle Spring,
> Veil'd in a show'r of roses and perfumes,
> Refulgent Summer in the pride of youth,
> Mild Autumn with her wain and wheaten sheaf,
> Or sullen Winter, loud, and tyrannous;
> Let nobler poets sing.
>
> (1–10)

It is interesting that after breaking away from *Paradise Lost* (awkwardly done by the jerk of an unwarranted dash), Hurdis begins to be interpretive of his next literary source rather than literal in his repetition. The phrase "gentle Spring" is lifted directly out of Thomson's *Seasons* (line 1 of *Spring*), but "Veil'd in a show'r of roses and perfumes" is Hurdis's condensation of "one white-empurpled shower / Of mingled blossoms" (*Spring*, 110–11) and "Shower every beauty, every fragrance shower, / Herbs, flowers, and fruits" (*Summer*, 127–28). In "Mild Autumn, with her wain and wheaten sheaf," Hurdis has quoted the last two words (*Autumn*, 1) but invented the wain—an allusive contraction of Thomson's long descriptive apostrophes to Industry and ripe harvests. Apparently Hurdis was less threatened by Thomson's genius than by Milton's and felt free to interweave a few of his own perceptions with those of the poet of the English year.

But even for Hurdis, word-for-word repetition for more than a few lines is unacceptable. His choice of an as-yet-untreated subject—"Be mine the task to sing the man content, / The Village Curate" (19–20)—is meant to declare, in dutiful epic-georgic fashion, his own originality. In any case, liturgical rehearsal does not really work as sacramental praise, because it sets the source text further away from the reader. Its failure to capture the original with notable energy only emphasizes the gap between a minor late talent and an earlier genius.

A second Renaissance strategy denies special privilege to any single author or text or literary period, and so also more vigorously denies historical gaps, by plundering an assortment of originals at will. In this strategy, which Greene calls "eclectic imitation" (the rhetorical name is *contaminatio*), allusions, echoes, fragmented quotations, topoi, motifs, images, philosophical ideas, stylistic devices, and structural elements from heterogeneous models jostle one another. The purpose behind the heterogeneity of *contaminatio* seems to be the poet's desire to express a feeling of being connected to the whole of his cultural history. He uses eclectic imitation in a way that gives delight in recall and a sense of liberating power through manipulation. Successful poems in this vein also seem to communicate to the sympathetic reader an atmosphere of authority transferred from the original texts.

According to Greene, the "eclectic mingling of heterogeneous allusions recurs repeatedly in [Petrarch's] Italian poems throughout his entire career" (39). In the mid-eighteenth-century poets of England such mingling was rampant. It was a prime aspect of poetic composition among the major voices of the period—Gray, Collins, Akenside, Smart in his public Augustan manner, the Wartons, and to a much lesser extent Goldsmith and Gay. John Philips at the turn of the century had started it with his playful use of Virgil and Milton in *Cider* and "The Splendid Shilling," though his method was conceived as a mocking version of the profound, formally sustained imitations of a single source developed by Dryden and bequeathed to the Augustan Age. This Drydenian technique, which makes the imitating poem a freely conceived parallel of its source, was the staple Restoration and Augustan method of fashioning strong poetry. The great achievements of Dryden and Pope assured this, and assured continued use of the method in the eighteenth century. W. K. Wimsatt, in fact, thinks the conceptual mode of imitation was exhibited in peculiar concentration in the period between the deaths of Pope and Johnson (1744–84). It was

> the method, the bondage, and the main freedom of all English neo-classic and preromantic poetry—the principle of imitation or free-running parallel. Imitation not only of the full, ancient, and classical models, Homer or Pindar, Horace or Juvenal, but also, increasingly, as the classical models became, or may have seemed to become, used up, imitation of the whole British tradition and especially of the English poets who had already best imitated or paralleled the ancients—Spenser and Milton especially, and, though he was still very near, Pope. (119).

Wimsatt notes that the fourth Asclepiadean meter, used by Milton in his translation of Horace's *Odes* 1.5 ("What slender youth bedewed with liquid odours"), was used again by Collins and the Wartons, and that in Collins's "Ode to Evening" it becomes a "novel extension of a

classic form to enclose or shape the stuff of a newly intensified landscape melancholy" and create a mood "that subsists purely in its symbols, with no real motives." The novelty is richer and more inclusive
when we realize that

> whereas the dim landscape images and pensive mood are mi-
> nor Miltonic, the movement of the phrases through the tiny
> stanzas is not cut or segmented, as in "*Penseroso*" couplets, but is
> like the actual movement of Horatian odes and at the same
> time like Milton's *Paradise Lost* style and his sonnet style too,
> continuous from line to line, and even from stanza to stanza.
> (123)

Wimsatt elucidates other kinds of imitation explored for the first
time in English poetry under the aegis of eighteenth-century anti-
quarianism and primitivism: ballad forms and modes, the "Ossianic"
or Homeric-Miltonic-Celtic blend of Macpherson, the "expressionist"
mock-antique language of Chatterton, the unique mixture of Scots
literary dialect and traditional poetic English in Burns. Whether the
immediate embodiment was good or bad, these provided a liberating
draft which could infuse vigor and scope into the efforts of the young
poet of the later eighteenth century. Bowles to a degree, Blake, Southey, Coleridge, and Wordsworth all drank of this spirit. But it depended, always, on a more or less subtle bondage: "The expressive
freedom of eighteenth-century English poetry is born only in virtue of
the mimetic and repetitive tradition under which the poets labored"
(Wimsatt 72). And Wordsworth earned his own freedom by accepting
the same principle of bondage.

He altered the character of this bondage, however, by carrying
further changes already occurring within it. Wimsatt has noted the
enlargement of the scope of things imitated, but he has not emphasized the fragmentation—the paralleling of more minute and more
varied elements drawn from a wider range of sources. In Collins's
"Ode to Evening," for instance, there are, in addition to the things
Wimsatt mentions (Miltonized classical meter, penseroso imagery and
allegorizing, the epic Milton's drawing out of sense from line to line), a
host of words and phrases imitated from other authors. The "folding
star" of line 21 parallels the "unfolding star" of *Measure for Measure*
IV.ii.218 and "the Star that bids the Shepherd fold" in *Comus*, line 93
(Milton probably took his image from Shakespeare and inverted it,
and Collins probably imitated the line in *Comus*). Collins's phrase is not
an allusion, not even a "virtual allusion"; that is, it is not asking us to
compare two contexts. The time of day is the same, but Comus's brief

description of evening is a prelude to his gross invitation: "Meanwhile welcome Joy and Feast, / Midnight shout and revelry, / Tipsy dance and Jollity" (lines 102–4). This is hardly consonant with Collins's soft-shadowed, innocently sensual picture of the "genial loved return" of his "maid composed." If anything, that maid reminds us of the Lady in *Comus*, rather than one of Comus's train. The confusion only deepens when we bring the two texts side by side. The line is a reworking of a phrase, an "echo" which need not, probably ought not, call attention to the full context of its source in order to achieve its designated effect. It is a product of poetic training in a "mimetic and repetitive tradition." So is "paly circlet" in line 22, an appropriate evening change wrought in the morning star's "bright Circlet" described in *Paradise Lost* V.169. So too is the first line of the poem, "If aught of oaten stop or pastoral song," in which a Spenserian phrase ("if aught of") has been used to vary a line of *Comus* ("Or sound of pastoral reed with oaten stops," line 345).

In Collins's lines,

> . . . while now the bright-haired sun
> Sits in yon Western tent, whose cloudy skirts,
>   With brede ethereal wove,
>   O'erhang his wavy bed . . .
>
>   (5–8)

we may agree that the "wavy bed" of the sun "inevitably recalls Milton, *Nativity Ode*, 229–31: 'So when the Sun in bed, / Curtain'd with cloudy red, / Pillows his chin upon an Orient wave. . . .' " (Lonsdale 463–64, note to line 8). On the other hand, the locating of this Miltonic bed where the sun "sits in yon Western tent" may not inevitably recall an inverse image from Shakespeare, but the prominent position of Shakespeare's image at the end of the first scene of *Hamlet* makes a deliberate imitation by Collins plausible: "the morn in russet mantle clad / Walks o'er the dew of yon high eastward hill" (I.i.166–67). "Brede" may be ascribed to current poetic diction; however, since it was rare and not part of the primary Spenserian bequest of terms, its use in two prominent poems—by Philips in *Cyder* ([1708], II.295) and by Akenside (imitating Philips) in *The Pleasures of Imagination* ([1744], II.118)— suggests a succession of prelusive imitations. "Skirts," no doubt, was "a common poeticism for the edge of a cloud," and Lonsdale in his edition of Collins quotes or cites passages in Spenser, Milton, Pope, Thomson, and Akenside which employ it (463, note to lines 5–6). "Skirts" may thus lie beyond the pale of allusion; yet among his citations Lonsdale omits a more celebrated passage that seems to me an "inevitable" parallel and one that in fact informs the construction of the sun image in the "Ode to Evening":

> Fountain of Light, thyself invisible
> Amidst the glorious brightness where thou sit'st
> Thron'd inaccessible, but when thou shad'st
> The full blaze of thy beams, and through a cloud
> Drawn round about thee like a radiant Shrine,
> Dark with excessive bright thy skirts appear,
> Yet dazzle Heav'n, that brightest Seraphim
> Approach not, but with both wings veil thir eyes.
>   (*PL* III.375–82)

Despite the relevance of a larger context, one is not dealing with an allusion here. Collins's sun is Apollo-like, beclouded, and inaccessible, but there are no other significant interconnections. It would confuse the effect of his ode to approximate evening's "calm vot'ress" to an eye-veiling seraph or anything other than a natural divinity, for in the felt presence of such a divinity inheres the main energy of the verse, and the aura of Milton's God would annihilate her. What the passage from *Paradise Lost* offers is a number of "authenticated elements" that can be reworked to make a new description of the sun as a bright contrast and prelude to evening—or rather, a description at once new and old that carries with it not a precise meaning but a dim yet palpable feeling of grandness, of Miltonic weight and pressure.

This imitation of minute elements is of course as old as literature and as recent as the most contemporary piece. But carried out in such dense series and so often with little meaningful relevance to sources, it was also something new, a technique characteristic of the fragmentation of thought and feeling in the period following the high Augustan age. In addition to fragmentation, it involved an expansion of imitative practice to new kinds of subtexts. It can be seen as the recovery of a Renaissance mode, but with an awakening to England's cultural past and literary traditions rather than to those of antiquity. Love of Spenser, Shakespeare, Milton, Dryden, Pope, and Thomson, of ballads, of Gothic ruins and rural Britain, has nudged to one side the love of Homer, Virgil, Ovid, and Horace, of the Greek and Roman lyric poets, of classical ruins and pastoral Italy. Though the central figures of antiquity still press forward from the sidelines, in the search for voice and authority it is mainly the phrases of English precursors which are woven into the still basically Augustan texture of the poetry of the Age of Sensibility. The result may be a particolored web, in the pattern—*mutatis mutandis*—of Petrarch, who in his "Triumph of Eternity" "brings together allusions or echoes of Cicero, Horace, Saint Matthew, the *Apocalypse,* Saint Augustine, and Dante" (Greene 39).

The most reductive form of *contaminatio,* returning toward sacramental imitation, is the cento. Wordsworth's note to the cento he published in the 1835 edition of his poems tells us that he "sometimes indulges" in "this practice . . . of linking together, in his own mind, favourite passages from different authors," claiming for it only the value of *"private* gratification."[2] But the cento is simply one infertile terminus of what proved to be, often, a fertile process for certain eighteenth-century poets and later for Wordsworth. The later-eighteenth-century forms of imitation evolved from a struggle for voice. If this struggle involved an attempt to call voice out of nature, it also involved—particularly in the eclectic form—an attempt to wrest it from the poetic tradition. The focal points were Spenser, Shakespeare, Milton, Thomson, and the pastoral Pope (*Windsor Forest* and other minor poems). All these poets, with the aid of willful selectivity and distortion, were treated as nature poets in the picturesque or sublime mode, so the project of drawing a voice out of nature was blended with that of drawing a voice out of the power centers of British poetry. Echoes of the natural scene and of past poets were functionally similar devices of representation for the minor poets of the Age of Sensibility oppressed and exhilarated by the great talents of the English tradition.

The eclectic mode of imitation tries to deny any historical separation from the past even as it tries to deny the overwhelming importance of any single figure in the tradition. As a creative method of the poet of sensibility, it was hypothetically aimed at making him a fellow of (for example) Milton in stature, engaged in the same enterprise, but not a slave to the Miltonic, since that was only one of many keys in which the agile manipulator of traditional tonalities could play. At the same time the method could strengthen a new piece with Miltonic power and authority (or Shakespearean, or Thomsonian) while declaring the manipulating poet's independence of the Augustan mode, tyrannically ruled by Pope's presence. The later-eighteenth-century poet also declared his freedom simply by his power to imagine a vehicle in which he could bring together and carry into contemporaneity so many strong past voices.

This is the main method of the Age of Sensibility ideally understood. But the eclectic mode of imitation did not often work out well in practice. The better talents among the poets of the Johnsonian era did manage to color their verse with the intense and even seductive quality of their sensibilities, yet they could seldom manage a strong, coherent voice or form. The fragmentation caused by their desultory impressing of phrases and tonalities from the masters was too insistent, the seams where separate elements were joined were too lumpy, the purposiveness of the echoes was too feeble. The strongest way to form such pieces into a whole is to engage in an allusive dialogue with the subtext, but that is precisely what these poets, in their self-conscious weakness, avoided: They tried to increase their substance by suckling at rather than wrestling with their sources.

If this failure of nerve, or simply talent, constituted a flaw in the method of *contaminatio*, the method nonetheless had its successes. The possibility of a syncretic welding of many subtextual elements into a forceful unity, which Greene finds happily achieved in certain works of Petrarch and Politian, was opened in the later eighteenth century because of the dominant presence of Milton. Despite the implicit declaration of independence in the juggling of heterogeneous sources, many non-Miltonic poetic elements were bent in his direction or seen through Miltonic spectacles, including at times even Shakespeare, whom Milton himself had incorporated into the world of "L'Allegro" by means of an aggressive distortion that has the dramatist "Warbling his native Wood-notes wild." Furthermore, the subtexts lumped together were mostly not from Greece and Rome—two distant, different, and now, in the associative consciousness of poets, moribund cultures—but from a single, living culture which was nearer, more homogeneous, and more familiar: the ebullient tradition leading, with a glance back at Chaucer, from Spenser to Pope.

This is precisely the span of echoes, allusions, and mere references in Joseph Warton's "Ode to Fancy." Spenser, Milton, Dryden, Thomson, Pope, and Akenside are all evoked in one way or another. It is a smorgasbord, yet there is a unity of tone and feeling in the poem because it is most essentially an imitation, in a broad sense, of "Il Penseroso." The Miltonic tetrameter couplets sound Augustanized on account of the high degree of end-stopping, the apostrophizing rhetoric of Augustan pastoral, and the frequent appearance of poetic diction and stock images. The poem as a whole exudes the non-Miltonic odor of sensibility through the poet's personal stance, his gothicism, his appeal to emotion and spiritual enthusiasm, and his typical mid-century use of abstract personification. Nonetheless, we can read it as a version of the minor Milton, the extra-Miltonic references being subsumed into the frequent transpositions of his original words. Warton draws on other poets in the English tradition to support his restatement of the Miltonic view, and the very act of pressing these sources into service gives a certain authority to Warton's idea—an authority not merely arbitrary, though for the most part references remain a parade because Warton has failed to capitalize on the subtexts.

Using the same method, Collins achieves a greater intensity of effect in his "Ode to Peace." The appeal to authority and for vocal support is less blatant because the echoes have been more fully transformed, and the subtextual parading is diminished by the greater unity of conception and the deeper level at which the voices are blended. The central subtext is Milton's Nativity Ode, which perhaps imposed itself principally because it too describes the substitution of a new peaceful order for an old oppressive one. The link is mainly one of mood, but it is concrete to the extent that Collins draws directly on Milton's image of "meek-ey'd Peace," who comes

>   softly sliding
> Down through the turning sphere,
> His ready Harbinger,
>   With Turtle wing the amorous clouds dividing,
> And waving wide her myrtle wand,

to strike "a universal Peace through Sea and Land" (Nativity Ode 47–52). However, while keeping her gentle and erotic characteristics, Collins changes her from a disguised Venus to Astraea. And he revises Milton's plan by using extended classicizing personification to change the Venusian descent to an Astraean return, the birth to a marriage, and the casting out of the pagan order to the restoration of a heathenish golden age:

> O Peace, thy injured robes upbind,
> O rise, and leave not one behind
>   Of all thy beamy train:
> The British lion, goddess sweet,
> Lies stretched on earth to kiss thy feet,
>   And own thy holier reign.
>
> Let others court thy transient smile,
> But come to grace thy western isle,
>   By warlike Honour led!
> And, while around her ports rejoice,
> While all her sons adore thy choice,
>   With him for ever wed!
>   (13–24)

Although making full use of his source, Collins declares, unlike Warton, the independence of his own conception. And, unlike Warton, he shapes his conception with care so that the elements will blend.

The pattern of escape and return structures the poem: Peace flees upward to escape the rape-minded, earthward-bent god of War, turns with the turning spheres, and then, in a vision of possibility, comes back down in state ("by warlike Honour led") to enter into a royal marriage with the genius of Britain. Granted that the primary purpose of the poem is to express a longing for peace and to image it as possible, it is nevertheless a version of the progress poem, whose underlying concept is strongly supported by the poets (all of major stature) whom Collins echoes. Lonsdale notes the verbal presence of Spenser (through the image of the lion, which recalls the beast that fawned before Una in the *Faerie Queene* I.iii.6.1–3, and through the diction: "upbind," "beamy"); of Milton (*PL* I.787: "with jocund Music charm his ear" [see "Ode to Peace" 11], as well as the Nativity Ode); of Pope ("Eloisa to Abelard" 126: "charm my partial eyes" [also "Ode to Peace"11]); of Dryden (*Palamon and Arcite* I.109–10: "the God of War / Was drawn triumphant on his iron car" ["Ode to Peace" 5]); on of Thomson ("Nuptial Song Intended for Sophonisba" 27–28: "the furious god of war / Has crushed us with his iron car" ["Ode to Peace" 5], and, more vaguely, elements used to describe the storms of *Winter*, such as Thomson's cormorant [*Winter* 144–45]).

All these poets spoke for a high English poetic culture, either by celebration or by satirical attack, and the specific poems Collins echoes deal in one way or another with redemption, union, and justice. They thus come in aid of the poet who asks (I take it to be a forceful question): "What sounds may charm thy partial ears, / And gain thy blest return!" (11–12). By echoing them, Collins can levy on the command of classical and British themes they embody, wooing Astraean Peace back to Britain simply through the authority of their vocal presence. They are harmonized by being subordinated to Milton's Nativity Ode voice, which in turn is subordinated by Collins's transformation of that poem's plan. The echoed voices join to become a wedding choir, as it were, at the visionary nuptials of Peace and Britain.

The "Ode to Peace" is better than Warton's "Ode to Fancy," but it is certainly no masterpiece. Like Wordsworth's "Remembrance of Collins," it is rather engaging than strong. And this is usually the case even with the more successful eclectic imitations, in which the hard task of finding a proper alliance of sources and a unifying purpose is accomplished, unless the borrowings function dynamically. When they do, we encounter the third kind of imitative strategy, which Greene calls "heuristic imitation." This strategy is built on conflict— conflict that recognizes the otherness of the subtext, the pastness of the past. Eclectic imitation suppresses this awareness of historicity because it wants to assimilate, to swell its notes with the harmonies of its originals, and otherness would add dissonance. It is a way of finding a voice to suffice, so that wholeness of vision can be achieved. The modern view that authenticity and originality are sisters makes us resistant to the idea that eclectic imitation can really succeed. Even Greene feels that at best it can manage only a surface success, an order able to "tolerate the counterpoint of the voices it [brings] together," but unable to "find out the drama of that counterpoint at a deeper pitch of conflict" (p. 40). Embodying the drama of contrapuntal voices at a deeper pitch is what heuristic imitation can do.

Though many texts may stand behind the poem written in this mode, one is singled out as its supposed point of origin, and the later poem then defines itself as an effort of growth away from its origin to a limited but genuine independence. It thus becomes, in Greene's terms, something of a *rite de passage* from the past to a freer, more creative present, involving "a double process of discovery: on the one hand through a tentative and experimental groping for the subtext in its specificity and otherness, and on the other hand through a groping for the modern poet's own appropriate voice and idiom" (p. 42). Rather than seeking power through assimilation, then, this method seeks power through painful, judicious self-distancing.

In his discussion of Ben Jonson's "On Inviting a Friend to Supper," Greene notes that Jonson "Englishes Martial in order to work over English, to thicken its texture and complicate its resonance. The text cannot simply leave us with two dead dialects. It has to create a miniature anachronistic crisis and then find a creative issue from the crisis" (42). The successful resolution of this crisis produces "a fresher, more polysemous [literary] code." The practitioners of this polysemous style closest in time to Wordsworth were the neoclassicists, whose referential devices can be superficial but generally operate as rich allusions. These allusions are not only of a phrasal but also of a structural sort, so that, as in Pope's *Imitations of Horace,* both the architecture of the whole building and the details on the capitals are brought over and transformed to fit their new setting.

Transformation is essential to the act of distancing, though recognizable features must be left standing. The freedom to transform flowed out of the conviction or deeply satisfying pretense of the neoclassical writers that, although the world might be going downhill, the high culture they were arbitrating was the equal of Roman Augustan culture and therefore complete enough to give them genuine, even easy, mastery over their medium and their sources. Paradoxically, they at once recognized and denied the historical differences between their art and the art of Rome. The recognition was openly asserted in the brilliant strategies of transformation they employed; the denial was embodied in the air of ease which seemed to claim—and suppress any anxiety about—the complete accessibility of the classical texts they drew on and the mythico-cultural world these texts projected.

Thus, a full appreciation of Clarissa's speech in Canto V of *The Rape of the Lock* (lines 9–34) depends on the reader's close acquaintance with Sarpedon's speech to Glaucus in Book XII of the *Iliad* (lines 371–96 in Pope's translation). The rhetorical structure is kept intact: Why are we heroes so great in pomp and power, Sarpedon asks, unless it is because we follow the honorable path of courage? If we could attain fullness of life by avoiding the risk of our lives, then we should avoid that risk and simply seek our pleasure. But since this cannot be, for life is in every case a journey into disease and death, let us take the high road of honor toward our inevitable end: Honor alone can prevail over fate by bringing us fame. Following this pattern closely, Clarissa asks why we beauties are so valued unless it is because our reputations are buttressed by good sense. If we could fulfill our potential merely by pursuing the round of pleasure, then we should pursue it. But since this cannot be, for disease and death inevitably intervene, let us follow the road of "good Humour": That alone will enable us to prevail over the pettiness of life and achieve something enduring.

The architecture of the two passages being the same, so that the reader in a sense comes to inhabit a Homeric space while reading Pope, a mock-heroic effect is produced by the sharp contrast in situations, which the transformed details are devoted to establishing. The Greek heroes' ample possessions in lands, herds, and harvest crops for feasting guests become the glittering ornaments of modern beauties, "deck'd with all that Land and Sea afford" (*The Rape of the Lock*, V.11). The parallel in *The Rape of the Lock* is close enough to place the emphasis crucially on the difference between fruitful possessions and superficial adornment. This emphasis is pursued by Pope through expansion of details. In his translation of Homer, Sarpedon asks, "Why on those Shores are we with Joy survey'd, / Admir'd as heroes, and as Gods obey'd?" Clarissa asks why beauties are

> Angels call'd, and Angel-like ador'd?
> Why round our Coaches crowd the white-glov'd Beaus,
> Why bows the Side-box from its inmost Rows?
>
> (V.12–14)

Sarpedon, considering the possibility of escaping the common fate, states his conditional clause in a general way—"Could all our Care elude the gloomy Grave" (*Iliad*, XII.387)—while Clarissa elaborates:

"Oh! if to dance all Night, and dress all Day, / Charm'd the Small-pox, or chas'd old Age away . . ." (*The Rape of the Lock,* V.19–20).

These and other similar transformations of detail form part of the way Pope gives recognition to the difference between the cultural world of eighteenth-century England and the cultural world of the ancients, dominated by the heroic ideal. And of course the power of *The Rape of the Lock*'s mock-heroic mode comes from exploiting that difference. But there is also in this passage a denial of the historical gap between the two cultures. Pope identified Clarissa's speech as the moral center of the poem, though it was a late addition, and the tone indicates that we are to take its message seriously. The crucial part of it is introduced by a precise repetition of a phrase used at a parallel point in Pope's translation of Sarpedon's speech, and the ensuing words are close in spirit. Sarpedon says,

> But since, alas! ignoble Age must come,
> Disease, and Death's inexorable Doom;
> The Life which others pay, let us bestow,
> And give to Fame what we to Nature owe.
> (*Iliad* XII.391–94)

And Clarissa:

> But since, alas! frail Beauty must decay,
> Curl'd or uncurl'd, since Locks will turn to grey,
> Since painted, or not painted, all shall fade,
> And she who scorns a Man, must die a Maid;
> What then remains, but well our Pow'r to use,
> And keep good Humour still whate'er we lose?
> (*The Rape of the Lock* V.25–30)

Various touches bring Hampton Court back into focus, and the difference between good humor and glory is self-evident, yet the underlying issues to be faced and the perception of the human condition are identical, brought over whole from the *Iliad*. This assumes that Homer's values are easily accessible in the original passage and remain valid, able to be transferred by simple parallelism. Without this assumption the weight of Clarissa's view would not be great enough to establish it in the center of Pope's poem. Here Homer, Pope, and nature are the same.

Wordsworth's relation to Milton was often of this sort, emphasizing and eliding difference. Though it is possible to demonstrate anxieties in Wordsworth about not measuring up to or being able to get out from under Milton, it is also possible to find instances of Wordsworth's sense of assurance in relation to him. In Book III of *The Prelude* (lines 284–93), the young St. John's resident, after evoking the master in all his alien sublimity (with the aid of echoes from *PL* V.901, VII.27, and XI.704 in "uttering odious truth, / Darkness before, and danger's voice behind"), brings him back toward his earthly origins in a way that makes him seem suddenly not only small and slight but almost Wordsworth's protégé:

> Bounding before me, yet a stripling Youth,
> A Boy, no better, with his rosy cheeks
> Angelical, keen eye, courageous look,
> And conscious step of purity and pride.
> (290–93)

The reduction is in fact delightful, but it teeters on the edge of undermining subterfuge.[3] Not only does Wordsworth allow the suggestion that Milton was a prig, but his "stripling Youth" and "rosy cheeks / Angelical" echo Milton's "stripling Cherub" and "Youth smil'd Celestial," which describe the false disguise Satan puts on to fool Uriel (*PL* III.636, 638). What can be made of this? The context does not suggest a merely trivial quotation, yet we cannot say that the approximation of Milton and Satan is seriously intended. The Romantic conception of Milton as an archrebel, later a commonplace, makes the approximation plausible, and it is true that the "lady of Christ's College" threw off his cherubic disguise when he became a controversialist and propagandist for Cromwell's rebel government. The turn might be seen as a Bloomian "transumption" or overgoing driven by unconscious anxiety, but nothing else in Wordsworth's context supports this reading. Perhaps one can conclude that in the passage Wordsworth is halfway between the eclectic and the heuristic modes, in his playful mood expending the same imaginative energy in transforming Milton from an "awful soul" to an innocently proud angelical boy that Milton did in transforming Satan to a stripling cherub.

   An example from a different context is Wordsworth's set of marginal commentaries in his edition of *Paradise Lost* (quoted in Wittreich 103–9). Sometimes perceptive, his annotations are often disruptingly picky and dismissive. There are no sustained expressions of awe. One is tempted to see this cocksureness as the result of unconscious anxieties, for though the grounds for such a view are unprovable, the sense of a comfortable *maîtrise* over so powerful a text intimated by the annotations fails to explain why *Paradise Lost* haunted him, continually pressing him toward creative responses in his poetry. Indeed, his heuristic relation to Milton typically appears in his strongest verse.

Suppressing anxiety in relation to his great models is something Wordsworth shares with Pope, although in one way or another Wordsworth lets the anxiety show, while Pope never does. That a suppression was involved in the ease of the neoclassical manner seems likely, because we know that figures as masterful as Petrarch and Milton experienced anxiety in relation to classical literature.[4] As Greene notes, the painful breaking away that leads to poetic identity is an impoverishment as well as an enrichment. It fails to satisfy a need for exchange with one's source. The object of one's primary love, the subtext, cannot respond, blessing or cursing the transformation as a living father might: "The sub-text or its author cannot even appear to verify the interpretation that the imitative text presumes. The filial gesture of critical affection never truly reaches its destination" (43). Thus growth away from the subtext expressed in the heuristic text always threatens to become a solipsistic exercise, for "intercourse with the cultural other always [comes] to a point where intuition [has to] replace historical consciousness" (43).

Despite pretenses, then, the sense of easy filial contact with one's sources obtaining in eclectic imitation is lost in heuristic imitation, traded for a gain in independence and creative excitement. A heightening of the heuristic mode into a "dialectical" one (as Greene calls it) leads to strenuous and almost paradoxical attempts at making a new kind of connection without sacrificing the gain in independence. In dialectical imitation, the imitating text moves further away from its sources in order to make a full revisionary statement, but does so in a way that lays it open to a critique by the subtext and invites a dialogue between the two texts. Greene cites Erasmus's *Praise of Folly,* among whose "authenticating models" are the humorous dialogues of Lucian. Though Erasmus mimes Lucian only to take quite a different position, expressed fully in the hymn to Venus that ends his work, he nonetheless leaves himself "open to criticism from the irreverent Lucianic spirit that [he] had begun by invoking." Thus, Greene says, "by entering into a conflict whose solution is withheld, the humanist text assumes its full historicity and works to protect itself against its own pathos" (45).

It is true, as Greene notes, that "every imitative work which is not [sacramental] initiates this process of mutual criticism" and that the "strife" recognized already by Longinus involves, "when it truly engages two eras or two civilizations at a profound level . . . a conflict between two *mundi significantes*" (46). But it is a matter of intensity and degree, and relatively few works manage a truly dialogic relationship with their source texts. In mid- and later-eighteenth-century poetry and in Wordsworth, the dialectical mode of imitation on a large scale is rare. I am not aware of any sustained examples on the order of *The Praise of Folly*. In the Age of Sensibility the scarcity of dialectical imitation can be explained in part by its poets' inability to create large forms of inventive power, Blake excepted, and in the Romantic period by the continual urge of poets other than Wordsworth to be free from or to triumph over models, rather than hold a dialogue with them.

If one takes passages instead of whole works, however, dialectical imitation can be found. One rather subtle dialogue is carried on in a famous passage of the *Prelude*, the meditation on the meaning of the Mt. Snowdon vision (XIII.66–119). There are parallels to Young's *Night Thoughts* (IX.1061–66), to Shakespeare's Sonnet 64 and to Akenside's *Pleasures of Imagination* ([1744] I.121 and other lines), but these are all used assimilatively, in the spirit of eclectic imitation. The most profound model here, the one from which Wordsworth is distancing himself, is an equally famous passage in *Paradise Lost* expounding the Chain of Being (V.451–505). The appositeness of the Miltonic passage lies in its being a definition of the relation between the created universe—especially, of course, man—and transcendent being. Wordsworth's purpose is to displace Milton's conception with his own, but without losing the sublimity, power, and authority of the Miltonic statement or controverting the idea of transcendent being, of which Wordsworth has just had a vision.

The allusive markers are not obvious. The only direct echo is Wordsworth's "discursive or intuitive," which repeats exactly a phrase from *Paradise Lost* (V.488). However, the context surrounding this phrase in *The Prelude* evocatively supports the central thrust of Milton's passage placing the origin of things in God: For Wordsworth, the highest minds, those capable of using imagination, or "Reason in her highest mood,"

> are truly from the Deity,
> For they are Powers; and hence the highest bliss
> That can be known is theirs, the consciousness
> Of whom they are habitually infused
> Through every image, and through every thought,
> And all impressions; hence religion, faith
> And endless occupation for the soul
> Whether discursive or intuitive;
> Hence sovereignty within and peace at will [,]
> Emotion which best foresight need not fear [,]

> Most worthy then of trust when most intense.
> Hence chearfulness in every act of life [;]
> Hence truth in moral judgements [,] and delight
> That fails not in the external universe.
>   (XIII.106–19)

The expression of liberating joy in this passage, the "delight / That fails not in the external universe," parallels Milton's "enjoy / Your fill what happiness this happy state / Can comprehend, incapable of more" (V.503–5). The limitation which most obviously differentiates the parallels, Raphael's "incapable of more," is a temporary, or temporal, one; the "winged Hierarch" has just held out the possibility of man's rising higher to a spiritual existence alongside the angels. However, the reduction of this differentia reveals a deeper one; for while man's elevation would not entail actually abandoning the "external universe," by making the physical frame of things optional Milton denies it the indispensable role Wordsworth assigns it:

> Your bodies may at last turn all to spirit,
> Improv'd by tract of time, and wing'd ascend
> Ethereal, as wee, or may at choice
> Here or in Heav'nly Paradises dwell;
> If ye be found obedient, and retain
> Unalterably firm his love entire
> Whose progeny you are.
>   (*PL* V.497–503)

This is precisely where the later poet is revising the earlier. He does so in several ways which finally dovetail. Wordsworth's higher minds are habitually conscious whose progeny they are, but they express themselves through their power of creativity, not through obedience. Furthermore, they recognize in nature a permanent, not a temporary or optional, mediator of a higher life. What natural energy accomplishes too is not the maintenance of a progressive hierarchy but an awakening from the sleep of death to which Wordsworth's simple dipolar order, made up of consciousness and unconsciousness, makes man liable.

Milton wonderfully expounds the progressive hierarchy:

> So from the root
> Springs lighter the green stalk, from thence the leaves
> More aery, last the bright consummate flow'r
> Spirits odorous breathes: flow'rs and thir fruit

Man's nourishment, by gradual scale sublim'd
To vital spirits aspire, to animal,
To intellectual, give both life and sense,
Fancy and understanding, whence the Soul
Reason receives, and reason is her being,
Discursive or Intuitive; discourse
Is oftest yours, the latter most is ours,
Differing but in degree, of kind the same.

(V.479–90)

Wordsworth overgoes Milton by realizing the promise offered in the last line. He allows his higher minds intuitive powers, makes imagination (Milton's "fancy") the crown of reason, and envisions a creative interchange between fully conscious men and the highest reality:

Willing to work and to be wrought upon,
They need not extraordinary calls
To rouze them, in a world of life they live,
By sensible impressions not enthrall'd,
But quicken'd, rouz'd, and made thereby more fit
To hold communion with the invisible world.

(XIII.100–104)

The natural universe has become a permanent frame for man's existence, and the hierarchy of the Chain of Being has, in one imaginative pass, been flattened, compressed to a single plane where all that is not human participates in being—the "world of life"—and where man either responds to being simply through the creative exercise of consciousness or falls into unconsciousness, the sleep of death. Even in the second case the sleepers are not doomed by position to disconnection from the world of life, since nature under certain circumstances works to rouse them. When she puts forth "That domination which she oftentimes / Exerts upon the outward face of things," she

So moulds them, and endues, abstracts, combines,
Or by abrupt and unhabitual influence
Doth make one object so impress itself
Upon all others, and pervade them so
That even the grossest minds must see and hear
And cannot chuse but feel.

(XIII.77–84)

Yet if Milton has been revised by transumption here, so that low and high, enduring and transient, spiritual and natural are all made to participate in being as elements on the same plane (whereas before participation was parceled out by degrees on a vertical scale), he has not been silenced. Wordsworth's revision shows sympathy (intensified in the 1850 version) toward its subtext and a certain dependence on it, thereby opening itself to a Miltonic critique. The sympathy lies mainly in a parallel sense of the sublime, which Wordsworth elsewhere asserts he has developed through early experiences of nature but admits to having learned also, at the level of poetry, from Milton. The dependence is a dependence on Miltonic terms for the sublime. His revisionary view prompts him to do without them, but he cannot.

"One Almighty is, from whom / All things proceed, and up to him return" (V.469–70), according to the Puritan visionary. Wordsworth rejects this neo-Plotinian movement for one that has something in common with life-sustaining biological exchanges (thus the mind feeding upon infinity, creating its own conditions or catching them when created for it) and also with political exchanges like those experienced by middle-class insurgents in the French Revolution (the willingness "to work and to be wrought upon," which "alone is genuine Liberty" [XIII.100, 122]). But in so rejecting Milton's view, Wordsworth's sublime order—the "greatest things" built up from "least suggestions," the "invisible world" and "highest bliss" (lines 98, 99, 105, 107)—has become vague in definition and structure. "The highest bliss / That can be known" is the "consciousness of whom" one has one's being, yet God hardly functions in any traditional sense, seeming to be a verbalism for the life that permeates the universe. The interchanges of life with life are all inwardly diffused. Though the distinguishing terms are kept, it is hard to see what distinguishes lower from higher, since Wordsworth's lesser and greater consciousnesses differentiate only degrees of intensity in exchange, not qualities of spirit or life. We know what Wordsworth is talking about in terms of his own experience, but what is the fundamental or metaphysical difference between the "greatest things" and the "least suggestions"? This is the question the Miltonic subtext poses. The difference must exist for sublime experience to be more than a solipsistic emotional turbulence, yet if the difference is conformed to the recognition of a personal God, hierarchical structure must reemerge. The imperious presence of hierarchical structure would defeat the Wordsworthian concept of sodalitarian interchange; the elimination of hierarchical structure would leave sublimity without a solid foundation.

The blurring, diffusing, and naturalizing of a personal God in passages like the Snowdon meditation laid Wordsworth open to inaccurate but not wholly false charges of pantheism. In confrontation with a Miltonic concept emphasizing the power and goodness of a personal, all-creating God from whom man earns his freedom by obedience, these potential impieties of Wordsworth's vision stand out. And there is no doubt that they worried him. In the earlier versions of *The Prelude*, he was willing to risk them; and in the 1805 version of the Snowdon passage he gains energy by not resolving the Miltonic critique, because it makes his statement seem won out of tension, at once more daring and more authoritative. In the 1850 version, however, his need to provide more traditional expressions of piety, his loss of confidence in the comprehensiveness of poetic vision, and his increasing dislike of unstructured daring all led him to revise this part of the Snowdon material in favor of the Miltonic subtext.

Thus in the later version "this world" is now clearly distinguished from an implied next world. The elevated mind now knows "the highest bliss / That flesh can know" (not "That can be known"; compare Milton's "happiness this happy state / Can comprehend, incapable of more"), and knows it as only a subordinate consciousness may by holding "fit converse with the spiritual world" rather than "communion with the invisible world." The term "spiritual" has reintroduced something of the vertical order embedded in Milton's exposition of the Chain of Being; in this respect "invisible" (1805 version) is more neutral. Separation between the human and the divine, a separation that barely existed in the 1805 version, has become distinct. The Snowdon scene had appeared to Wordsworth, in his first formulation,

> The perfect image of a mighty Mind,
> Of one that feeds upon infinity,
> That is exalted by an under-presence,
> The sense of God, or whatsoe'er is dim
> Or vast in its own being.
>
> (69–73)

As an image, the scene could be a reflection of the divine mind, but since the mind it images may be "exalted" by other things than "the sense of God"—by "whatsoe'er is dim / Or vast in its own being"— one cannot so easily identify the underlying power. It reflects a vague process, a mode of being, in which man, God, and nature all participate.[5]

In the 1850 version it has become an "emblem" instead of an "image," an allegorical representation of a "majestic intellect," which, if still not wholly explicit, clearly enough represents the divine mind exerting unmediated power. In the 1805 version, the terms "sense of

God" and "under-presence," though they can be taken argumenta-
tively as supporting the idea of God as the ground of things, function imagistically to blur the focus and keep the divine being from
commanding stage center in the scene. The representation in the
1850 version directly manifests divine consciousness. Gone is the
blurring of relationships which allowed the "Mind" to be shared
among man, nature, and God, gone is the earlier Wordsworthian
distaste for God seen as the maker of things. With the unsubtle help
of the familiar biblical and Miltonic verb "broods," the depicted
mind is placed above creation, and the visionary observer is invited
to climb a Platonic ladder toward ideality. This alien Platonizing
pulls against the idea of mutual exchange that gives a peculiarly
Wordsworthian visionary life to the passage, drawing the poet into
an explicit and abstract reinforcement of hierarchical order, as in the
new phrase "interchangeable supremacy" (1850 version, line 84).[6]
The Platonic ladder fuzzily presupposed here is a recognizable analogue of the Chain of Being:

> There I beheld the emblem of a mind
> That feeds upon infinity, that broods
> Over the dark abyss, intent to hear
> Its voices issuing forth to silent light
> In one continuous stream; a mind sustained
> By recognitions of transcendent power,
> In sense conducting to ideal form,
> In soul of more than mortal privilege.
> ([1850] XIV.70–77)

The cap of this process of separating the human and divine orders
is reached at the end, where the permanent speaking frame of things
encountered in the 1805 version, affording "delight / That fails not in
the external universe," drops from view. It is replaced by the familiar
"this world" of Christianity, with its "ills that vex and wrongs that
crush / Our hearts" ([1850] XIV.124–25), against which must be pi-
ously placed its higher counterpart, God's free gift to man:

> if here the words of Holy Writ
> May with fit reverence be applied—that peace
> Which passeth understanding, that repose
> In moral judgments which from this pure source
> Must come, or will by man be sought in vain.
> (XIV.125–29)

These revisions identify more clearly the dialectical nature of the original "imitation" of 1805 by showing how Wordsworth became uncomfortable with the Miltonic critique he had incorporated. But neither this nor the other extreme of imitation described by Greene, sacramental imitation, is common in the poet's allusive practice. Though it is useful to recognize the distinctions between each type of imitation and see that they are still current in the eighteenth century, we can get closer to an overall schematic understanding of Wordsworthian echoing by collapsing Greene's four classes into two.

Taking sacramental and eclectic imitation together, one can define a class of imitative techniques whose goal is to achieve a connection with the past by assimilation. Assimilation may involve connaturalizing one's text with its originals (sacramental imitation) or connaturalizing the originals with one's text (eclectic imitation); but since Wordsworth almost never uses sacramental imitation, I shall ignore this distinction and call all borrowings which seek a connaturalization of text and subtext *assimilative echoes*. The counterpart class—heuristic and dialectical imitation considered together—can then be said to involve *comparative echoes*. If the goal of the borrowing is closure or self-assertion through distancing one's insight from that of the subtext, the mode of imitation is heuristic; if the goal is to initiate a process of self-disclosure in which the subtext plays a role, the mode of imitation is dialectical. This distinction has some practical value, though it is not crucial.[7]

The classification into assimilative and comparative echoes is a pragmatic rather than logical dichotomy, because the two classes are not exclusive. Comparative echoing necessarily involves some assimilation between text and subtext, just as the assimilative process involves some comparison. I have therefore based my categorical assignments on practical judgments about the complexity of echoic effects in each instance. Nonetheless, I think my classification outlines something real in Wordsworth's allusive practice, pointing to its several goals and suggesting reasons for particular executive acts in composition.

When we step back from the level of compositional choices to assess Wordsworth's general aims in borrowing, we find that the poet was guided by a threefold sense of purpose. His first goal was a normative one. It was no doubt instinctive in part, yet it also involved deliberate choice, prompted by his conscious dedication in an Enlightenment spirit to a poetic career: He saw himself as chosen, because of the gift of speech vouchsafed him, to renew and hand on a language of instruction in how to live, a vehicle of truth—the spiritual law laid down in past writings whose authors he must emulate and confront. This is not to deny his sense of his own originality. He recognized that he had things to say known to no one else; but the way in which he describes this side of his creativity shows that it is simply an opposite pole of his normative impulse:

> Possessions have I that are solely mine,
> Something within which yet is shared by none,
> Not even the nearest to me and most dear,
> Something which power and effort may impart [.]
> I would impart it, I would spread it wide,
> Immortal in the world which is to come.
> (*Home at Grasmere*, PW5.336, lines 686–91)

In other words, it provides the force behind his desire to renew what he knows he must preserve.

Wordsworth's strong emphasis on renewal, however, is not a claim laid, even in playful hyperbole, to wholly original language. He does attempt to shed or transform eighteenth-century poetic discourse, and in his early prefaces he asserts his intention to ally the language of his poems with various new models—rural speech, the conversation of the middle class, the talk of men in action as recorded in travel books—but these models provide unsatisfactory explanations of his style, and the conclusion can be drawn that "the real language of men" often meant for him in practice the language of Milton and other impassioned poets. Like the disciples of early Christianity, who were bound both to an ancient textual tradition and to the sayings of an unprecedented new voice, Wordsworth was proclaiming the good news in a revolutionary age; and though his avowal that the poet is "a man speaking to men" has a strong Enlightenment ring, it is also an echo of St. Paul arguing for prophecy over ecstatic speaking in tongues:

> For he that speaketh in an unknown tongue speaketh not unto men but unto God: for no man understandeth him; howbeit in the spirit he speaketh mysteries. But he that prophesieth speaketh unto men to edification, and exhortation, and comfort. (1 Corinthians 14.2–3)

"Edification, and exhortation, and comfort": It is in this vein that Wordsworth addresses Coleridge at the end of *The Prelude*. The words are not precisely the same, but the same meanings reign. The speaker prays that he and his fellow poet may be to men, in an atmosphere of new revelations not wholly unlike that surrounding Paul,

joint-labourers in a work
(Should Providence such grace to us vouchsafe)
Of their redemption, surely yet to come.
Prophets of Nature, we to them will speak
A lasting inspiration, sanctified
By reason and by truth; what we have loved,
Others will love; and we may teach them how.

(XIII.439–45)

That so proclaiming the good news necessarily involves echoing and revising the literary past can be supported by a number of twentieth-century critical insights into literary practice from the Renaissance on, whether one relies on Frye's view that all significant poetry must be allusive, or on such current views as Bloom's that later poets clear a space for themselves through misprision of their predecessors' texts, or Michael Riffaterre's that significance, as opposed to merely referential meaning, can only arise from intertextuality.[8]

Even among the early Christians, the atmosphere of proclaiming the good news, in addition to having the normative purpose of reaching the spiritual ear of Everyman, includes a kind of allusiveness as well. The early Christian oral tradition included the Old Testament and Apocrypha, memorized by or well known to the illiterate among the Jews, and a significant dimension of both Christ's teaching and the apostolic spreading of the good news was pointed reference to Scripture in order to affirm both the continuity and the revolution involved in the new spiritual order. This practice assisted in the speech revolution recorded in the New Testament and was itself partly modeled on a long series of revisions of one Old Testament prophet by another. It became in turn for later Western literature a major stylistic and conceptual model of the revisionary process. Critical to this process was the deliberate, defiant redefinition of what was sacred and what was profane. As Harold Stahmer notes:

> Before fixed forms of celebration with their attendant linguistic formularies had been developed, the power of the good news was proclaimed, simply shouted amid ecstatic joyous enthusiasm. . . . Ordinary human qualities were suddenly consecrated, made sacred vehicles of the New Creation. The profane, in this setting, was simply that which the Word must yet touch and transform. The profane, in the sense of an absolute which is opposed to the sacred, no more existed for the early Christians than it did for the early Israelites.[9] (25–26)

Mutatis mutandis, this sort of reconceiving of sacred and profane was inherent in Romantic enthusiasm; and many commentators, most persistently M. H. Abrams, have drawn parallels between Wordsworth's validation of the ordinary and the revolution of early Christianity. But Geoffrey Hartman has seen this kind of redefinition as a general principle of literary change. Noting in one place that the Romantics, "though they belong to the Enlightenment and believe in a progress of consciousness, . . . were not for bigger and better minds but for a finer magic, a more liberal participation of all in the imaginative life" (*Beyond Formalism* x), he states in another that this sort of literary program is a version of a typical process which "moves us toward a new sense of the profaned word. The history of literature, in its broadest aspect, appears to be a continual breach of levels of style (high style being profaned, low style elevated), or a history of metaphorical transference (sacred attributes being secularized, and vice versa)" (*Beyond Formalism* 22–23).

The strong poet has to breach the levels of style in a way that accomplishes three things at once: the manner he develops must answer to the spirit of the times and so enable him to "[create] the taste by which he is to be enjoyed" (Wordsworth, "Essay Supplementary," *PW* 2.426); it must solve problems of diction, figuration, or conceptualization which seem to hinder his creativity, thus providing a self-propelling vehicle; and it must reinvent or alter the prior mode of poetic speech so as to cut that speech free of dead weight while putting it in possession of seemingly "natural" energies hidden in, or by, the tradition. This is the norm of poetic change, whether evolution or revolution. It cannot be fully accomplished without deliberate comparison, subtle or overt; and the main instruments of literary comparison are echo, quotation, allusion, and allied kinds of paralleling. Wordsworth felt he had to emulate and surpass models (Chaucer, Spenser, Shakespeare, Milton), and he trained himself to trade on all the voices that told him things, or hints of things, that he wanted to tell to mankind.

Developing an art of allusion was therefore part of his normative goal. But since developing one's art is naturally inseparable from the normal egocentric desire to distinguish oneself, a second goal guiding Wordsworth's allusiveness was the intention to become a genuine prophet. Translated into poetic practice, this meant developing a strong voice. Because for Wordsworth the strongest voice he knew was Milton's, this required his taking on Milton as a vital inheritance while distancing himself from him.

One means of grappling with a predecessor, as Harold Bloom has shown so forcefully, is the strong mode of allusion. Here one authoritatively differentiates oneself from the master and perhaps "transumptively" triumphs over him so as to claim self-origination or, more courageously, to initiate an open-ended dialogue with him. However, this process also engages and seems to authenticate issues of importance to the *modus operandi* of the imitating poet—in Wordsworth's case, creating an English poetry of prophetic power while holding inviolate his independence of vision, and developing the equivalent of a theodicy (with nature at the center), among other "Miltonic" concerns. Hartman has noted that for Milton "the possibility of an English or Western poetry was not conceivable . . . without Virgil's guidance. Virgil was the great literary mediator who showed (together with Horace) that poetry could be written even at a distance from the [archaic, naive, directly prophetic] source." But what Milton imitates in Virgil "is not Virgil's style as such but a method of mediation, the self-conscious acceptance of a secondary, 'translating' function" (*Beyond Formalism* 198–99). Thus, while confronting Milton in order to wrestle away his own strong voice, Wordsworth also evokes him in order to possess himself of Miltonic priorities and master a method of mediation. It is for him the most natural way of both appropriating and breaking away from tradition.

Inevitably, though, there is more than one master. One original may assume the greatest importance in a writer's work, but few strong poets owe their whole style and matter to a single predominant influence; and so it is with Wordsworth. Not only Milton, but Spenser, Shakespeare, Thomson, and Coleridge also initiated self-differentiating references in Wordsworth's texts. On the other hand, there is a large group of poets from whom he feels no need to differentiate himself, because he knows he has transcended them in power and vision. Yet he feels free to use them as sources of poetically substantiated attitudes, feelings, or images, since he understands himself to be properly transforming and thereby fulfilling what they had attempted with incomplete success or dim awareness. He uses them as inditers of revisable matter, intuitive but not fully enlightened visionaries, freer but not-yet-freed manipulators of poetic language, authenticating though not superior voices.

Authenticating, for he did after all need support: Even though he had a firm faith in himself as a voice of mankind, he knew that the attitudes and products of his nature-consciousness seemed unheralded. If the "prime and vital principle" was already his, and his alone "In the recesses of [his] nature, far / From any reach of outward fellowship" (*Prelude*, XIII.194, 195–96), he still needed the community of his eighteenth-century predecessors. For it was not strictly true that "No other [could] divide with [him] this work, / No secondary hand [could] intervene / To fashion this ability" (ibid., 191–93). This fashioning required the assimilation of a corpus of pre-Romantic poets.

When he was calling a voice out of the landscape, whether shaping a vision of nature or human consciousness, he used spot quotations, nonallusive echoes, gestalt-establishing structural mirrorings of little connotative consequence, and similar elusive re-representations of these minor poets' texts. It was a poetic parallel of his self-rescuing act during moments of childhood vision, clasping a tree to break his internal fall—in this case the tree of substantiated poetic discourse linked historically with his own. The assimilative mode was something he had learned from the very poets he echoed, but because it was intimately associated with his naturalizing vision of things, his use of it embodies what I would call his distinctively Wordsworthian goal.

In pursuing these three goals—the normative, the Miltonic, and the Wordsworthian—Wordsworth often adopted different echoic strategies for each. It remains to show how the goal-oriented application of these strategies worked in practice and what functions they performed.

Part II

The Art of the Borrowings

4

The Principles of
Wordsworthian Allusiveness

Do Wordsworth's various ways of borrowing from other poets constitute a conscious art or do they express a merely instinctive, ad hoc
application of a casual gift informed by voluminous reading and a
capacious memory? The question is particularly pressing when we
consider the poet's assimilative mode of echoing, which has struck
readers as an often-unconscious process. In the case of the comparative mode we may assume that his classical education and his study of
the English poets taught him the refinements of an art powerfully
instituted by Virgil, richly developed by England's Virgil, Milton, and
adopted as the primary method of composition by Dryden and his
followers. Even in this case, though, the question of whether or not
Wordsworth had a conscious art of allusion arises, because in his
revolt against Augustan methods and textures he seems in all but a
few passages (and these appear exceptional through being especially
central) to eschew the full use of rich allusion.

The number of poems or passages in which rich allusions can be
found has begun to be extended, because newer hermeneutical approaches have fostered a collective interest in intertextuality. Yet it is
still true that many critics "read Wordsworth unconscious much of the
time of his place in the history of ideas or the polemical history of
style" (Hartman, *Fate of Reading* 161), and that they are not interested
in "assimilative" allusion or see it as evidence of the poet's insufficiencies. These apparent insufficiencies are generally associated with a
lack of surface art and thus of overt clues to underlying artistic methods that might help explain the baffling strength of Wordsworth's
poetic presence.

Noting this difficulty, Hartman tries to resolve it by redirecting
critical attention to the ways in which Wordsworth incorporates the
image of a voice in his poetry (*Fate of Reading* 160–63). His model
instance is the progression from quoted to "fully internalized speech"

(162) encountered in the Lucy poems as one goes from the overt exclamation, "Strange fits of passion have I known," to the subterranean voicings of "A slumber did my spirit seal." He shows how this internalizing reduces the "rhetorical glitter" of the verse to an even, demythologized discourse, and the traditional modes (in "A slumber," idyll and elegy) to "shadows of moods only" (163), while it deepens the structure into a psychologically balanced paradigm of loss and gain. Though Hartman's demonstration of this post-Enlightenment art, an art predicated on rescuing poetic speech from the inescapable predations of rationalist attitudes, concerns the poet's use of imagery, it suggests how one might also treat an art of borrowing in Wordsworth. Here, too, the poetic strategy tends to reduce the more visible marks of craftsmanship. Traditional comparative allusion asks us to stop, recognize the borrowed elements, measure the distance between the borrower and the lender, and then close the momentary gap by a hermeneutical act which affirms both the poetic intention and the higher standpoint of the borrower. Wordsworth's art often turns away from the brilliance of interruptive allusion, directing us instead toward the contextual deepening of the voice addressing us, accomplished by the overpassing shadow of a mood.

Suppose, for example, one attempts a confrontation of texts, following up the hint of an allusion to "Il Penseroso," line 126 ("rocking Winds"), in the first verse of what Wordsworth called "almost his only sonnet 'of pure fancy' " (PW3.425; Robinson 1: 94): "How sweet it is, when mother Fancy rocks / The wayward brain, to saunter through a wood!" (PW3.21). The confrontation will not enrich the hermeneutical act, because there is no interplay of textual meanings. Yet that this slight link is real and not a forced critical invention is suggested by various consonances between the two texts. As so often in Wordsworth, a penserosan echo is embedded in a poem of allegrian mood describing life in a moment of peculiar détente and plenitude. But the final lines reestablish the voiding spirit of "Il Penseroso": The happy flow of the speaker's thoughts prompted by the scene becomes so overwhelming "that at last in fear I shrink, / And leap at once from the delicious stream." Furthermore, vignettes as well as phrases from "Il Penseroso" are gathered into Wordsworth's sonnet. Upon completing his turn on rocking winds, rustling leaves, and minute-drops, Milton shifts to flaring day and enters a wood that is a darker cousin to Wordsworth's place of "Tall trees, green arbours." Milton's wood has

> arched walks of twilight groves,
> And shadows brown that *Sylvan* loves
> Of Pine or monumental Oak . . .
> (133–35)

There, by "Waters murmuring," we encounter the poet's dream, echoed by Wordsworth, though his is a waking impression ("Such place to me is sometimes like a dream"), as well as the equivalent of the later poet's "delicious stream" in the "Airy stream" in which Milton's dream unfolds. Perhaps the coincidence of terms is dictated by the poverty of rhymes in English, but it seems equally reasonable to conclude that Milton's words have floated to the surface of Wordsworth's coursing poetic ideas. Even Wordsworth's untypically heterogeneous simile comparing the "wild rose tip-toe upon hawthorn stocks" to

> a bold Girl, who plays her agile pranks
> At Wakes and Fairs with wandering Mountebanks,—
> When she stands cresting the Clown's head, and mocks
> The crowd beneath her . . .

seems prompted by the heterogeneity of imagery in Milton's companion poems.

What, then, is the point of the initial allusion? Part of the answer lies in recognizing that the key term, "rocks," represents an echo rather than a true allusion. John Hollander states that in principle the distinction between echo and allusion "seems to be drawn with respect to the degree, and kind, of incorporation of the vocal source in the response, and to the subtlety and profundity of the mode of response itself" (*Figure of Echo* 63). In terms of Carmela Perri's apt definition of allusion as a referential marker which requires construal, Wordsworth's "rocks" is not allusive.[1] His poem as a whole, though it plays with elements of the Miltonic original, makes no implicit call for a contrastive or comparative recourse to "Il Penseroso." To adduce Milton's poem in this way would disappoint; it would produce no more information than the affirmation that the two texts resonate in some vague fashion.

But the question then arises whether this resonance has any special value, and what that value is. If we hold by Hollander's statement, we must allow that the echo is less subtle and profound than an allusion in the same place might have been. In addition, we may have to allow that the echo is unconscious, or at least has been produced without a conscious intention. Hollander, in a passage quoted earlier, remarks on this:

> In contrast with literary allusion, echo is a metaphor of, and for, alluding, and does not depend on conscious intention. The referential nature of poetic echo, as of dreaming . . . may be unconscious or inadvertent, but is no less qualified thereby. In either case, a pointing to, or figuration of, a text recognized by the audience is not the point. (*Figure of Echo* 64)

This is insightful and seems perfectly valid. Yet accepting its validity need not condemn Wordsworth's habit of echoing as artless, lacking in intention and subtlety, as it might seem to. There are, of course, enough weak or inert Wordsworthian borrowings to embarrass faithful readers, but generally the process of echoing in Wordsworth's poetry has a peculiar power of its own, a power inherent in the full internalization of speech. The "transitive figurational connection" between quotation, allusion, and echo is parallel to the movement from quotation to mute reference in the Lucy poems as defined by Hartman, and the "rhetorical glitter" of Spenserian or Miltonic or Popean allusion has been reduced to the "shadow of moods only."

It is precisely the instauration or thickening of a mood that directs Wordsworth's main art of borrowing. The echoic process is the natural method for a poet who sees it as his prime task to lead poetry from "an institution easily infected by *ratio* . . . back to its source in *oratio*," constituting an image of voice which will give "Breathings for incommunicable powers"—powers "That touch each other to the quick in modes / Which the gross world no sense hath to perceive, / No soul to dream of." The poet finds inspiration by roaming "in the confusion of my heart, / Alive to all things and forgetting all," so that he may feel "whate'er there is of power in sound / To breathe an elevated mood, by form / Or image unprofaned." He embodies these elusive fundamental realities in structures which allow us to experience "feeling consecrating form, and form ennobling feeling"—a new kind of poetic experience because the form is not form as his readers encounter it in the tradition but a power of "spreading the tone, the *atmosphere,* and with it the depth and height of the ideal world." The poet who "wants his poetry to be like nature in function and effect" must make his voice work atmospherically, "like some natural produce of the air," and therefore will translate "those fleeting moods / Of shadowy exultation" which inspirit him with poetic insight into "shadows of moods."[2]

Wordsworth tells us that in his most percipient moments he stood in the presence of nature "not / In hollow exultation, dealing forth / Hyperboles of praise comparative" but feeling that "whate'er / I saw, or heard, or felt, was but a stream / That flow'd into a kindred stream, a gale / That helped me forwards" (*Prelude* VI.662–64, 672–75). This passage in a sense defines the "delicious stream" out of which he leaps in fear at the end of the sonnet on fancy, showing us why it is reminiscent of Milton's "Airy stream." Wordsworth wants to establish the sense of this stream as a vision of imaginative activity so rich it can annihilate flesh and blood. And because he comes here to a negative realization of what it is, he is reminded of "Il Penseroso," which explores insight achieved by negation in opposition to the affirmativeness of allegrian plenitude. He does not, however, confront penserosan attitudes, and therefore he is not making an allusion by contraposition. He is incorporating a mood by drawing on the atmospheric quality, the tone of another voice. This added element authorizes and enriches his own voice.

The late-Enlightenment project of recovering poetic voice is the distinctive project of Wordsworthian composition, as loss and recovery of self-as-voice is a version of the central subject in his poems, redeeming past reality. Looked at through the lens of the Enlightenment, the past reality seems a time when the natural, the spiritual, and the rational were blended:

> Youth maintains, I knew,
> In all conditions of society,
> Communion more direct and intimate
> With Nature, and the inner strength she has,
> And hence, oft-times, no less, with Reason too,
> Than Age or Manhood, even.
> *(Prelude* X.605–10)

The key to redeeming it lies in "the vocation and survival of imaginative power. The question facing Wordsworth is whether this power is dead or obsolete; and if not, how the enlightened mind can accommodate it" (Hartman, *Fate of Reading* 184). This question had grown steadily more insistent in the pre-Romantic period without being resolved:

> The tension between prophetic voice and fictive word becomes acute after Milton. Not only is paradise understood to be lost (that is, understood to have been, or now always to be, a fiction) but the great voice seems lost that knew itself as logos: as participating in real influence. The *philomel moment* of English poetry is therefore the postprophetic moment, when the theme of loss merges with that of voice—when, in fact, a "lost voice" becomes the subject or moving force of poetic song. (*Fate of Reading* 164)

Wordsworth takes over this "philomel moment" and begins to resolve it. He sees, or feels his way to the view, that the enlightened mind can accommodate the imaginative power if *ratio* is brought back to *oratio*, and that this may be accomplished by the management of poetic technique to recover genuinely poetic voice—to generate a voice that is truly bardic or prophetic but not stentorian, so that it speaks as "a man speaking to men" and *of* "nothing more than what we are":

> Perhaps Wordsworth comes to reveal rather than teach, and so
> to free poetry of that palpable design which Keats still charged
> him with. All truth, said Coleridge, is a species of revelation.
> Revelation of what? The question cannot be answered with-
> out a certain kind of pointing, as if truth were here or there, as
> if life could be localized, as if revelation were a property. Yet
> Wordsworth's concepts of nature, of natural education and of
> poetry, are all opposed to this reduction. . . . Pointing is to en-
> capsulate something: strength, mind, life. It is to overobjectify,
> to overformalize. It implies that there is a fixed locus of revela-
> tion or a reified idolatrous content. (Hartman, *Beyond Formalism*
> 49–50)

The avoidance of pointing leads to the deepening of structure by fully
internalizing speech, and this process is served by the assimilative
mode of borrowing.

The art of borrowing in Wordsworth, then, is in great part the
foster child of his desire to avoid pointing and so to internalize poetic
speech. It is a risky art, involving the constant possibility of falling flat
or dying away into muteness, because it substitutes a gestalt of feeling,
a field in which mood, tone, and atmosphere can spread, for a nodal
gathering of textual lines that sets the intellect to construing overt
clues formed by intertextual pressure. At times the gestalt is so near to
formlessness, the echoic suggestion so vague, that we are dealing with
an empty or trivial poetic turn and feel embarrassed, or we pass on
without noticing any thickening of texture or hearing another voice.
Is there any force, even the most attenuated gravitational effect, in
Wordsworth's echo of Moses Browne's "Sunday Thoughts" in these
lines of "Stray Pleasures": "In sight of the spires, / All alive with the
fires / Of the sun going down to his rest" (*PW*2.160, lines 13–15)?[3]

At other times the assimilative echo is highly pointed, as in the case
of the first line of the "Ode to Duty" (*PW*4.83), "Stern Daughter of the
Voice of God," which recalls *Paradise Lost* (IX.653): "Sole Daughter of
his [God's] voice" (that is, the command not to eat of the Tree of
Knowledge). This is the keynote of a series of references in the "Ode
to Duty" to Milton's epic. None of them requires construal by a heuristic confrontation of the two texts, however. Instead, this series of
references (to Books III and VIII, as well as to *The Doctrine of Discipline
and Divorce*) atmospherically underlines the central Miltonic view that
obedience to a higher power is human freedom: Because "Reason also
is choice" (*PL* III.108), submission to the dictates of Duty does not
prevent the later poet from acting freely, as he requires, "according to
the voice / Of my own wish" ("Ode to Duty" 42–43), but rather breeds

"a second Will more wise" (48; "lowly wise" in *PL* VIII.173 and "Ode to Duty" 61).

The assimilative mode may also verge on or blend with the comparative, making classification difficult. In "Composed upon Westminster Bridge" (*PW*3.38), for instance, Wordsworth prepares for the final epiphany, transforming London from a baleful industrial "anthill" (which like its emblem in Book VII of *The Prelude* lays "The whole creative powers of man asleep" [654]) to a "mighty heart," by alluding to Spenser's "Prothalamion." Wordsworth's line, "The river glideth at his own sweet will," with its crucial personifying possessive, recalls the celebratory personification of the Thames in the refrain of Spenser's poem, subtly enriching the mood of the borrowing poet's epiphany: "Sweete Themmes, runne softly, till I end my song." Spenser's setting for a prespousal celebration of a noble marriage becomes an undersong that supports Wordsworth's celebration of the marriage of the city and natural life. It provides a contrast as well, since by evoking London in the preindustrial era, the atmosphere of "Prothalamion" reminds us of what has changed—of the very matter Wordsworth has set about resolving in his industrial-age vision of the city. By using the echo both to support and to contrast Spenser, Wordsworth creates a hybrid with more intellectual content than the purely assimilative type of echo but with less energy than the purely comparative type.

When the assimilative mode dominates, we can only perceive the containing form by responding to the voice buried in it, for it is a feeling structure, and feeling is the informing principle of tone, mood, atmosphere, utterance-in-process. Wordsworth is preeminently the poet of feeling, his poems arising from "fleeting moods," "shadowy exultations," delayed responses, hauntings of the mind, glimpses, "vanishings." His poems turn on articulated thoughts, but the dynamic is feeling—feeling that moves, ripens, transforms mentation. We are teased, through the systole and diastole of meditation informed by the heart, not into Being itself or the idea of Being but into the sentiment of Being.

The relatively discursive texture of the verse, so well defended by Donald Davie in *Articulate Energy* as having its own species strength, may at first glance seem to belie the feeling, and the persistent reader of the canon must be trained to penetrate it; for the surface manner of speech is at once Wordsworth's mechanism of control over sentimentality and his concession to Enlightenment habits of mind. But where the feeling is sufficient, the restrained surface speech also works in the poet's favor because it places the burden of response on the reader. The reader must unbury the buried voice, listening to the undertone to recover the fused product of thought and feeling.

It is here that Wordsworth, as the first readers of *Lyrical Ballads* immediately recognized, is in full revolt. The polished texture of Augustan verse organizes the thought in a much bolder way and submerges the feeling. It concentrates on the structure of thought, and we must follow the thought rather than dig through to find it. The feeling, often attached to a vision of culture, is brought back to the surface through the polysemy of the terms and their embedding in a polysemous imitative mode. Imitation provides a dynamic thought structure. "The method, the bondage, and the main freedom of all English neo-classic and preromantic poetry" (Wimsatt 119) provided complexities and disjunctions which enriched the thought both emotionally and intellectually, especially by generating an ironic power of sameness-in-difference.

The only thing that Wordsworth never did, once his maturity was gained, was to attempt a full imitation in the eighteenth-century sense. He was, in Herbert Lindenberger's formulation, the fountainhead of an age which lay between the ideals of imitation and creation through genre and the ideals of sincerity and originality of expression (32). Renouncing the previous ready-made formal system, he had to find his way by what Hartman has called "reflective encirclement."[4] This meant groping his way through interanimation of thought and feeling to a structure in which feeling consecrated form (that is, thought) and form ennobled feeling. If we take this creation of feeling structures as "the method, the bondage, and the main freedom" of Wordsworth's poetry, we may see his art of borrowing as a modification of an intellectually guided allusive process into a mood-guided echoic one. Wordsworth himself saw this shift beginning to occur in those pre-Romantic poets he was attached to—Collins, for instance—and he turned it into a revolutionary process by making it a method. (Art in Wordsworth still means "nature methodiz'd," though the meaning of each term has changed from what Pope intended.) But if it is mood-guided, his art has *not* thereby become anti-intellectual: Paraphrasable thought still structures the movement of mind in his poems and articulates itself as voice; but feeling gains a new leverage in this method of making art "a means to resist the intelligence intelligently" (Hartman, *Beyond Formalism* 302).

Early in his career, Wordsworth seems to have understood this shift from an intellectual-pathetic toward an intuitive-feeling structure as part of a general movement from fancy to imagination. This is supported by his striking definition of imagination in *The Prelude* as "reason in her most exalted mood" (XIII.170)—a phrase which could be said to encapsulate the shift. Imagination operating as a mood of the intelligence is the fundamental principle determining the referential source of his assimilative borrowings. Mood acts like a gravitational field, organizing lines of force that flow between localized concentrations of the elements we can recognize and talk about as constitutive matter: images or statements of the poet's experience of external nature, his presentations of persons or conceptualizations of character, discovered or rediscovered feelings, events, general ideas, psychic processes, texts (his own as well as others')—all that Barthes and others refer to as the intertext.

These elements can be seen as themselves fields, concentrated to a node in the mood-organized net of feelings governing a whole poem. This can be true of both comparative and assimilative borrowings, but in the latter case the organizing mood of the original text is more significant as a determinant than the echoed terms which function as markers in Carmela Perri's sense. We are stimulated to experience the spirit of the original. If we do this through a cognitive construal depending on the comparison of texts, the borrowing becomes a traditional allusion whose intensity is governed by the complexity and aptness of the intertextual relations set up. If the possibility of construal is highly attenuated, its cognitive character fades and the borrowing becomes a mere echo, constituting a gestalt of feeling that we grasp by an intuitive process. Of course, because in poetry we are dealing with a highly organized form of discourse, the cognitive process never entirely ceases. We must still think about what can be articulated in the relationship between Wordsworth's text and his source. But the construing activity is more intuitive and synthetic than analytical. The answer, then, to the question of whether Wordsworth's habit of borrowing is a conscious art or an intuitive act is that it is both. It is a conscious attempt to use an intuitional mode of intertextual relationship.

5

Mapping the Intertext I: Comparative Allusion

Wordsworth's borrowings present us with a continuum of techniques, from full comparative allusions to assimilative echoes that are the merest whispers. Wordsworth employs clear-cut allusions most often when he wishes to shape and resolve a discontinuity. One purpose of deliberately introducing a sense of discontinuity—always a striking maneuver in this poet of continuities—is to define his poetic enterprise and distinguish it from that of his predecessors. He does this by establishing a complex interplay of joining and disjoining forces, since allusion creates a link at the same time as it enforces a difference, thus satisfying in a subterranean way his mental urge to affirm continuity. Despite inevitable anxieties engendered by literary rebellion and fear of capture by strong influences, he was not weighed down by the past like his mid- and late-eighteenth-century predecessors. He for the most part abandoned classical reference and treated the English tradition as a whole, playing down its historical character and treating its four greatest voices as contemporaries, whom "I must study, and equal if I [can]" (see note 14, page 226). He was not consciously disturbed by that deep sense of separation from favorite sources which characterized Renaissance figures in relation to the classical heritage they rediscovered and made into a ground of "conflict between acceptance and denial of distance" (Greene 36).

Nevertheless, self-definition evoked in Wordsworth feelings of stress, often expressed by an aggressive mood which led him into both explicit and more subtle acts of confrontation. He continually defines himself by comparison with Milton, and for that reason the bulk of his rich allusions are to Milton's works. Though Chaucer is not the foil we might expect him to be from Wordsworth's singling him out as a master to be emulated, Spenser and Shakespeare are. Many of the forty-odd echoes of Spenser I have noted are used with genuine allusive force, and the same is true of the more than one hundred borrowings from Shakespeare. The Bible, principle subtext of Western culture as a whole, Thomson, progenitor of eighteenth-century nature poetry, and Coleridge, Wordsworth's alter ego and rival, are the other most frequent sources of comparative allusion.

Wordsworth's use of comparative allusion essentially embodies the techniques presupposed by Greene's category of heuristic imitation, though the acts of confrontation are more often segmental than total (total in the sense of involving one subtext in the whole structure of the later text, as in true imitation). Heuristic imitation, in Greene's definition, works by bringing into focus the otherness and specificity of the subtext in such a way as to establish the imitating text as an *aggiornamento* of the original, an evolution of insight that sustains the discovery of the later poet's distinctive voice. The *locus classicus* of this sort of allusion in Wordsworth is the "Prospectus." Here the twenty-odd echoes of Milton refer us to more than half the books of *Paradise Lost* (I, II, III, V, VII, VIII, and IX), *Comus*, the fifth *Elegy*, and "At a Solemn Music." There are, in addition, references to or suggestions of Spenser's *Epithalamion*, Young's *Night Thoughts*, Thomson's *Spring*, *Summer*, and *Castle of Indolence*, Gray's "Progress of Poesy," Beattie's *Minstrel*, the 1744 version of Akenside's *Pleasures of Imagination*, Dyer's *Ruins of Rome*, and even perhaps Herbert's "The Temper, I" and Michael Bruce's *Lochleven*. Of all these, the only true comparative allusions are to Spenser, Shakespeare, Milton, and Thomson. Milton, of course, is central, Wordsworth's defiance of the Miltonic Jehovah in order to assert a new ground for poetry being a signal embodiment of the heuristic process.

Though critics look exclusively to Milton in explicating the "Jehovah" passage of the "Prospectus" (lines 24–41), it is also in some measure a reworking of Thomson's expostulation on philosophy in *Summer*. Simply setting Thomson's lines alongside Wordsworth's can make the links obvious and demonstrate that it is a lesser allusive subtext. Philosophy, Thomson says, rises heavenward, "intent to gaze / Creation through":

> With inward view,
> Thence on the ideal kingdom swift she turns
> Her eye; and instant, at her powerful glance,
> The obedient phantoms vanish or appear;
> Compound, divide, and into order shift,
> Each to his rank, from plain perception up
> To the fair forms of fancy's fleeting train;
> To reason then, deducing truth from truth,

And notion quite abstract; where first begins
The world of spirits, action all, and life
Unfettered and unmixed. But here the cloud,
So wills Eternal Providence, sits deep.
Enough for us to know that this dark state,
In wayward passions lost and vain pursuits,
This infancy of being, cannot prove
The final issue of the works of God,
By boundless love and perfect wisdom formed,
And ever rising with the rising mind.

                                                    (1787–1805)

In the "Prospectus," when it is compared with this passage, there is an initial reversal of directions and an extension of limits, a revaluation of large concepts (the divine, the Chain of Being), and a displacement of similar terms ("sits deep" : "sink Deep"; "cloud" : "veil"; "dark state": "shadowy ground"; "gaze Creation through" : "look / Into our Minds"; "ideal Kingdom" : "The Mind of Man— / My haunt"; "To reason, then, deducing truth from truth": "breathe in worlds / To which the heavens of heavens is but a veil"; "By *boundless love* and *perfect wisdom* formed, / And ever *rising* with the *rising mind*" : "such *fear and awe* / As *fall upon us* when we look / Into our *Minds*"). By this reversal Wordsworth has captured the spirit of philosophic exaltation and quite altered its referents in a way that overgoes Thomson and the Augustan world order he is celebrating to establish the personal order of Romantic vision:

        So prayed, more gaining than he asked, the Bard—
In holiest mood. Urania, I shall need
Thy guidance, or a greater Muse, if such
Descend to earth or dwell in highest heaven!
For I must tread on shadowy ground, must sink
Deep—and aloft ascending, breathe in worlds
To which the heaven of heavens is but a veil.
All strength—all terror, single or in bands,
That ever was put forth in personal form—
Jehovah—with his thunder, and the choir
Of shouting Angels, and the empyreal thrones—
I pass them unalarmed. Not Chaos, not
The darkest pit of lowest Erebus,
Nor aught of blinder vacancy, scooped out
By help of dreams—can breed such fear and awe
As fall upon us often when we look

Into our Minds, into the Mind of Man—
My haunt, and the main region of my song.

(24–41)

Wordsworth's use of Shakespeare in the "Prospectus" is typically double: He at once rewrites him by comparative allusion and makes him a poetic ally in order to revalue Milton. Shakespeare's Sonnet 107 ("Not mine own fears, nor the prophetic soul") reorders medieval Christian values. It does so, on the one hand, by avoiding any traditional image of them. Their presence is implied by a conspicuous absence: Fate is dissociated from its usual links with Christian Providence and made the "prophetic soul / Of the wide world, dreaming on things to come"; the eclipsed moon, the augurs, and the olives of peace are notably classical images. On the other hand, the reordering of values is shown in the familiar Renaissance assertion of the ability of the poet's personal gift (and therefore his love) to transcend time, a claim associated with classical poets. This strategy leads Shakespeare to demote the mystical world soul, equating it with the deceived augurs: Both are incapable of power over or insight into life. Wordsworth in part reverses this valuation, taking the "prophetic soul" (which he renames "Spirit") as a literal presence, a power oriented toward man which can bestow vision on him:

> Descend, prophetic Spirit! that inspir'st
> The human Soul of universal earth,
> Dreaming on things to come; and dost possess
> A metropolitan temple in the hearts
> Of mighty Poets: upon me bestow
> A gift of genuine insight . . .
>
> (83–88)

By also accepting Shakespeare's term "soul" but not devaluing it, rather giving it an effective role as a mediating human presence on earth, he creates a humanized hierarchy that leans on Shakespeare to evoke and contrast with the invocation in Book III of *Paradise Lost*. Milton asks the "Celestial Light" to make his soul prophetic:

> Shine inward, and the mind through all her powers
> Irradiate, there plant eyes, all mist from thence
> Purge and disperse, that I may see and tell
> Of things invisible to mortal sight.
>
> (52–55)

Wordsworth's terms catch up as well lines 17–19 of the invocation to Book I ("And chiefly Thou O Spirit, that dost prefer / Before all Temples th'upright heart and pure, / Instruct me . . ."). He then completes his thought by alluding transumptively to VII.374–75 ("the *Pleiades* before him danc'd / Shedding sweet influence") and X.661–62 ("and taught the fixt [stars] / Thir influence malignant when to show'r"). Wordsworth images his song as a heavenly body that

> With star-like virtue in its place may shine,
> Shedding benignant influence, and secure,
> Itself, from all malevolent effect
> Of those mutations that extend their sway
> Throughout the nether sphere!
>   (89–93)

These lines act transumptively because Wordsworth suddenly allies himself completely with the vision of Shakespeare, asserting that his poetic gift has the ability to transcend the devastations of time. The Romantic poet thereby sets his more earthbound spiritual claim over Milton's in the invocations. And he devalues Milton's purpose in Book VII of confronting Adam with the original creation of the world to show that he can achieve selfhood only by accepting his subordinate place in the divine scheme—or, after Adam has thrown away his original possibilities, that he can achieve redemption only through the divine creation of a new order (Book X). By evoking Shakespeare, Wordsworth is proposing the opposite: the possibilities of redeemed selfhood for man through the affirmation of his own inner gift in the here and now.

In dramatizing an insight that surmounts the vision of a predecessor, Wordsworth may at the same time express deep respect for his source. This renders his allusion dialectical, able to "[measure] its own signifying habits with those of the subtext" in a way that celebrates the source and invites its criticism (Greene 46). Such dialectical allusions almost exclusively refer to Milton, Shakespeare, or Spenser.

Leslie Brisman has subtly worked out Wordsworth's dialectical relationship with Milton. In discussing *"A little onward lend thy guiding hand"* (*PW*4.92), he shows how this poem, written to celebrate Wordsworth's recovery from one of his bouts of eye inflammation (which interfered with his reading) and to express his gratitude for his daughter's reading aloud to him, uses *Samson Agonistes*, *Paradise Regained*, *Paradise Lost*, and "Il Penseroso" to measure the distance between himself and Milton (213–18). One measure of the distance is a mild naturalizing of the Miltonic stance: a satanic impulse to leap into the "abrupt abyss" (*PL* II.405 ["infinite Abyss"] and 409 ["vast abrupt"]) is seen first as an "intense desire for powers withheld / From this corporeal frame" ("*A little onward*," 27–28) and then is imaged, with softening details, as the familiar compulsion to leap from a height—a "strong incitement to push forth / [One's] arms, as swimmers use, and plunge . . . / Where ravens spread their plumy vans at ease!" (29–32; compare Satan's fall and Christ's rescue in *Paradise Regained* IV.581–87). But this curious turn is finally converted into an expression of thanks that, his sight restored, the speaker can once again draw directly on his literary sources:

> Now also shall the page of classic lore,
> To these glad eyes from bondage freed, again
> Lie open; and the book of Holy Writ,
> Again unfolded, passage clear shall yield
> To heights more glorious still, and into shades
> More awful, where, advancing hand in hand,
> We may be taught, O Darling of my care!
> To calm the affections, elevate the soul,
> And consecrate our lives to truth and love.
>   (49–57)

The forcing upon the speaker's mind of the first two lines of *Samson Agonistes* makes him wonder "What trick of memory to *my* voice hath brought / This mournful iteration?" Brisman comments that while this uncalculated recall invokes "the potential awesomeness associated with the sublime in hearing Milton's voice in '*my* voice' " (213), the ensuing discourse leads to what appears to be a "transumptive" moment:

> Secured by his knowledge that his setting is a natural landscape, not a theological trial, Wordsworth moves a little further on in the brinkmanship of the Miltonic moment of choice. Precipitous height "Kindles intense desire for powers withheld / From this corporeal frame." The desire is to be airborne—not suicidally plunged; or, perhaps more accurately, the desire itself is for a metaphoric rather than literal power of flight. . . . to be able to plunge into the "abrupt abyss," which he wants us to recognize as the void in which Milton's Satan did not fear to tread. The literary echo would point to the satanism of poetic freedom, when a poetic son turns his back upon Milton-as-God-the-Father and asserts his power, like Wallace Stevens' angel, freely to leap from heaven to heaven of his own creation. (214–15)

And yet the transumption is not consummated. Wordsworth draws away, visualizing the figure on a spiritual peak as a swimmer under compulsion: This course of action is rejected as "too self-prompted," the speaker inviting "milder confrontations with 'Heaven-prompted Nature' " (217).

The gentler act of setting aside Milton is opposed, as Brisman points out, by an influx of other Miltonic elements. We see "in the images of nuns not an aspect of landscape but an appeal to Milton's penseroso mode; and in the final image of [father and daughter] 'advancing hand in hand' to learn of paradises within, . . . a version of Adam and Eve at the close of *Paradise Lost*, but with the stings of sexuality and unobedient female will removed" (217). It is the restoration of the speaker's sight which has brought about this openness to Milton:

> To the "glad eyes from bondage freed" a new receptivity will be granted. Influence will flow from the everlasting gates of the "Fane of Holy Writ" and the temples of classic lore (1827 version). Milton's image of the "everlasting Gates," opened to let in "The great Creator from his work return'd," implies future commerce: God will visit men "and with frequent intercourse / Thither will send his winged Messengers" (*PL* VII.565–73). So Wordsworth's poem . . . looks forward to an easy commerce with the ancient texts. . . . But it retains from Wordsworth's initial reaction to the quotation from *Samson Agonistes* the sense of awe before visitation of higher voice, and the expectation that, for all the discontinuities such intervention may imply, the "trick of memory" that finds Milton's voice now will prove redemptive of the intervening time . . . [making it] no vacancy but a gap creative of self-consciousness. (217–18)

Brisman's paradigm allows us to see clearly how the resolution of "*A little onward*" establishes an easy commerce with Milton but leaves itself open to criticism from its Miltonic subtext. Samson regained not his physical sight but his inner vision of God—a vision higher than that of the speaker in Wordsworth's poem, withheld from him because he cannot contemplate sacrificing his earthly existence to obtain it. Indeed, though Wordsworth envisions "Time, / The Conqueror" as crowning "the Conquered, on this brow / Planting his favourite silver diadem," he is cheered by the thought that neither time nor time's minister, "intent / To run before him, hath enrolled me yet, / Though not unmenaced, among those who lean / Upon a living staff, with borrowed sight" (4–6, 7–10). If it should bring the terrible dependence of a Samson-like blindness, the forerunning minister would be

the forerunner of death, and death, despite the crown, is refused
here. The evasions consequent upon this refusal of a spiritual confrontation with death are limitations of Wordsworth's vision, and the
Miltonic subtext illuminates them.

These evasions are also illuminated by echoes of *Hamlet* (III.i.89) at
a crucial moment in "*A little onward*." After contemplating the possibility of his reduction to blind helplessness (read, death) and then breaking off ("Should that day come—but hark! the birds salute / The
cheerful dawn, brightening for me the east"), Wordsworth affirms his
role as his daughter's guide through life. The mazy syntax, repeated
in the imaging of this journey, incorporates terms linking Dora to
Ophelia. Wordsworth says his part is

> to curb
> Thy nymph-like step swift-bounding o'er the lawn,
> Along the loose rocks, or the slippery verge
> Of foaming torrents.
>   (17–20)

This life-saving role is a displacement of his wish to rescue himself from
that bourne whence no traveler returns. The poet at this point allies
himself with Hamlet's refusal to plunge, but Shakespeare's context
makes an ironic comment: We know that Hamlet's puzzled will is a
consequence of his failure to understand himself, so that "enterprises
of great pitch and moment . . . lose the name of action" (III.i.86–88).
And we know too that Hamlet, whose apparently compulsive insensitivity toward Ophelia hides deeper feelings, is fully conscious of the erotic
nature of his relationship with his nymph, unlike the speaker of "*A little
onward*." He is thus able to request Ophelia to be a spiritual help—
"Nymph, in thy orisons / Be all my sins remembered" (89–90)—while
the paterfamilias of "*A little onward*" seeks, by an allusive turn which
suggests that she ignore his sins, an almost opposite relationship:

> From thy orisons
> Come forth; and, while the morning air is yet
> Transparent as the soul of innocent youth,
> Let me, thy happy guide, now point thy way,
> And now precede thee, winding to and fro,
> Till we by perseverance gain the top
> Of some smooth ridge, whose brink precipitous
> Kindles intense desire for powers withheld
> From this corporeal frame; . . .
>   (20–28)

He will again draw back, in affirmation of life but also to evade his incestuous feelings. The path that led to this point, though physically surrounded by a transparency like the soul of innocent youth, winds through an adult darkness allied to that which has enveloped Hamlet and given him pause. We know this because Shakespeare talks back through Wordsworth's allusion to *Hamlet*.

This example may imply that dialectical allusion in Wordsworth is typically fulfilled through evasions and unconscious elements. But while the dialogue with Shakespeare operates covertly, the openness to Milton seems explicit. Wordsworth clearly rejects the sort of sacrifice to the divine order which Milton exalts. His statement to Crabb Robinson that he had no need of a Redeemer (1: 158) implies that he was little affected by the sacrificial element in Christianity, even as embodied in Jesus' death. Yet his views are often contradictory, accommodating sacramental attitudes as well as opposing them and hence furthering genuine dialogue with Milton grounded in deep respect for this individualistic Protestant precursor.[1]

Wordsworth can also engage in overt dialogue with the ideological stance or literary kinds of his major precursors—Miltonic and Shakespearean views, Miltonic epic, Thomsonian and Youngian sermonic forms or visions of order—through "generic" dialectical allusion. This sort of dialectical discourse is encouraged by the lack of cultural authority and publicly representable systems of thought in Wordsworth's bolder revaluating conceptions. In "The Function of Criticism at the Present Time," Matthew Arnold asserts:

> The grand work of literary genius is a work of synthesis and exposition, not of analysis and discovery; its gift lies in the faculty of being happily inspired by a certain intellectual and spiritual atmosphere, by a certain order of ideas, when it finds itself in them; . . . life and the world being in modern times very complex things, the creation of a modern poet, to be worth much, implies a great critical effort behind it; . . . English poetry of the first quarter of this century, with plenty of energy, plenty of creative force, did not know enough. This makes Byron so empty of matter, Shelley so incoherent, Wordsworth even, profound as he is, yet so wanting in completeness and variety. . . . surely the one thing wanting to make Wordsworth an even greater poet than he is—his thought richer, and his influence of wider application—was that he should have read more books, among them, no doubt, those of that Goethe whom he disparaged without reading him. (3: 261–62)

Arnold could not fully grasp the adventurousness of Wordsworth's poetry, which depended on revisionary process and the presentation of mind in act; nonetheless, he has focused on a matter of concern to Wordsworth himself. The poet, who frequently apologized that his wide reading was not wider, worried that his revisionary concepts rested on too narrow or subjective a base. Generic allusion provided one way of dealing with this, engaging the worldview and genres of his predecessors in dialogue. If the method was largely instinctive because of his eighteenth-century training, the result could nevertheless be objective and deliberate.

Critics have discussed the ways in which *The Prelude* invokes the epic genre, in which each work, as Brian Wilkie has shown, is by definition engaged in dialogue with its central predecessors (Wilkie, chap. 1 and passim). A less-discussed source of generic allusion in *The Prelude* is the philosophical sermonizing poem, such as Pope's *Essay on Man*, Young's *Night Thoughts*, Akenside's *Pleasures of Imagination*, or Thomson's *Seasons*. These poems, particularly the first two, aim to teach man who he is—what his powers and place are—through an evolving argument. The last lines of *The Prelude* openly declare that Wordsworth's long poem shares these aims, for all its subtle pretensions to epic form.

Seen at a sufficient distance, one that blurs details, it resembles most particularly *Night Thoughts* in tone and organization. Young's long sermon, mazily structured out of periodically heightened insights into the workings of the human mind and a central movement toward a clarified outlook that has power to redeem the confusions of life, is transitional between Pope and Wordsworth. Though Young in the end champions reason, the Chain of Being, the heaven-derived mental impulse over the sensual natural one, and a traditional surrender of pride, he makes certain revisions in Popean emphases and the Miltonic conceptualizations on which they depend. He castigates Pope for his lack of passion in argument—the apparent insensitivity of his philosophical stance to the painful vexations of the human condition—and changes the fundamental ground of his argument from the Popean one of appealing to the divine plan to a consideration of the human psyche. He alters Pope's tone from cool to hot and his strategy from philosophy to psychology. At the same time, he claims continuity with his elected predecessors: Homer, Milton, and Pope. His extravagant apostrophes, bounding between bathos and genuine pathos, center on psychological experience, for all their trappings of rationalization and gnomic utterance; and he embodies this experience in a personal poetic vehicle which dramatizes the biographies of his speaker and the speaker's one-man audience, the disso-

lute youth Lorenzo, whom he wishes to convert. Young insists on his
poetic adventurousness, the originality of his theme, his techniques,
his gifts as a poet. While he exalts reason, he valorizes strong feeling;
while he drives his addressee toward ascetic choices, he gives physical
pleasure a valid role; while he envisions spiritual insight as necessarily
displacing natural insight, he delights in nature and sees it as an
intermediate teacher.

Though in some respects he Miltonizes avidly and imagines a universe even more rigidly vertical than Milton's, he also inverts Miltonic
vision: He sees man not as a disemparadised wanderer (wandering for
him is a failure of an unfallen reason to exert itself), but as a winged
soul properly tending to heaven. The fallen world is defined not as a
place in which we necessarily labor in pain but as one in which we too
easily remain wedded to the instability and shadowiness of instinctual
gratification. His vision of mankind suggests that all men are in essence poets and by an exertion of creative will can redeem themselves,
in the sense that they can open themselves to a higher reality: "The
more our spirits are enlarged on earth, / The deeper draught shall
they receive of heaven" (Night Ninth, 578–79). His vision is optimis-
tic, promising joy and emphasizing growth:

> Embryos we must be, till we burst the shell,
> Yon ambient azure shell, and spring to life,
> The life of Gods, O transport! and of man.
> . . . .
> The world, that gulf of souls, immortal souls,
> Souls elevate, angelic, wing'd with fire
> To reach the distant skies, and triumph there
> On thrones, which shall not mourn their masters changed,
> Though we from earth; ethereal, they that fell.
> (Night First 132–34; Night Second 349–53)

The professing poet himself is seen as a Dionysian figure guided by
rapture, a God-inspired and god-like creator who

> can grasp whate'er th'Almighty made,
> And wander wild through things impossible!
> What wealth, in faculties of endless growth,
> In quenchless passions violent to crave,
> In liberty to choose, in power to reach,
> And in duration (how thy riches rise!)
> Duration to perpetuate—boundless bliss!
> (Night Sixth 470–76)

This has links with Wordsworth's vision of the poet in *The Prelude* (XIII.84–119), despite central differences. There are so many passages of Young in which the terms and spirit recall Wordsworth, though the referential context is altered (sometimes radically), that *Night Thoughts* seems to hover dimly over the creation of *The Prelude* and *The Excursion*. Its poetic pressure on *The Prelude* is rarely recognized explicitly, but it exerts itself as an "underpresence" in moments when the commonality of purpose in the two poems comes to the fore.

One of these moments is the Snowdon vision in Book XIII of the 1805 *Prelude*. The commonality in these very different visions of order lies in the fact that however much Young may assert his allegiance to the Chain of Being and its architect, thereby downgrading this world of sense experience and mental limitation, his goal is to dignify man. In frequent sermonizing iterations he sustains didactically an image of universal hierarchy; and yet in particular passages he elevates the possibilities of the human spirit by seeming to collapse the architecture of the cosmos even as he describes it. In Night Ninth, for instance, where he undertakes a climactic journey through the heavens "In ardent Contemplation's rapid car" (1715), he clearly states the littleness of creation in comparison with the Creator, using architectural terms:

> Stupendous Architect! Thou, Thou art all!
> My soul flies up and down in thoughts of Thee,
> And finds herself but at the centre still!
> I AM, thy name! Existence, all thine own!
> Creation's nothing; flatter'd much, if styled
> "The thin, the fleeting atmosphere of God."
> (1586–91)

Yet despite the doctrinal absoluteness of this humbling picture, in the same canto Young presents the creature man as having exceptional powers, such that he can overleap the limiting bounds of instituted order by creative mental acts which approximate him to his maker. The speaker, careering through the upper firmament—"the noble pasture of the [human] mind" and "garden of the Deity" (1039, 42)—exclaims to Lorenzo about grandeur:

> As yet thou know'st not what it is: how great,
> How glorious, then, appears the mind of man,
> When in it all the stars, and planets, roll!
> And what it seems, it is: great objects make

> Great minds, enlarging as their views enlarge:
> Those still more godlike, as these more divine.
> (1061–66)

And though the "wondrous space" of the heavens "quite engulphs all human thought" (1105–6), it awakens in the observer's mind a sense of infinite reality in which potentially immortal man may participate. Speaking of the panorama of stars, he says:

> The boundless space, through which these rovers take
> Their restless roam, suggests the sister thought
> Of boundless time. Thus, by kind Nature's skill,
> To man unlabour'd, that important guest,
> Eternity, finds entrance at the sight.
> (1174–78)

Man can overleap the structure of creation because of the peculiar nature of his mind—its character as "the boundless theatre of thought" (1392). This character is the key to the essential nature of man and shows him how to link desire and potentiality:

> The mind that would be happy, must be great;
> Great, in its wishes; great, in its surveys.
> Extended views a narrow mind extend;
> Push out its corrugate, expansive make,
> Which, ere long, more than planets shall embrace.
> A man of compass makes a man of worth;
> Divine contemplate, and become divine.
> As man was made for glory, and for bliss,
> All littleness is in approach to woe;
> Open thy bosom, set thy wishes wide,
> And let in manhood; let in happiness;
> Admit the boundless theatre of thought
> From nothing up to God; which makes a man.
> (1381–93)

Behind the glorification of human potential stands Milton's passage on the Chain of Being in *Paradise Lost* (V.469–505). Though the principal purpose of Raphael's speech to Adam is to ensure his acceptance of his limited condition in full obedience to God, the Archangel holds out the promise that the emparadised human body "may at last turn all to spirit, / Improved by tract of time, and wing'd ascend / Ethereal, as wee, or may at choice / Here or in Heav'nly Paradises dwell." Implied is the idea of an increase in mental happiness, of which Adam and Eve are not yet capable. Young makes specific allusions to this passage—for instance, when his speaker says of the vast night scene through which his imagination is flying, "A banquet, this, where men, and angels, meet, / Eat the same manna, mingle earth and heaven" (1224–25). In speaking of what Raphael holds to be future possibilities as already there, Young is imagining that collapse of vertical cosmic architecture which provides the most original element of his vision. It is evident, too, that despite his Deism, he is in revolt against Pope's view of things, so much more static than Milton's and so bent on fixing man in severe limitation.

Young's reworking of the tradition of poetic sermonizing in the direction of what were to become Romantic conceptions makes it more available to Wordsworth as a genre, and the genre is alluded to in his express interpretation of his vision on Mt. Snowdon. In the far background stand the hill-prospect poems and the loco-descriptive genre with which the poet began his career; in nearer view stands a series of meditations on the Chain of Being comprising Raphael's discourse, the *Essay on Man*, *Night Thoughts*, and Akenside's *Pleasures of the Imagination*. But the chief entryway into the spirit of these poems is Young's grand sermon. The Snowdon meditation begins as a night thought: "A meditation rose in me that night / Upon the lonely Mountain" (XIII.66–67). Wordsworth achieves full understanding "when the scene / Had pass'd away," unlike Young, who is immediately exalted by what he sees. Like Young, though, Wordsworth makes his central theme the potentiality of the mind. In Young's Night Ninth, the heavens provide not an image of the mind but a "pasture" for it; yet the essential function of the scene is the same: to make nature mediate between divine and human consciousness.

Of course the difference is of signal importance, too, since God in Wordsworth is submerged in the scene, existing as an underpresence, and nature, as is not the case in Young, becomes an active agent of insight. However, the continuity of the two poets' visions is sustained by the similar focus on the centrality of the human response, the creative act through which the mind becomes glorious. For Young, when the soul of man is able to "stretch to that expanse / Of thought" and "give her whole capacities that strength, / Which best may qualify for final joy" (573–74, 576–77),

> How glorious, then, appears the mind of man,
> When in it all the stars, and planets, roll!
>
> (1062–63)

For Wordsworth, nature may act in such a way "That even the grossest minds must see and hear / And cannot chuse but feel" (XIII.83–
84). Then,

> The Power which these
> Acknowledge when thus moved, which Nature thus
> Thrusts forth upon the senses, is the express
> Resemblance, in the fulness of its strength
> Made visible, a genuine Counterpart
> And Brother of the glorious faculty
> Which higher minds bear with them as their own.
>
> (84–90)

Many of Young's terms and phrases resemble Wordsworth's. At
times, granting the difference between Young's overly exclamatory
poetic persona and Wordsworth's quieter, more deeply meditative
one, the tone of address is similar; and in the passages just cited there
is a degree of convergence, guided by likenesses in the general conception. But there is nothing specific enough to establish a direct allusion
to Young in Wordsworth's passage. The allusion is generic.

Thus we are not surprised to find in the Snowdon meditation
allusive echoes of other grand sermonizing poems. The words
"catch" and "powers" resonate with Akenside. In the 1744 version of
The Pleasures of Imagination, Akenside tells us that, as Nilus cast
Memnon's image in bronze to respond to the sun's rays with "unbid-
den strains,"

> even so did Nature's hand
> To certain species of external things,
> Attune the finer organs of the mind:
> So that the glad impulse of congenial powers,
> Or of sweet sound, or fair proportion'd form,
> The grace of motion, or the bloom of light,
> Thrills through Imagination's tender frame,
> From nerve to nerve: all naked and alive
> They catch the spreading rays; till now the soul
> At length discloses every tuneful spring,
> To that harmonious movement from without
> Responsive.[2]
>
> (I.113–24)

He goes on to show how the nervous system produces an equivalent of
what Wordsworth is describing when, comparing them to nature in

her sublime moments, he says that higher minds "can send abroad / Like transformation"—"for themselves create / A like existence, and, whene'er it is / Created for them, catch it by an instinct" (XIII.93–96).

It is true that Akenside, with his tendency to fusty classicizing and fustian rhetoric, creates a merely decorative picture ("love and joy / Alone are waking," 130–31), suggestive in the light of his successor's ideas but falling far short of the Wordsworthian vision of the interchange between the mind and nature. It is significant for the generic context Wordsworth is invoking, however, that Akenside, impelled in part by his strong anti-authoritarian attitude, defends even more vigorously than Young the creative freedom of the mind. Why, he asks, "was man so eminently rais'd / Amid the vast Creation" (151–52), why is he ordained to think so far beyond his circumstances, to aim so high for justice and truth?

> wherefore burns
> In mortal bosoms this unquenched hope,
> That breathes from day to day sublimer things,
> And mocks possession? wherefore darts the mind,
> With such resistless ardour, to embrace
> Majestic forms; impatient to be free,
> Spurning the gross control of wilful might;
> Proud of the strong contention of her toils;
> Proud to be daring?
>
> (I.166–74)

Although what follows is a Thomsonian (and hence un-Wordsworthian) ride on the sublime, the tenor of this passage undermines the chain-of-being order it seems to accept and, rather, promotes, in a near-Romantic vein, the satanic virtues of pride, freedom, defiance, self-generated order. Akenside even has the aspiring soul, on completing a Young-like career through the heavens, plunge like Satan into the vast abrupt—"the eternal depth below," "that immense of being" (208, 211)—in order to explore the whole universe and "enlarge her view, / Till every bound at length should disappear, / And infinite perfection close the scene" (219–21). Here is an early expression of the sublime infinity-consciousness that will ultimately depose the concept of the Chain of Being.

The capacity of the human soul to overleap its limitations and enlarge itself seems to be the basis for Wordsworth's echo of another text in the sermonizing tradition, Gray's "Alliance of Education and Government." Lines 59–83 of Gray's poem are an exhortation to defend European political freedom on the basis of his conviction that the

individual soul is by nature free. It is Gray's verbalizing of this assertion, with its emphasis on the reserve of energy available to the soul
when it is aware of its divine origin, which leads directly to Wordsworth's echo. Speaking of those who "build up greatest things / From
least suggestions, ever on the watch," Wordsworth says that

> Such minds are truly from the Deity,
> For they are Powers; and hence the highest bliss
> That can be known is theirs, the consciousness
> Of whom they are habitually infused
> Through every image, and through every thought,
> And all impressions; . . .
>
> (XIII.106–11)

The parallels in Gray, while far from exact, are striking:

> what seasons can control,
> What fancied zone can circumscribe the Soul,
> Who, conscious of the source from whence she springs,
> By Reason's light on Resolution's wings,
> Spite of her frail companion, dauntless goes
> O'er Libya's deserts and through Zembla's snows?
> She bids each slumbering energy awake,
> Another touch, another temper take,
> Suspends the inferior laws that rule our clay:
> The stubborn elements confess her sway;
> Their little wants, their low desires, refine,
> And raise the mortal to a height divine.
>
> (72–83)

The two distinctively Wordsworthian turns in the *Prelude* quotation
above are expressed in side-by-side terms that make a single verbal
phrase, "habitually infused." Infusion points to a different kind of
consciousness from the discrete state of awareness embodied by
Young, Akenside, and Gray. And habitualness suggests another revisionary difference: These three authors state or imply that extraordinary, not habitual, responses drive the soul into knowledge of its
divinity. The same is true of Thomson, whose *Summer* seems to have
provided another echoic source in its description of "the enlightened
few, / Whose godlike minds philosophy exalts." In this passage the
narrator, tremulously "drinking" the effulgence of the evening star,
says of these higher minds,

> They feel a joy
> Divinely great; they in their powers exult,
> That wondrous force of thought, which mounting spurns
> This dusky spot, and measures all the sky.
>
> (1716–19)

Wordsworth tells us that these minds are great precisely because they do not need special circumstances—either apocalyptic perceptions that, in Young's words, allow them to hear "at once, in thought extensive . . . / Th'Almighty fiat, and the trumpet's sound" (Night Sixth, 464–65), or the call of "higher scenes" (Night Ninth, 1217)—to find and put forth their powers. Wordsworth's "great minds" are different from ordinary minds only in being more intensely and steadily able to remain open to life:

> Willing to work and to be wrought upon,
> They need not extraordinary calls
> To rouze them, in a world of life they live,
> By sensible impressions not enthrall'd,
> But quicken'd, rouz'd, and made thereby more fit
> To hold communion with the invisible world.
>
> (XIII.100–105)

All these sources are spawned or poetically informed by the parent subtext which Wordsworth distinctly echoes in the phrase "discursive or intuitive," from Book V of *Paradise Lost*. One can restate what was previously said about Wordsworth's reworking of his Miltonic original as his making accessible in the ordinary present what Milton imagines as the future interchange between man and angel, and redefining the meaning of "Your bodies may at last turn all to spirit" (497) in terms of the imagination and its relation to nature. Wordsworth subsumes the parent text and its derivatives by alluding to them generically as well as specifically, collectivizing them as a body of literature sermonizing on the Chain of Being—on man's nature and its relation to "Great Nature." It is important to see that in the temporal evolution of this body of literature the Chain of Being continues to be relied upon to provide an image of cosmic structure, while being steadily undermined, for Wordsworth can be seen as capping this evolution with a grand assertion of a subject-object model based on new Romantic modes of relational consciousness, especially imaginative interchange.

If this were all, I should assign the generic allusiveness of the passage to the heuristic category; but I think there is a dialogue between the sources, seen collectively, and the text. What Wordsworth's model lacks and the others have is architecture, and architecture provides a metaphor for objective validity and a shareable order. Wordsworth's new imaginative order is, at an ultimate level—that of the transformations which are its life—not clearly objective or shareable. This is maintained by Albert O. Wlecke, who has tried to show that the poet's acts of perception depend on apperceptions of inner consciousness. He states that "Wordsworth's experience of the act of apperception latent in every act of perception is the ultimate source of [his] hope for a vision of a paradise to be regained in the 'common day' " (131). No supernatural agency or system is needed to achieve this vision, only a transformation of consciousness; and the poet helps bring this about by inditing words that "speak of nothing more than what we are," with such force that he arouses an apperceptive activity in his readers parallel to his own. He hopes that in this manner a great work of his, "Proceeding from the depth of untaught things, / Enduring and creative, might become / A power like one of Nature's" (*Prelude* XII.310–12). "But," Wlecke comments,

> this transforming function both of nature and of poetry, ultimately proceeds "from the depth of untaught things" inside the poet himself. For the paradox of *humilitas-sublimitas* takes its origin in that "depth" of subjectivity, that abyss of idealism, which is immediately intuited in the act of apperception. And such an intuition by its very nature can never be taught. (133)

Noting Wordsworth's articulation of this position—"The prime and vital principle is thine / In the recesses of thy nature, far / From any reach of outward fellowship, / Else is not thine at all" ([1850], XIV.215–18)—Wlecke concludes with an analytical summary that underscores its solipsism. In *The Prelude* Wordsworth shows

> the autonomy of his own mind, a mind that by itself can undertake the labor of redemption without the "extraordinary" call of a Christian vocation. . . . [But the "communion with the invisible world" on which this labor depends] must finally be understood as indeed a form of self-communion whereby the poet apperceives the presence of his own consciousness at the very heart of every act of perception. . . . [His] visionary mind sits alone, in a solitude of sublime self-consciousness which is

both the ultimate threat to the world of perception and the exclusive source of that world's transfiguration. (136–37)

I am not convinced that the paradox of apperception (apparently objective perception as self-projection) is so absolute, ultimately closing off the poet's spiritual experience from the kind of communion he sought, but certainly the poet himself was aware of the problematic element in his approach. The triumph he experiences in the Mt. Snowdon meditation and embodies in the passage as a new model of life lived according to the imagination is tempered by his silent knowledge of its extreme subjectivity, its lack of that "architecture" on which prior understanding of human potential had been founded and made shareable. He therefore draws what for him are the significant texts embodying the architectural-objective view into his account, at once to show the extent of his revision of that order of ideas and to open his revision to criticism by it. This is the fundamental office of dialectical allusion. It may seem here to be something like having one's cake and eating it too, but it is not, because, as Greene avers, it "creates a kind of struggle between texts and between eras which cannot easily be resolved" (45).

6

Mapping the Intertext II: Assimilative Allusion

When he used this mode of echoing, Wordsworth *was* in a sense trying to have his cake and eat it too. He put into his rhetorical mix the attitudes and imaginative atmosphere of preceding poets, or poetic communities, in order to enrich it. The effect of this blending, when successful, is either to adsorb the old taste—to make cling to the surface a flavor at once familiar and piquant—or to absorb it, mixing it in so thoroughly that it adds only a subtle essence. When the process is unsuccessful, the echoed ingredients remain inert and merely disturb the smoothness of the texture.

If these assimilative methods of composition are instinctive, like the experienced cook's use of spices or pinches and handfuls of ingredients, they are not without a plan. The plan is based on the poet's urge to acknowledge and reinforce the mood of his piece, the tone of voice or attitude with which he wishes to speak. Using a principle as vague as this, it is possible to sort Wordsworth's selection of sources into innumerable groups, but I believe there are four that usefully organize the spectrum of his actual practice. It is difficult to find natural names for these four groups, as they do not simply embody common feelings and are the product of a highly literary mind measuring itself against the minds of other poets. Since mood in Wordsworth is always the resultant of meditation and has a conceptualizing force, I have chosen names for the moods that indicate their underlying concepts as well as their spirit: "moralizing," "anthropologizing," "naturalizing," and "poeticizing."

THE MORALIZING MOOD

In the moralizing mood we find Wordsworth trying to evoke or test certain "philosophical" orientations to the world. In his need to draw

on prior voices to help him establish the texture or feel of these orientations, he almost exclusively turns to Elizabethan and seventeenth-
century poets (Burns is a major exception) or the genres in which they
worked. And his selectivity is further limited by temperament. By modern standards, he is fairly literal as an interpreter or critical reader,
guiding himself by the explicit argument and the apparently direct
referential elements in the pieces he read.[1] This literalism is particularly to the fore when he is in a moralizing mood, and in poems which
pursue this mood his echoic sources thus tend to be poets who themselves explicitly moralized. The sources can be further subdivided according to the particular moral mood guiding the writing.

THE STOIC MOOD. What may be loosely called a stoic orientation is
prevalent in Wordsworth's oeuvre. It moves into the foreground when
he deals with such things as pain and loss, pessimism, despair, the need
for fortitude, the vicissitudes of life or human history. He is then
likely to echo assimilatively writers who express stoic attitudes—
Daniel, Shakespeare, Milton, or Denham.[2] Daniel is a fairly frequent
source, found in various Wordsworthian contexts. These contexts
range from the well-known quotation of the prefatory sonnet to Fulke
Greville which Daniel included in *Musophilus* (Wordsworth uses the
first version of the sonnet to image the "humourous stage" on which
the growing child of the Immortality Ode cons the various parts he
will later play in life) to an obscure echo in the final lines of "Personal
Talk" II.[3]
     Daniel nicely defines the stoic fortitude of the conservative tempera-
ment Wordsworth was always prone to and increasingly adopted after
the death of his brother John. It is not surprising, then, that Daniel is
evoked in "The Character of the Happy Warrior" (*PW*4.86), an elegy
on Lord Nelson that is also a covert elegy on John. De Selincourt
quotes the apposite passages from Daniel's "Funerall Poem upon the
Earl of Devonshire" (*PW*4.420), but reading these makes it clear that
there is neither close imitation nor an interplay of text and subtext.
What is called up is an attitude toward life already fully developed by
the Elizabethan poet and here appropriated to cement the central
metaphor of Wordsworth's vision—his revision, really—of his brother's character. He saw his brother as representative of the man of
placid virtue able to face the ultimate challenge of death in a muted
Romantic spirit of joy. "Doomed to go in company with Pain, / And
Fear, and Bloodshed," this placable warrior, "endued as with a sense /
And faculty for storm and turbulence," is enlarged into jollity and
"attired / With sudden brightness, like a Man inspired" (lines 12–13,
57–58, 51–52). These lines, and the central segment of Wordsworth's

poem stating how such a man becomes "happy as a Lover" (51) in dealing with evil, power, and danger, strongly recall without actually echoing lines 107–14 and 139–45 of Daniel's elegy.

Spenser, for Wordsworth the great original of English poets who aimed to moralize their songs, is sometimes echoed in contexts of stoic acceptance. He hovers over the whole of *The White Doe of Rylstone* and is used directly in the "Dedication" to set up the tone of inward acceptance of loss. The poem is Spenserian in the sense of being a moral allegory about the spiritual capacities of human beings. The spirit's ability to rise above its animal circumstances without abandoning them is emblematized by the redemptive career of the white doe (the poem "starts from a high point of imagination, and comes round through various wanderings of that faculty to a still higher; nothing less than the Apotheosis of the Animal"); and the depth of its inner resources for mastering spiritual threats is measured by Emily's quietly harrowing growth, which allows her "To abide / The shock [of loss], AND FINALLY SECURE / O'ER PAIN AND GRIEF A TRIUMPH PURE." The high moral road the poem takes made Wordsworth at once immensely proud of it (he thought it, "in conception, the highest work he had ever produced") and concerned about its failures on the level of action ("Everything that is attempted by the principal personages in 'the White Doe' fails, so far as its object is external and substantial"). He clearly wanted it to be read in the same spirit as he read Spenser, as a fantasy whose imaginative freedom allowed it to address directly the most fundamental realities, producing "Notes . . . as of a faery shell / Attuned to words with sacred wisdom fraught."[4]

The wisdom with which Wordsworth freights his words can hardly be called sacred in any traditional sense, however. He plays upon traditional Christian conceptions of the ascent of the soul, but Emily's spiritual development is won through a long naturalizing and humanizing process, and her feminine version of stoical patience and fortitude is not supported by anything that can be felt dramatically as a leading from above. The guidance of the white doe is rather a leading from below. Thus if the hovering presence of Spenser's epic is pushed to the level of an interpretive intertext, puzzling disharmonies appear. Direct allusions to *The Faerie Queene* occur in the "Dedication," and the most overtly moralizing of these forms part of Wordsworth's assertion that he and his wife "by a lamentable change [the death, in 1812, of their children Catherine and Thomas] were taught / That 'bliss with mortal Man may not abide'" ("Dedication" 22–23, quoting with a slight change Spenser's "That blisse may not abide in state of mortall men," *Faerie Queene* I.8.44.9). The functional value of the quotation in taking Spenser's central stance as emblematic of the Christian version of stoic fortitude is clear; but the poem that follows is intent on demonstrating that a genuine bliss—Emily's "triumph pure"—may indeed abide with mortal consciousness. Setting the original alongside the passage from the "Dedication" will not help elucidate or enrich this apparent subtlety.

The original words are Arthur's, spoken to Una after he has rescued the Red Cross Knight from the dungeon of Pride, and immediately preceding his urging the fallen knight to "take to you wonted strength, / And maister these mishaps with patient might" (*Faerie Queene*, I.8.45.1–2). The thrust of Arthur's speech is away from resolution in the order of nature, and nothing in Wordsworth's straightforward parallel context indicates that we are to take his presentation as revisionary. Hence we have to fall back on the concept of a "spot quotation" invoking only the general atmosphere of stoic-Christian moralizing that attends Spenser's allegory. It is not a heuristic reference but an assimilative device that helps Wordsworth educate the reader how to read his poem. His incorporating an aspect of Spenserian voice justifies and sustains the quasi-allegorical moralizing approach of *The White Doe of Rylstone*.

Shakespeare and Milton crop up often in stoic contexts. *Macbeth*, V.iii.23, is called up in "Upon the Same Occasion [September, 1819]"— "my leaf is sere / And yellow on the bough." Milton's sonnet on his blindness is quoted in *The White Doe*, 1069 ("*Her duty is to stand and wait*"). More complex is a reference to both poets together in "Personal Talk" (*PW*4.73). The four linked sonnets, which include other references to Shakespeare, Spenser, Daniel, Collins, and Coleridge, may be seen as an expression of the power of poets to redeem the ravages of time into "genial seasons" ("Personal Talk" IV.5). In the first sonnet the poet tells us that he prefers to make his fireside a place of solitude rather than sociability, maintaining a long, barren silence in which he can

> sit without emotion, hope, or aim,
> In the loved presence of my cottage-fire,
> And listen to the flapping of the flame,
> Or kettle whispering its faint undersong.
> (11–14)

This evident allusion to the "film, which fluttered on the grate / . . . the sole unquiet thing" in "Frost at Midnight" enhances the meaning of the silence as a creative pause. But it is hard to explain why Wordsworth should have included among the list of those whose presence he avoids in this pause not only friends and neighbors and chance-met

"ladies bright, / Sons, mothers," but "maidens withering on the stalk."
The inclusion of this refined company suggests a satirical thrust, but
the context of the whole tells us to discard this idea. The mention of
the unfulfilled maidens may be explained, though, by hints in the
poem that the poet is dealing with the presence found in absence—
silence, solitude, life beyond the daily round so universally controlled
by social (sexual and familial) roles. Yet the subtexts invoked by the
phrase describing the maidens would confuse us if we took them as a
comparative allusion. Shakespeare, drawing on the venerable poetic
argument about the inferior value of the unplucked rose, has Theseus
tell Hermia in *A Midsummer Night's Dream:*

> earthlier happy is the rose distilled
> Than that which, withering on the virgin thorn,
> Grows, lives, and dies in single blessedness.
>   (I.i.76–78)

Comus, Wordsworth's proximate source, gives this honestly argued
advice a wickedly seductive turn in repeating it to Milton's variant of
Hermia. He says to the Lady, "If you let slip time, like a neglected rose
/ It withers on the stalk with languish't head" (*Comus,* 743–44). This
double-barreled source is too powerful to bring to bear on Wordsworth's casual reference with direct allusive force; it would explode
the atmosphere of quiet fireside chat into which we have been invited.
And though there is a mild paradox here (in keeping away familiar
visitors to his hearth the poet is inviting to it the wider company of his
readers), it is not capable of incorporating in terms of genuine textual
interplay the stronger paradox of the poet's allying himself, in his
celebration of "barren" solitude, with two seductive promoters of social engagement. We have to read the echo more simply as an atmospheric inclusion of poetic voices which affirm social norms that
Wordsworth is here setting aside in something of a stoic spirit.[5]
    Wordsworth's stoic voices are clustered among the English poets of
the Renaissance in part because the era's poetry represented for him a
font of dramatically enunciated wisdom, and in part because he had a
will to defy his Augustan heritage, which embodied the most discur-
sively moralizing poetry in the English tradition. He can fully respond
to eighteenth-century moralizing only in Burns.[6] In "To the Sons of
Burns" (*PW*3.69), his aim is Burns-like—to fulfill a paternal duty by
giving direct moral advice; and he plays off Burns's "A Bard's Epitaph" in a straight way, using his predecessor's verse form and com-
menting overtly on Burns's overt moral comments. In the flatly didactic context of "To the Sons of Burns," Wordsworth must reject the

Burnsian paradox of "The Vision," which asserts that "the *light* that led astray / Was *light* from Heaven" (lines 239–40, in Burns; quoted by Wordsworth, with slight changes, at lines 41–42). He even empties his first and more important model, "A Bard's Epitaph," of its wistful complexity. Burns allows for a poet of "judgment clear" who yet is ruined by "thoughtless follies" and so, with a barely effective dramatic irony, makes his concluding bit of straight advice—"Know, prudent, cautious *self-controul* / Is Wisdom's root"—the cry of a lost voice beyond the grave. Wordsworth's having taken the role of the catechizing *senex* seems to cancel out his attempt to call up that anguished verse in his final lines: "But be admonished by his grave, / And think, and fear." One wonders if the essential spirit of Burns, which, by way of balancing severe moral comment with praise, Wordsworth recommends his sons to seek at the sanctified cottage fire, can in fact inhabit that lustral spot. In such a context, two further echoes of Burns ("To J. S****" 51, 53) lie inertly in the too-smooth texture of a poem attempting to capture the grainy and self-contradictory genius of the Scottish peasant bard.

THE EPICUREAN MOOD. Another group of poets, also Elizabethan and Jacobean, is called upon to substantiate an opposite strain of moralizing, which for the sake of symmetry I label "epicurean," in its vulgarized sense. Here the emphasis is on asserting the values of simple pleasure, on expressing a joyous attitude or celebrating what is given, on light-hearted spectatorship which recognizes the picturesque or stage-like character of life. Most of the poets Wordsworth echoes in this vein are minor figures and appear only once or twice: Thomas Churchyard, Henry Constable, Richard Corbet, Charles Cotton, Sir John Davies, Richard Lovelace, George Wither. But he draws more regularly on Drayton, Herrick, Jonson, Spenser, Shakespeare, and Milton's allegrian voice. His most frequent source is Drayton, who holds a position in the epicurean pieces somewhat parallel to Daniel's among the stoic ones. Ten of eleven echoes I have noticed refer to the high-spirited *Nymphidia*, to *The Muses' Elysium*, or to a passage in Song XXX of *Polyolbion* describing the titanic gaiety of the Cumberland mountains pursuing their game of tossing echoes back and forth (125–64.)

The image of mountain echoes created in the last source seems to have had a strong hold on Wordsworth's imagination. We can find references to mountain echoes in the Intimations Ode (line 27), "Yes, it was the mountain Echo" (*PW*2.265), and other pieces that develop the poet's concern with resonance. The image seems to represent the responsiveness of the sublimely permanent other in nature to human presence. In "To Joanna" (*PW*2.112) it is initiated by skeptical laughter on the part of the title personage, who is amused by the speaker's ravishment with the harmony of details on the face of a tall rock—details which create "one impression, by connecting force / Of their own beauty, imaged in the heart" (49–50). The laughter, taken up by the very mountains pictured in Drayton's poem, is replicated as it is amplified and tossed about between their giant heads into a great emblem of natural joy; but so sublime does it become, and so admonitory to Joanna's mildly alienated skepticism, that she is first astonished and then frightened. The image occurs again, divested of its fearful sublimity, in *Home at Grasmere* (*PW*5.313ff.) at the end of a passage in which Wordsworth asserts that the great good place he discovered in childhood has now become his physical and spiritual center, "a haunt / Of pure affections, shedding upon joy / A brighter joy" (50–52). He concludes:

> And now 'tis mine, perchance for life, dear Vale,
> Beloved Grasmere (let the Wandering Streams
> Take up, the cloud-capt hills repeat, the Name),
> One of thy lowly Dwellings is my Home.
>
> (56–59)

The echo of *Polyolbion* is slight, but the juxtaposition of vale, stream, and hill with the idea of naming, the location of Grasmere in Westmoreland (treated along with Cumberland in Drayton's Song XXX), and the atmosphere of play (looking back to Drayton's mountain nymphs chasing each other in "wondrous meriment") all seem to fix it. The movement in Drayton from "grim Hills . . . / From clouds scarce ever cleer'd" to the mountains conversing in joyous shouts, "with Ecchoes loud and long," has its parallel in Wordsworth's image of his haunt "darting beams of light" through "such damp and gloom / Of the gay mind, as ofttimes splenetic Youth / Mistakes for sorrow" (*Home at Grasmere* 53–55). But the links are all atmospheric and operate under the general license of the epicurean mood.

A resonance of *Paradise Lost*, Book XI, flashes fishlike through the phrase "damp and gloom / Of the gay mind" with an ironic twist that suggests a consequential comparison. In the penultimate book of Milton's epic, the archangel Michael explains to Adam the postlapsarian process of death, closing his discourse by representing its degradation of life energies:

> and for the Air of youth
> Hopeful and cheerful, in thy blood will reign

A melancholy damp of cold and dry
To weigh thy Spirits down, and last consume
The Balm of Life.

(XI.542–46)

In Wordsworth the essential reference of Michael's terms is reversed, the melancholy becoming the false spleen of youth and the balm of life being rescued and sustained.[7] On the other hand, the spot quotation of Shakespeare's *Tempest* in Wordsworth's "cloud-capt hills" works in the epicurean mode of assimilative borrowing, for there is no incorporation in either a direct or ironic spirit of Prospero's sense in describing the dissolution of

the baseless fabric of this vision,
The cloud-capped tow'rs, the gorgeous palaces,
The solemn temples, the great globe itself,
Yea, all which it inherit . . .

(IV.i.151–54)

What is incorporated is the general conception of imaginative play Prospero elaborates in his speech, released here by Wordsworth's joyous conviction that he has at last come home.

This same sense of play is at work in "The Power of Music" (*PW*2.217). Though Wordsworth said it was "taken from life" (*PW*2.507), much of it is in fact taken from Sir John Davies's "In Philoneum." Not a true imitation, Wordsworth's version is a loose rewriting in a spirit of effusive pleasure at observing how music may redeem listeners from their driven urban existence, from the weary weight of an all-too-intelligible world. In Davies's poem, the author's ironic perception of the same power, through which he sees night-world victims and oppressors—all the cats and dogs of the city—curiously suspended from their activities and bonded only by their abstraction from normal consciousness, is elaborated into a satirical point about a spellbinding mountebank's brilliantly ignorant practice of medicine. This is quite different from what Wordsworth does. The later poet eliminates Davies's "point," alters "the Ballad singer's auditory" to innocent representatives of city trades (Davies's cutpurse is explicitly excluded), adds transforming details from the repertory of Romanticism (the brightening moon, which renders the singer "a centre of light"), and makes the spellbinding quality of music not an analogue of cheating but a redemptive instrument which, suspending life's compulsive train, binds by presence instead of absence. Of all this there are only imaginable hints in Davies, and textual comparisons show only differences. What links the two poems is Wordsworth's feeling of being in tune with Davies's apperception, his sense that life, when heightened by acts of imagination, is like a scene in a theater (spectators included), something other than "life as it is." That one author uses this awareness to affirm the dominion of life as it is and the other to defy its power to grind down becomes irrelevant in the assimilative mode: Wordsworth levies on his source echoically to fill out the gestalt of a mood, not to imply a confrontation of meanings.

In some epicurean borrowings, Wordsworth seems to be moving back toward the mode of Augustan imitation, or establishing a generic intertext, in the interest of giving an explicit revisionary turn to his allusiveness, until a kind of playfulness disperses the movement in a gesture of freedom. "To the Daisy" (*PW*2.135), for instance, composed during the period of his most joyous poems, is nearly identical in meter and rhyme scheme to Drayton's *Nymphidia.* And *Nymphidia* is directly echoed. Speaking of poets who delight in the lore of "Fayries," Drayton tells us that

> No Tales of them their thirst can slake,
> So much delight therein they take,
> And some strange thing they faine would make,
>   Knew they the way to doe them.
>   (13–16)

Wordsworth, converting the subject to the lore of flowers, is more confident:

> But now my own delights I make,—
> My thirst at every rill can slake,
> And gladly Nature's love partake
>   Of Thee, sweet Daisy!
>   (5–8)

Wordsworth's naturalizing thrust and the reversal of Drayton's image from unslaked to slaked desire seem to represent a heuristic allusion, but there is really no purposive engagement of Drayton's themes. The hidden echoes engage, rather, the spirit of fancifulness played out in the original text (and underlined in the placement of the later piece among *Poems of the Fancy*). As Wordsworth's note indicates ("See, in Chaucer and elder Poets, the honours formerly paid to this flower," *PW*2.138), he is reworking a traditional topic, but the references are merely atmospheric. The poem invokes Chaucer's *Legend of Good Women,* with its palinodic displacement of the rose by the daisy, especially lines 89–184 and 506–22 of text G. Song XXX of *Polyolbion* appears again, this time a different section of it which describes the sport of the nymphs inhabiting the landscape, as they "skip from Crag to Crag, and leape from Rocke to Rocke" (Song XXX, line 136). This Drayton echo forms a background for the restless natural hungerings of Wordsworth's youth, when "from rock to rock I went, / From hill to hill in discontent / Of pleasure high and turbulent" ("To the Daisy" 1–3).

The foreground is held by another poet. In his present calm, all passion not quite spent, Wordsworth approaches the daisy in the spirit of George Wither, from whose *Shepherd's Hunting*, Eclogue IV, he extracts an epigraph:

> Her [the muse's] divine skill taught me this,
> That from every thing I saw
> I could some instruction draw,
> And raise pleasure to the height
> Through the meanest object's sight.

These lines sound Wordsworthian, and are made to sound more so by Wordsworth's substitution of "instruction" for Wither's "invention" (line 3). The latter term surfaces, though, in line 48 of the main text, where Wordsworth asserts that the daisy has inspired "some chime of fancy wrong or right; / Or stray invention." Like other poems written in 1802, which Jared Curtis has shown in careful detail to reflect Wordsworth's reading of seventeenth-century poets, this representative of "Poems of the Fancy" is colored by what one might call, following Curtis, metaphysical playfulness. But in its celebratory mood it avoids finally allying itself with the metaphysical mode by leading the fancy into direct enjoyment of nature, not through nature to some wittily unconventional statement about the human condition:

> An instinct call it, a blind sense;
> A happy, genial influence,
> Coming one knows not how, or whence,
> Nor whither going.
>
>   (69–72)

That is why the echoes in "To the Daisy" are predominantly Elizabethan or earlier, except those from the unmetaphysical Puritan, Wither.

THE APOCALYPTIC MOOD. The third moralizing mood does incorporate speculation about the human condition, minus the wit. I call it "apocalyptic" because it transcends stoic and epicurean attitudes to focus on final things or revelatory experience. This mood generally calls up comparative allusions in the high style, but there are instances of assimilative echoing in the same vein. We find atmospheric borrowings from Spenser, Shakespeare, Milton (particularly the Nativity Ode and "Il Penseroso"), Herbert, the King James Bible, and minor figures like William Habington—again sources in the orbit of the English Renaissance. These borrowings are embedded not only in grand statements and aporetic meditations but in heart-colloquies, explorations of naturalized religious feelings, and mild turns on Christian thought, where they work to "spread the tone."

The tonal effect of Milton's "Penseroso" in the last line of "Remembrance of Collins" (*PW*1.41) has been noted in Chapter 1. Hovering over the whole is an idea expressed by the wizard Indolence in Thomson's *Castle of Indolence:* "What, what is virtue but repose of mind?" (Canto I, stanza 16). The speaker of Wordsworth's piece, suspending his oar, invokes that repose and meditatively projects it on to his image of the poet who "Could find no refuge from distress / But in the milder grief of pity." Playing on the sense of crepuscular calm created in Collins's "Ode to Evening," Wordsworth's act of projection becomes a natural blessing in which the dead poet is exalted as one of Virtue's train: "—The evening darkness gathers round / By virtue's holiest Powers attended" (25–26). But the closing advent of Virgilian shadows evokes, in the light of the Christian centuries which have distanced that poet's pastoral voice, a subtle threat requiring more than a merely natural blessing to undo it (the combined stoic and epicurean morality of Thomson's Indolence is after all false counsel). The blessing has to be pressed through natural imagery to a higher pitch, in which "old experience [might] attain / To something like Prophetic strain" ("Il Penseroso" 173–74), and this is accomplished by the vague echo of "Il Penseroso."

The same implicit upward turn is implied in an echo of Milton's Nativity Ode fleetingly heard in the last canto of *The White Doe of Rylstone*. We have seen that the main theme of this Wordsworthian version of historical romance is the familiar one of the great decade: compensation for loss through the "strange discipline" imposed by nature.[8] The Miltonic echo comes just at the point where Emily has contained her loss as far as she can with the help of stoic fortitude. Now, seeing her paternal home again, she puts "her fortitude to proof":

> The mighty sorrow hath been borne,
> And she is thoroughly forlorn:

> Her soul doth in itself stand fast,
> Sustained by memory of the past
> And strength of Reason; held above
> The infirmities of mortal love;
> Undaunted, lofty, calm, and stable,
> And awfully impenetrable.
>
> (1621–28)

She is about to encounter the doe, through whose agency she will be fully restored to life from her forlorn state. Her acceptance of this "gift of grace" binds once more the "Pair / Beloved of Heaven" and resolves the devastations of time wrought on the innocent woman, while raising the doe above its natural condition. (Appropriately, the final lines are shot through with suggestions of "Il Penseroso.") The echo of the Nativity Ode thus occurs at a pivotal moment. It is subtly conveyed in the last two lines of the quotation: the homonymic carrying over of "stable" (the denotation has changed) and the re-creation of the same deliberately naive deformation of normal pronunciation Milton used to make up his rhyme—a peculiar chime no reader of the Nativity Ode is likely to forget because of this deformation and its terminal position in the poem: "And all about the Courtly Stable, / Bright-harness'd Angels sit in order serviceable" (243–44).

At this point in Wordsworth's poem the pure and innocent Emily rests under "A self-surviving leafless oak" (1630) in a quite different state from that of the Christ child in Milton's poem, the focal difference being her bondage to depressed spirits. Yet the echo marked in the rhyme, carrying over the original mood, implies that angels sit invisibly about her—that, guided by some greater power, she will be penetrated by the "kindliest intercourse" of nature and thus, when "The weak One [the doe] hath subdued her heart" (1782), may be "Uplifted to the purest sky / Of undisturbed mortality" (1852–53), set free to die.

This elevation of condition, with the echo-borne suggestion of angelic presence, is reinforced by another echo from another Miltonic context. When Wordsworth tells us that Emily's "soul doth in itself stand fast" (1623), the climax of *Paradise Regained* opens momentarily to view—Christ in his "uneasy station" on the pinnacle of the temple, taking the whole weight of his human reality on himself by resisting the ultimate Satanic temptation to force the Father to act on his behalf: " 'Also it is written, / Tempt not the Lord thy God'; he said and stood" (IV.560–61). Here there is consonance of meaning at one level between text and subtext, though of course the larger contexts present opposed attitudes (Christ's coming in the Nativity Ode, for instance, is the death knell for all natural concepts of redemption).

But Wordsworth's echoes of Habington's "Description of Castara" in "She dwelt among the untrodden ways" (*PW*2.30) lack even this mediation. He draws on Habington's first stanza:

> Like the Violet which alone
> Prospers in some happy shade:
> My *Castara* lives unknowne,
> To no looser eye betray'd,
> For shee's to her selfe untrue,
> Who delights ith' publicke view.

The borrowings of image and situation are unmistakable, but in setting, rhetorical character, form, and movement the poems seem to have nothing to do with each other. The only connection beyond mere resonance is the thematic idea of using description to transform the beloved into a religious object. Habington concludes:

> Her pure thoughts to heaven flie:
> All her vowes religious be,
> And her love she vowes to me.
> (40–42)

In the context of his poem it is a logical conclusion, the capping vision of the woman's tested and inviolate virtue. Wordsworth's conclusion involves a sudden shift, surprising even if we take it in the context of all the Lucy poems. It is prepared for rhetorically, however, by the abrupt change of images in the second stanza—the movement from Habington's violet (which Wordsworth has made a metaphor rather than a simile) to a star. Lucy is

> A violet by a mossy stone
> Half hidden from the eye!
> —Fair as a star, when only one
> Is shining in the sky.
> (5–8)

But this change involves more than imagery. There is a movement across the dash from earth to heaven, from metaphor to simile, from exclamation to calm statement, from a thing rich but dark in color and half in view to one brilliant and in plain view, from simple syntax to syntax complicated by subordination, and from an image of some natural freshness to an old Petrarchan standby for the beloved. Furthermore, the movement is asyndetic, disjunction being enforced by the dash. The speaker has indeed dashed to heaven, as if he were impatient to reach Habington's conclusion. But the heavenly translation of Lucy to a Hesperidean presence, looked at from a naturalizing perspective outside the Petrarchan tradition, suggests dying, and that suggestion is taken up: "But she is in her grave." Castara, the "chaste altar" of the speaker's love in Habington's poem, can be compared to a violet because she is in fact inviolate; her holiness is natural, the effect of inborn virtue rationally developed. Lucy's natural holiness—her violet-like life among the untrodden ways—cannot prevent and even seems to lay her open to violation by death. She becomes a religious object in a new sense: She is a numen awakening the speaker suddenly to deeper thought about the interinvolvement of his naturalizing consciousness, which has seemed to make vows upon the altar of nature, with the idea of death. This awakening is the subject of all the Lucy poems.

The relation between Wordsworth's poem and Habington's is not developed in direct intertextual terms. Even the links in imagery are merely echoic, not truly referential on the level of meaning. The echo simply thickens the atmosphere of false confidence in normal descriptive continuity set up by Wordsworth in the first six lines. The false confidence is going to be roughly broken, but first it must establish itself; and this is accomplished by Wordsworth's bringing forward a smooth seventeenth-century voice that uses rational progression of imagery to work an old trick, a variant of Petrarchan or Cavalier praise treating the beloved as a religious object. What is established is then subjected to a demystification, but this demystification is not a specific overgoing of Habington's poem and indeed could be effected without it. The earlier piece is merely a foil that helps bring out what is already there. Thus even the lingering echo that initiates the final movement of Wordsworth's poem ("She lived unknown," recalling Habington's "My *Castara* lives unknowne") does not work as a genuine allusion: Readers who do not catch the intertextual reference are not missing any vital elements of meaning.

A similar concern for the mortal liabilities of an innocent wedded to nature governs "To H. C. Six Years Old" (*PW* 1.247), though it leads not to a meditation on death but a fear that the child's character may be incapable of meeting the normal shocks of life. This apostrophe to Hartley Coleridge consciously undermines Coleridge's earlier rumination on his son as a baby in "Frost at Midnight." There the father becomes confident that the growing boy, by wandering "like a breeze /

By lakes and sandy shores, beneath the crags / Of ancient mountain, and beneath the clouds" (54–56), will "see and hear / The lovely shapes and sounds intelligible / Of that eternal language, which thy God / Utters" (58–61) and so be molded and protected by Providence. Wordsworth translates Hartley's conning of "shapes and sounds intelligible" into his making "a mock apparel" that clothes "unutterable thought." The boy's aeolian wandering becomes the "breeze-like motion" of a "faery voyager" whose boat (in an image borrowed from Carver's *Travels*) "may rather seem / To brood on air than on an earthly stream";[9] and though this presents a "blessed vision," it inspires fear for what may happen to the boy in the future.

The poet's troubled thought is then overtly rejected as his godfatherly concern leads him into a redemptive movement parallel to that in "Frost at Midnight." Like the ambiguous opening imagery, however, the movement is far more compromised than Coleridge's, betraying the same proto-tragic sense of nature's duplicitous relation to innocence as is seen in "She dwelt among the untrodden ways." Hartley will not experience the common lot of slow temporal degradation through the twin actions of pain and grief, but will be subject to an all-or-nothing fate. The passage expressing this prevision turns on Coleridge's line, "Therefore all seasons shall be sweet to thee" (65):

> O vain and causeless melancholy!
> Nature will either end thee quite;
> Or, lengthening out thy season of delight,
> Preserve for thee, by individual right,
> A young lamb's heart among the full-grown flocks.
> (20–24)

This prophecy is in fact opposite to that of "Frost at Midnight" in one important respect: Hartley's preservation depends not on a natural development *tout court*, one based on experience open to all and evolving like the growth of muscle and bone, but on the lack of it, on a sustaining of the status quo granted by providential exception ("individual right") and mediated by a nature responsive to personhood.

The contrast in view between the two poems comes about ultimately because in Wordsworth's imagination God as an active agent has been replaced by nature. In Coleridge nature is only an instrument of divine Providence; here it is providence itself. Yet Wordsworth in this case is not ready to go as far in a naturalizing direction as he was in the Lucy poems, undoubtedly because Hartley is an actual person and the child of his friend, and the poet does not wish to reduce the current of hope to so narrow a channel. He therefore picks up Coleridge's aim of connecting his son to a divine reality by echoing Marvell's "On a Drop of Dew." Marvell wittily elaborates the paradox of an evanescent natural phenomenon that through its very structure embodies a heavenly existence:

> See how the Orient Dew,
> Shed from the Bosom of the Morn
>   Into the blowing Roses,
> Yet careless of its Mansion new;
> For the clear Region where 'twas born
>   Round in its self incloses:
> And in its little Globes Extent,
> Frames as it can its native Element.
>   (1–8)

Wordsworth ignores the metaphysical wit and its paralogical demonstrations (particularly Marvell's perorating comparison of the drop of dew to the soul), invoking only those parts of the poem which resonate with the idea of the dewdrop's tenuous hold on its earthly surroundings. His echo catches up lines from the beginning and from the middle:

> Restless it roules and unsecure,
>   Trembling lest it grow impure:
> Till the warm Sun pitty it's Pain,
> And to the Skies exhale it back again.
>   (15–18)

In Wordsworth this becomes:

> Thou art a dew-drop, which the morn brings forth,
> Ill fitted to sustain unkindly shocks,
> Or to be trailed along the soiling earth;
> A gem that glitters while it lives,
> And no forewarning gives;
> But, at the touch of wrong, without a strife
> Slips in a moment out of life.
>   (27–33)

This amplification of Hartley's future under the aegis of natural providence accomplishes several things at once. By seeming to weight his fate on the side of a short life, it sustains the theme of disquietude which unfolds the central paradox in Wordsworth's view of natural innocence. Yet it does so in a way that accomplishes the poem's original aim of celebrating the boy. It also preserves the naturalizing force of Wordsworth's vision by undoing Marvell's "demonstration" of the heavenly nature of dew; yet, at the same time, by the very fact of echoing Marvell Wordsworth is able to create the impression that he is supporting the father's view of his son as a child of God. The dodgy ten lines of the opening have prepared for this, so that the poem can be read as a meditation on what happens to the children of God—"the exquisitely wild"—under natural providence. It is in fact a demystification of "Frost at Midnight," but a tactfully hesitant and partial one through its cautious diction, its self-interrupting argumentative movement, and its selective echoing of Marvell's poem.

The preceding examples are interesting exceptions to the rule that Wordsworth's "apocalyptic" assimilative echoes play an obvious role in helping to further the mood. The echo of Herbert's "Sunday" and "Virtue" in Book VII, line 695, of *The Excursion* appropriately enhances the pathos of the burial of a child on an all-too-fair day. The misquotation of Jeremy Taylor's *Rule and Exercises of Holy Dying* in *Excursion* VI.532–33 by the Solitary (some men are "made desperate by 'too quick a sense / Of constant infelicity' ") curiously points the Solitary's implied accusation of God by using pastor against pastor. Taylor's original actually says, "This is a place of sorrow and tears, of great evils and a constant calamity," immediately followed by "Let us remove from hence, at least in affections and preparations of mind." The echo and its associated sequel give new authority to the Solitary, who is always the odd man out in the small group of discussants, and fresh weight to his argument and his choice of a retired life (Taylor I.v.2, pages 45–47).

Self-evident appropriateness is common in Wordsworth's borrowings from Scripture. The bulk of the biblical echoes occur in poems full of sententious comment, like *An Evening Walk* and *Descriptive Sketches*, in works or passages attempting grand statement, like the "Prospectus," "The Power of Sound," and parts of *The Prelude*, or in pieces that overtly involve religious discourse, like *The Excursion*, "*A little onward lend thy guiding hand*," and "Processions." These poems account for a large majority of the "apocalyptic" borrowings. I have already noted Richard Brantley's view that Wordsworth's language is pervaded by religious terms drawn from the evangelical discourse of his day, particularly those involved in its emblematic and typological methods of reading the natural world. Brantley argues that the poet was not simply a secularizer of inherited theology but engaged religious issues in a religious spirit. M. H. Abrams, on the other hand, has shown how central Christian insights are secularized in the revisionary process of Romantic compositions. Despite their opposing premises, however, the two critics agree in finding religious ideas to be deeply involved in the thematic, structural, and textural organization of Wordsworth's poetry.

Biblical references in Wordsworth's works are exceeded only by references to Milton, Shakespeare, Gray, and Spenser. But many are allusively inert echoes, highly familiar phrases which function as tags, decorative reminders, or slight sermonic turns. We expect to find this bland sort of echo in *An Evening Walk* ("Choked is the pathway, and the pitcher broke," line 256 [1793], drawing on Ecclesiastes 12.6) and *Descriptive Sketches* ("Deep that calls to Deep," line 433 [1793], drawing on Psalm 42.7; the turn on Genesis 42.38 in line 631 [1793], "Bows his young hairs with sorrow to the grave"; the restatement of "a new heaven and a new earth" in line 645 [1849], from Revelation 21.1). And we expect it in the many sermonizing speeches of *The Excursion* ("their place knew them not," quoting Psalm 103.16 at I.546; the quotation from the metrical version of Psalm 88.11 at II.381–82; the unresonant use of the common biblical phrase, "beauty of holiness," at VI.11; the description of Moses smiting the rock for water [Numbers 20.1–11] at VI.919–20). But we find similarly bland echoes in *The Prelude* (the turn on St. Paul's "armor of righteousness" [2 Corinthians 6.7] in IV.168–71 of the 1850 version, for example, or "that peace / Which passeth understanding," XIV.126–27, from Philippians 4.7). We find them in "Calais, August, 1802" (*PW*3.109): "Is it a reed that's shaken by the wind, / Or what is it that ye go forth to see?" (cf. Matthew 11.7), and in a variant of "The Old Cumberland Beggar" ("ye know not what ye do" [*PW*4.447], from "they know not what they do," Luke 23.34). These borrowings do not even seem to function atmospherically, as so many assimilative borrowings do; they act primarily as moral mementos.

A few, however, have atmospheric force, or accomplish still more. When the Wanderer in *The Excursion* attacks the excuses of rationalistic philosophers who lead us to "pore, and dwindle as we pore, / Viewing all objects unremittingly / In disconnexion dead and spiritless" (IV.960–62), he draws on Psalm 139 to deny that earth and sky and

>   that superior mystery
> Our vital frame, so fearfully devised,
> And the dread soul within it—should exist
> Only to be examined, pondered, searched,
> Probed, vexed, and criticized.
>
>   (IV.974–78)

The primary allusion is to verse fourteen of the psalm: "I will praise thee; for I am fearfully and wonderfully made: marvelous are thy works; and that my soul knoweth right well." But this carries with it the tenor of the whole psalm, which expresses the right kind of searching and the limitation of human vision:

> O Lord, thou hast searched me, and known me. Thou knowest my downsitting and mine uprising, thou understandest my thought afar off. . . . My substance was not hid from thee, when I was made in secret, and curiously wrought in the lowest parts of the earth.
>
> (vv. 1–2, 15)

Even richer is the Solitary's ironic use of "O death, where is thy sting? O grave, where is thy victory?" (1 Corinthians 15.55) to accuse religion with its "retinue, / Faith, Hope, and Charity" (V.332–33) of empty promises:

>   of you,
> High-titled Powers, am I constrained to ask,
> Here standing, with the unvoyageable sky
> In faint reflection of infinitude
> Stretched overhead, and at my pensive feet
> A subterraneous magazine of bones,
> In whose dark vaults my own shall soon be laid,
> Where are your triumphs? or your dominion where?
>   (V.340–47)

The echo of a related passage from 1 Corinthians 15.52—"for the trumpet shall sound"—though quite straightforward, adds a deep resonance to the last stanza of "On the Power of Sound" (*PW*2.323) by setting the thematically exact "last trumpet" in the widest context of the eternity of the word. The same kind of effect is achieved by the equally straightforward yet highly resonant "The Rain is over and gone!" in the final line of "Written in March" (*PW*2.220), the phrase being a direct quotation of the Song of Solomon 2.11. But exceeding these in allusive power is the subtle turn on Revelation 3.20, as well as Exodus 34.33–35 and its revision in 2 Corinthians 3.13–16, created in a familiar passage of *The Prelude*. The passage gives no obvious clues to its sources:

>   Gently did my soul
> Put off her veil, and, self-transmuted, stood

Naked as in the presence of her God.
As on I walked, a comfort seem'd to touch
A heart that had not been disconsolate,
Strength came where weakness was not known to be,
At least not felt; and restoration came,
Like an intruder, knocking at the door
Of unacknowledg'd weariness.

(IV.140–48)

These words represent a partial conversion and are a preparation for the culminating conversion of the "dedication scene"—Wordsworth's description of how he was inwardly bound to the career of poet. The passage is preceded by lines explaining how the speaker, just arrived home on his first summer vacation from Cambridge, feels a mixed sense of pleasure and embarrassment on entering again the scene of the old walks during which he had spouted aloud the inspirations of juvenile poeticizing. One implication of this embarrassment is that the creative fervor he used to feel, so awkwardly self-exposing even at the time, has lapsed, unconsciously covered over by more "sophisticated" mundane pursuits. In representing the unwilled rediscovery of this fervor, Wordsworth echoes the passage in Exodus where Moses, just descended from Mt. Sinai, must veil his shining face in order to give the people "in commandment all that the Lord had spoken with him in mount Sinai":

> And till Moses had done speaking with them, he put a vail on his face.
> But when Moses went in before the Lord to speak with him, he took the vail off, until he came out. And he came out, and spake unto the children of Israel that which he was commanded.

(34.33–34)

The word "vail" is the allusive link. Traversing the original ground of his poetic passion—sacred ground and, in a typically naturalizing Wordsworthian turn, flat—the poet comes into the presence of the divine commandment which is to rule his adult life. The moment, in contrast to Moses at Sinai, lacks intellectual articulateness, even depends on its lack, because the predominance of feeling over clear thought allows a richer exploration of what is at stake:

I had hopes and peace
And swellings of the spirits, was rapt and soothed,
Convers'd with promises, had glimmering views

> How Life pervades the undecaying mind,
> How the immortal Soul with God-like power
> Informs, creates, and thaws the deepest sleep
> That time can lay upon her; . . .
>
> (IV.152–58)

But the resonance of Exodus helps articulate the experience in a subterranean way. This text, first invoked in *The Prelude*'s opening lines ("a house of bondage" and "a wandering cloud," I.5–6 and 18 [1805], recall details of Exodus 13.3 and 21–22), is a symbolic overseer of the mental journey the poem represents. Furthermore, the part of Exodus echoed in *Prelude* IV.141 has its own biblical afterimage in 2 Corinthians, chapter 3, where St. Paul extends the meaning of Moses' veil. Christians, he says, "use great plainness of speech," unlike Moses, who

> put a vail over his face, that the children of Israel could not steadfastly look to the end of that which is abolished:
> But their minds were blinded: for until this day remaineth the same vail untaken away in the reading of the old testament; which vail is done away in Christ.
> But even unto this day, when Moses is read, the vail is upon their heart.
> Nevertheless when it shall turn to the Lord, the vail shall be taken away.
> Now the Lord is that Spirit: and where the Spirit of the Lord is, there is liberty.
> But we all, with open face beholding as in a glass the glory of the Lord, are changed into the same image from glory to glory, even as by the Spirit of the Lord.[10]
>
> (vv. 13–18)

This text too is caught up in Wordsworth's echo, helping to explain why the veil is a weariness and why it is not acknowledged. It is part of a habitual and unenlightened way of looking at the central issues of life. The Pauline passage also substantiates the linked feelings of comfort, strength, and enlargement, and it prepares for the succeeding lines asserting that the soul has "God-like power," since in the liberty of the spirit, Paul says, man becomes a mirror-image of God. In Revelation, this spirit, envisioned as "the Amen, the faithful and true witness, the beginning of the creation of God" (3.14), accuses the world-loving churchgoer, who "knowest not that thou art wretched, and miserable, and poor, and blind, and naked" (v. 17), of being "lukewarm, and neither cold nor hot" (v. 16). His lukewarmness is the equivalent of unacknowledged weariness, and the spirit comes to chasten and enlighten this impoverished worshiper, interrupting him in the same way that Wordsworth is interrupted:

> Behold, I stand at the door, and knock: if any man hear my voice, and open the door, I will come in to him, and will sup with him, and he with me. (v. 20)

In this inspired moment, Wordsworth's references to Daniel 5.27 ("Thou art weighed in the balances, and art found wanting") also become allusively alive, despite the familiarity of his source. For Wordsworth uses it to dismiss the divine threat depicted in the Book of Daniel (*mene, mene, tekel, upharsin*), arrogating judgment to himself and justifying his lowly status along with his dim awareness: "I took / The balance in my hand and weigh'd myself. / I saw but little, and thereat was pleas'd" (*Prelude* IV.148–50). But the norm of the borrowings in the apocalyptic vein is closer to the taglike "How are the Mighty prostrated" (2 Samuel 1.25), which Wordsworth attaches to *The Prelude* X.952. Thus, the apocalyptic echo is, on the whole, the least interesting of Wordsworth's assimilative borrowings.

THE ANTHROPOLOGIZING MOOD

Wordsworth draws on a different set of sources when his thoughts are occupied with the social nature of man. His lifelong project of speaking out philosophically "on Man, on Nature, and on Human Life" was a channel for a number of his natural propensities, however much its grand outlines may have been inflated in response to actual or internalized pressure from Coleridge's seductive and mutually self-serving imaginings about his friend's intellectual capacities. Constant brooding on the human condition led Wordsworth to invest his energies not only in introverted self-study, turning over his inward experiences of childhood consciousness, nature, or adult relationships, but also in what he thought of as studies of man's social and political nature. Despite a growing desperation over those deficiencies of intellectual knowledge which seemed to unfit him for authorship of a great philosophical poem, and despite intense spurts of directed reading, he was never able to make his studies as programmatic as he intended;[11] but his bent for probing social phenomena went beyond engaging in conversation the outcasts and fringe characters he met on his walks, or pursuing a picturesque interest in rural life. He read extensively in history and in books that we can see as treating life from an anthropological or sociological viewpoint.

It is well known that his favorite books were accounts of travels. The growth in travel books was a response to the steady rise in tourism, a late bourgeois flowering of impulses initiated in the Renaissance Age of Discovery and a further popularization of the love of the picturesque, which focused on ruins and rural life. But travel books had still other values. In Lane Cooper's view, these accounts embodied for Wordsworth "the real language of men," and the poet himself stated that "without much of such reading my present labors cannot be brought to any conclusion" (Cooper 109). These books, in addition to providing an imaginative outlet for his wanderlust and real-life examples of the journey as a metaphor for the discovery of the self, gave him information about the reactions of human beings tested in action, about social organization in other lands, about man more or less (as he and his age thought) in a state of nature.

The contemporary idea that one could get closer to the essence of man by observing humanity in a primitive state, along with the particular Wordsworthian variant of it that saw the study of nature leading to the study of man, also gave impetus to the poet's interest in the works of naturalists like William Bartram or James Grahame (usually presented as travel narratives, though sometimes also as guides or poems). Of the same nature, but turned toward the past, were the writings on antiquities, topographical poems, and accounts of local lore. Though he struggled against the popular impulse to seek out the picturesque scene, the melancholy ruin, or the local novelty, Wordsworth could never put it to rest because it was so closely allied with the idea that these objects were peculiarly revelatory of the nature of man, pages of a continuing anthropological study. If Wordsworth was, as Cooper asserted, a "poetical geographer," he was also by his lights a poetical anthropologist: "All things shall speak of Man."[12]

Another kind of anthropological trace, an antiquity of sorts, but one which had survived intact and by its very character resisted the merely picturesque while being vividly pictorial, was the ballad. To Wordsworth it spoke directly of man because its plain language embodied fundamental emotions and actions without adding anesthetic layers of tailored narrative, moralizings and dogmas, or overly artful description. Its peculiar economy and saltatory progressions demanded imaginative responses on the level of feeling to fill in the gaps, while its reliance on fragmentary remnants of pre-Christian religious or mythological beliefs suggested more fundamental yet still immediate reactions to the fate-laden life underlying civilized life. This mode of functioning embodied a demystification of the typical poetic study of mankind—the smooth exemplary tale, the moral essay, the confident meditation on a picturesque scene. Demystification of this sort meant humanization to Wordsworth, not rationalistic reduction. Through swift transitions, uncomplicated yet elusive symbolic imagery, subtly charged dramatic quotation, poignant ironies contrasting the abrupt workings of human passion with the continuity of natural life, and a "penumbra of folklore or . . . 'folk imagination,' " the ballad created a simple human order that resisted simple interpretation.[13]

Certain poets who relied on the spirit of the ballad, like Chatterton, Bürger, and of course Burns, also seemed to Wordsworth to incorporate this direct human voice, and we find echoes of them in poems concerned with man and social conditions. On the other hand, there are almost as many echoes of Pope as of Burns. To be sure, Wordsworth, who "could repeat, with a little previous rummaging of my memory, several 1000 lines of Pope," thought of the arch-Augustan as a poet who had refined away the direct human voice.[14] But his revolt against Augustan diction and genres did not prevent him from absorbing some of Pope's attitudes toward man or storing away in his mind the peculiar poetic power with which the neoclassical poet embodied them. Wordsworth, still in many ways a man of the Enlightenment, also shared some of Pope's Augustan sense that Roman literature was a profound respository of insights into man. He made this literature an important part of his reading, particularly the Roman historians, whose view that the cultivated virtue in each individual is the essential binding force of the polity was consonant with his own.[15]

Most of the borrowings from these oddly assorted sources are of the assimilative sort. Labeling the mood which calls them into play "anthropologizing" emphasizes its role in mediating Wordsworth's concerns with the psychosocial nature of man. It is not radically different from the moralizing mood, but to the extent that it is distinctive it carries the poet's impulse to evoke or test images of human cultural ways, of the existential condition of man (the shortness or disappointments of life, the weaknesses and strengths of choice), and of the structure of desire. It is the mood that ponders the still, sad music of humanity as it plays in the background of individual possibility, community, or fate. The echoed sources give glimpses into these areas of experience, and because they embody the simple givenness of experience, Wordsworth does not use them in a revisionary, allusive way. He tries to incorporate, not overgo, visions of the human condition.

"Ruth" (*PW*2.227) is permeated by the anthropologizing mood. The poem draws a complicated picture of the relations between man and nature. The lush wildness of Georgia seems to infuse the seductive "Youth of green savannahs" (68) with vital energy, yet it also assists his fall into the excesses which destroy his life and Ruth's. The more placid influences of the English landscape work some healing in the mad mind of the deserted and broken girl. Informing the Georgian scene is a force which Milton described in the Garden of Eden in *Paradise Lost,* a certain superabundance, difficult to control, that "Nature boon / Pour'd forth profuse on Hill and Dale and Plain" (IV.242–43). In the epic it is linked with those urges that separate Eve from Adam and lead her to dare the forbidden.

Details in "Ruth" which editors have ascribed to Wordsworth's reading of Bartram's *Travels* are also related to the Garden of Eden, such as the "plants that hourly change / Their blossoms, through a boundless range / Of intermingling hues" (55–57), recalling Milton's "Flow'rs of all hue" (IV.256). And the one direct echo of *Paradise Lost,* the Youth's assertion that the bliss of the Georgian paradise will be enhanced by the knowledge that the couple will have a privileged security—allowing them to live happily "in a world of woe, / On such an earth as this!" (83–84)—is allusively alive in its ironic prolepsis of the truth. Also generative of comparative energy is the use of *Othello* (I.iii.128–70) to show Ruth's captivation by the apparently heroic qualities of the Indian-fighter as he tells Ruth tales of his combats (lines 43–48). (The possible echo of Marvell's "Garden" in the "green shade" of line 47 adds still another interesting referential complexity.) Echoes of Ophelia's mad demise (*Hamlet* IV.v.21–74) in lines 196–98 are tamer and less artfully relevant.

These allusions develop the foreground of the poem's study of man's social nature. The borrowings from Bartram help shape the background. The poem is not "a close rendering of Bartram's narrative," as De Selincourt's note tells us, relying on E. H. Coleridge (*PW*2.510). Rather, Wordsworth generalizes and simplifies Bartram's details. Bartram describes in the manner of the naturalist the laurel magnolias along the San Juan River of East Florida:

> [They are] the most beautiful and tall that I have any where seen, unless we except those, which stand on the banks of the Mississippi; yet even these must yield to those of St. Juan, in neatness of form, beauty of foliage, and, I think, in largeness and fragrance of flower. Their usual height is about one hundred feet, and some greatly exceed that. (91)

Speaking of the Youth, Wordsworth writes,

> He told of the magnolia, spread
> High as a cloud, high over head!
> (61–62)

By the cloud image, which is his own, he emphasizes the lavish free-dom of Georgian nature, and by his simplicity and naive repetition of "high" he invokes the ballad atmosphere, which is further enhanced by the leaping-and-lingering manner in which he tells his tale, the common-yet-vivid imagery he uses throughout, and the almost imper-sonal presentation of the fateful circumscriptions laid on the girl.

At the same time his resonances pick up the mood of Bartram's psychological animadversions on human life, which show how our "higher powers" and aspirations to virtue are vulnerable because of our domination by moods emanating from our "inferior passions." But Wordsworth echoes only the character of these excurses, drawing in a tonal way on his original but not confronting it allusively. De Selincourt tells us that "the frontispiece of [Bartram's *Travels*] depicts a chieftain, whose feathers nod in the breeze just as did the military casque of the youth from Georgia's shore" (*PW*2.510): A military casque

> With splendid feathers drest;
> He brought them from the Cherokees;
> The feathers nodded in the breeze,
> And made a gallant crest.
> (21–24)

By thus approximating his youth to Bartram's chieftain (a typical "noble savage"), Wordsworth is able to put in the foreground the youth's energetic powers and daring pride while keeping in the back-ground Bartramian musings about the vulnerability of man's finest qualities.

Other references to Bartram, though slighter, work in much the same way. The naturalist's frequent references to the animating yet calming effect of the sun's return at dawn are compressed into a particular echo in "She was a Phantom of delight" (*PW*2.213): "And now I see with eye serene / The very pulse of the machine."[16] It is only one substantiating detail in the poem's attempt to explore and resolve the complexity of a personality by depicting its essence; but it fits exactly, since the woman described (Wordsworth's wife) is associated principally with the light of dawn and a quiet vivacity.

Wordsworth's attack in Book III of *The Prelude* on false pedantry, particularly as it corrupts "the plain Steeples of our English Church" (line 425), is driven home by a suggestion that the seat of learning "for our Country's Youth" be made into a sanctuary like "a Virgin grove, / Primaeval in its purity and depth" (442–43). This un-Miltonic naturalizing of an essentially Puritan attitude is supported by his use of a passage in Bartram. Interestingly, with its paradisal lushness Bartram's description is more Miltonic in spirit than Wordsworth's:

> magnolian groves, from whose tops the surrounding expanse is perfumed, by clouds of incense, blended with the exhaling balm of the liquidambar, and odours continually arising from circumambient aromatic groves of illicium, myrica, laurus and bignonia.[17] (64)

Bartram's specific details are not essential here; rather, it is the naturalist's continual emphasis on unspoiled nature as God's temple which Wordsworth assimilates in making a case for the naturalizing of learning. One instance of this natural learning is the "Boy of Winander" passage in Book V of *The Prelude,* and it is possible that the description there of the "concourse wild" of the hoots the boy raises to provoke a response from the owls was influenced by Bartram's description of "the cheering converse of the wild turkey-cocks . . . saluting each other":

> The high forests ring with the noise, like the crowing of the domestic cock, of these social centinels [*sic*]; the watch-word being caught and repeated, from one to another, for hundreds of miles around; insomuch that the whole country is for an hour or more in an universal shout.[18] (89)

The examination of the assimilative uses of travel books could be extended through echoes of Samuel Hearne's *Journey from Fort Prince Wales* in "The Complaint of the Forsaken Woman," of Wilson's *Pelew Islands* in "The Affliction of Margaret," and beyond to many other examples, but from the point of view of my argument, they all resemble one another. We encounter a different source of the anthropological spirit in the passage from Book III of *The Prelude* treated above. Lines 456–59 seem to echo Pope's *Dunciad.* In complaining that there is no true depth of commitment or insight in the plan and practice of English education, Wordsworth concludes:

> Our eyes are cross'd by Butterflies, our ears
> Hear chattering Popinjays; the inner heart

Is trivial, and the impresses without
Are of a gaudy region.

"Gaudy" helps give away the source of the poet's butterflies, for Wordsworth shared with Pope an aversion to glitter and similarly used it as a
metaphor for moral emptiness. Their common Enlightenment roots
are never more evident than when they are engaged in the defense of
true culture. Thus in the *Dunciad* Pope ends his condemnation of trivial
pedantry on a similar note, having his zoological specialist proclaim,

> "I tell the naked fact without disguise,
> And, to excuse it, need but shew the prize;
> Whose spoils this paper offers to your eye,
> Fair ev'n in death! this peerless *Butterfly*."
> (IV.433–36)

Although in Wordsworth the butterfly has become the pedant himself, the spirit of his remark is similar and allows the echo to assimilate
Pope to his context.

Wordsworth's sense of what fundamental objects should engage the
attention of man, as well as his expression of them, obviously evolved
away from Pope's, but a certain consonance of moral outlook persists
in a subterranean fashion. Evidence of this may come to the surface in
the form of an echo when Wordsworth makes direct statements about
man's situation or social duties. His favored sources in these cases are
The Rape of the Lock and the *Essay on Man*. It is not surprising to find in
his very first poem, "a tame imitation of Pope's versification" dominated by a confident Enlightenment outlook, an allusion to the *Essay
on Man:* "Go to the world, peruse the book of man, / And learn from
thence thy own defects to scan."[19] But Pope's verse tract is also engaged in *The Prelude*. In Book V, after defending the literature of
fantasy as a positive influence on the child and a spiritual resource to
counter the dull pressures of adult life—"Tales that charm away the
wakeful night / In Araby, Romances, Legends, penn'd / For solace"
(520–22)—Wordsworth says that an imaginative inner life allied to
this literature persists through the limiting yet humanizing changes
associated with mental growth. The terms of his statement recall a
passage in the *Essay on Man:*

> It might demand a more impassion'd strain
> To tell of later pleasures, link'd to these,
> A tract of the same isthmus which we cross
> In progress from our native continent

> To earth and human life: I mean to speak
> Of that delightful time of growing youth
> When cravings for the marvellous relent,
> And we begin to love what we have seen;
> And sober truth, experience, sympathy,
> Take stronger hold of us; and words themselves
> Move us with conscious pleasure.
>
> (V.558–68)

It is not only in accord with his theme of growth but characteristic of Wordsworth's Romantic orientation that Pope's image of turbulent fixity, "Plac'd on this isthmus of a middle state" (*Essay on Man* II.3), should become one of passage. But there is a consonance at a deeper level, where both see life as a struggle with, and their role as justifying, limitation. This is what governs the recalling of Pope's voice here.

Less philosophical and more concretely social is the mood which incorporates *The Rape of the Lock*. The imitation of the mock-heroic card game (III.25–100) occurs in a quite different context yet manages the same structure of reductive comment, showing how social life is typically an organization of aggression expended in an insufficiently self-conscious struggle for selfhood. Belinda's fierce desire to assert herself ("Thirst of Fame" makes her "[burn] to encounter two adventrous Knights") is satirized both for its disproportionate intensity and the triviality of the field in which she exerts it. And yet ironically the card game is more real than the social game at Hampton Court (until the cutting of the lock changes—or better reveals—its character).

Wordsworth's version in *The Prelude* is gentler, colored more by nostalgia than by satire, and of course his players are only boys who could not have known better. But the critique of aggressive excess remains, as does the emphasis on the triviality of its medium, asserted as much by the shoddiness of the defective card deck as by the mock-heroic sallies. And both poets set the final perspective by quick glimpses of the world outside. Pope prefaces his game by noting that it is the dinner hour, so that "The hungry Judges soon the Sentence sign, / And Wretches hang that Jury-men may Dine" (III.21–22). Wordsworth, though he too glances at the greater social world in which soldiers are "Neglected and ungratefully thrown by / Even for the very service they had wrought" (I.545–46), turns to the natural scene for counterpoise:

> Meanwhile, abroad
> The heavy rain was falling, or the frost
> Raged bitterly, with keen and silent tooth,
> And, interrupting oft the impassion'd game,

From Esthwaite's neighbouring lake the splitting ice,
While it sank down towards the water, sent,
Among the meadows and the hills, its long
And dismal yellings, like the noise of wolves
When they are howling round the Bothnic Main.

(I.562–70)

The spot quotation from *As You Like It*—"keen and silent tooth," recalling Amiens' winter wind, which is "not so unkind / As man's ingratitude: / Thy tooth is not so keen" (II.vii.175–76)—suggests that behind
Wordsworth's tone, an odd mixture of warm remembrance, gentle
satire, and proto-sublimity, the theme of man's ingratitude to man
hovers dimly. Along with more positive features of human nature, it
has its origin in "home amusements" such as these.

If one abstracts the echoes found in *Descriptive Sketches*, not many
assimilative borrowings from Pope are left.[20] In "Written in London,
September, 1802" (*PW*3.115), there is a generic echo of Pope's *Moral
Essays*, in which the central subjects are "Rapine, avarice, expense"
("Written in London" 9). The poem contains a specific allusion to
Milton's sonnet "On the Lord General Fairfax at the Siege of Colches-
ter," which ends, "In vain doth Valor bleed / while Avarice and Rapine
share the land"; but the condemnation of glitter in Wordsworth's
sonnet is Popean:

To think that now our life is only drest
For show; mean handy-work of craftsman, cook,
Or groom!—We must run glittering like a brook
In the open sunshine, or we are unblest:
The wealthiest man among us is the best.

(3–7)

So is the emphasis on the trivialization of goals and the fatuous idola-
try of money that seem to have taken over in England. The addressing
of an intimate friend (Coleridge is meant) and the impassioned moral
tone, on the other hand, are Miltonic—not surprising, since all of
Wordsworth's political sonnets are modeled on Milton. What brings
Pope and Milton together here is the underlying Roman attitude:

Plain living and high thinking are no more:
The homely beauty of the good old cause
Is gone; our peace, our fearful innocence,
And pure religion breathing household laws.

(11–14)

This seems almost to encapsulate the kind of statist piety that governs the outlook of Rome's historians and political writers, who as noted, are part of a highly argumentative substratum of Wordsworth's thought. Mill wrote that he "talks on no subject more instructively than on states of society and forms of government . . . [What] struck me was the extreme comprehensiveness and philosophic spirit which is in him. . . . [He] seems always to know the pros and cons of every question" (Mill 81). Perhaps because they are linked in his mind with prose debate, Wordsworth does not often echo them in his poetry; but when he does, it is in contexts dealing with human polities and allied matters. His sources in these instances are most frequently Plutarch and Livy, though there are allusions to or citations of Polybius, Cicero, and Curtius, as well as to writers outside this category, like Seneca, Pliny, and Herodotus.[21]

The poem "Dion," based on Plutarch's *Life of Dion,* liberally echoes phrases from Dryden's translation. Because he was trained to austere virtuousness by Plato and yet fell prey to both the subtle blandishments and gross perils of power, Dion became emblematic of the blend of fair and foul so generally fostered in public men, and this is a main reason for Wordsworth's echoes of *Macbeth.* Dion appears also in *The Prelude,* where he hovers over Wordsworth's memories of his conversations with Michael Beaupuy, in the Loire Valley, away from the turmoil of the French Revolution (IX.414–23). Only the positive aspects of Dion's career are represented, and they are meant, by reflection on what is *not* stated, to enhance our image of Beaupuy's virtue, proof in every way against the thirst for power. At the same time, the echo silently substantiates the poet's recoiling at the consequences of the Revolution, "the fate of later times." Other allusions to Plutarch in the 1805 *Prelude* (the *Life of Sertorius,* I.190–93, the *Life of Timoleus,* X.951) adduce similar apparently affirmative yet actually vexed considerations of the way in which virtue makes its perils-of-Pauline way through history.

An allusion to Plutarch in *The Excursion* bears on the way power corrupts by separating men from influences which nourish virtue.[22] But most often when Wordsworth is considering how virtue is nourished he turns to images of man in rural settings. In doing so he takes over a long tradition, at once current in the new naturalizing ideologies of the second half of the eighteenth century and informed by literary attitudes going back to Virgil and Theocritus. In relation to these older pastoral conventions, he takes a demythologizing stance, showing (to a readership which sees pastoral conventions as mere artifices subsuming away their very themes) how human nobility is built up out of quotidian elements accruing through a purposive connection with the simple and fundamental experiences of life—like the shepherd who

> feels himself
> In those vast regions where his service is
> A Freeman; wedded to his life of hope
> And hazard, and hard labour interchang'd
> With that majestic indolence so dear
> To native Man.
>
> (*Prelude* VIII.385–90)

His demythologizing of the pastoral figure prepares the ground for remythologizing: the creation of the Wordsworthian humble-sublime peasant or rural outcast. The action which produces this equal reaction may take the form of pushing against Virgil, though Wordsworth deeply respects the Virgilian sense of nature (which in fact involved a partial demythologizing of Theocritean fancy), so that he also echoes the Roman poet when he wishes to substantiate a naturalizing impulse. If opposing pastoral convention, he may echo the Virgil of the *Eclogues* in a negative spirit, using a form of assimilative borrowing that ends by rejecting or ablating its source. Thus in Book VIII of *The Prelude*, after setting down several magnifying images of the shepherd he encountered on walks—views of a figure "In size a giant, stalking through the fog," "glorified / by the deep radiance of the setting sun," or "descried in distant sky, / A solitary object and sublime" (VIII.401, 404–5, 406–7)—and telling us how these images provided him with an idea of human nobility, he takes care to repudiate the eclogue figure standing in the wings by comparing him with the shepherd:

> this Creature, spiritual almost
> As those of Books; but more exalted far,
> Far more of an imaginative form,
> Was not a Corin of the groves, who lives
> For his own fancies, or to dance by the hour
> In coronal, with Phillis in the midst,
> But, for the purposes of kind, a Man
> With the most common; Husband, Father; learn'd,
> Could teach, admonish, suffer'd with the rest
> From vice and folly, wretchedness and fear.
>
> (*Prelude* VIII.417–26)

The echo here is essentially generic, but there are similar, specific echoes of Virgil in the same book of *The Prelude*. In a long passage setting up the pastoral vision of human life for a passing appreciation and then a fall, the poet recalls both Virgil and Horace through references to "the Banks / Of delicate Galesus" and the "Smooth life" of the herdsman "on the inviolable Stream / Of rich Clitumnus" (VIII.313–14, 316, 318–19).[23] An allusion to the *Aeneid* (VIII.319–25) in lines 129–32 of the 1850 version plays a similar assimilating-ablating role.

Virgil is also called up through the workings of another aspect of the anthropologizing mood. Wordsworth seems to have been particularly struck by the sixth book of the *Aeneid* (in all, he echoes this book nearly half of the twenty or so times he borrows from Virgil, though several of these echoes are quite slight or are filtered through Milton), perhaps because it creates a picture not simply of the mysteries of the underworld but of an earth-centered moral order and a community of "The noble Living and the noble Dead" (*Prelude* X.970). One positive response to the fact of death, the final arbiter of separation and loss, involved this envisioning of a community of the living and the dead. It was founded on accepting the experience of separation as inevitable and thus recognizing that man had a duty to cultivate the subterranean link between that "mysteriously-united pair / . . . Death and Life," consecrating "the best affections that proceed / From their conjunction" (*Excursion*, V.903–6).

"Laodamia" (*PW* 2.267), picturing a woman who embodies the insatiability of human desire, dramatizes her failure to accept the inevitability of separation and cultivate the proper affections. Though it is shaped by Ovid's *Heroides* and Euripides' *Iphigenia*, the poem most frequently echoes the *Aeneid*. None of the Virgilian echoes involves a fruitful confrontation of texts; they simply help assimilate Virgil's underworld atmosphere, with its moral structuring of the relation between life and death. The opening speech of Laodamia, for instance, draws in details of *Aeneid* VI.243–54 to set the stage for an analogue to the descent into Avernus. As an analogue, it is ironic, since Laodamia will learn nothing and lose all in the most private of responses to death; but beyond this general contrast, Wordsworth does not push the specific details he borrows toward a revelatory confrontation.

If there is any such confrontation, it comes about through the evocation of Milton's twenty-third sonnet, with its spirit of anguished acceptance. "Laodamia," "Methought I saw my late espousèd Saint," and the relevant passage of the *Aeneid* have a common tie. Milton's final lines transform Virgil's description of Aeneas attempting to embrace Anchises in hell: "But O, as to embrace me she inclin'd, / I waked, she fled, and day brought back my night."[24] Virgil's submerged presence in Milton's poem subtly suggests that though there is nothing in the an-

guish of the moment to relieve the speaker, accepting the laws of death
will permit the solace of a reunion in heaven, just as Aeneas, after the
long trial of the Italian wars, will take his place beside Anchises in
Elysium. In contrast to Milton's poem, the Virgilian presence in
"Laodamia" is on the surface; Wordsworth uses it to strengthen his
characterization, opposing Laodamia's attitudes to Aeneas's without
suggesting any ironic subsurface links:

> Forth sprang the impassioned Queen her Lord to clasp;
> Again that consummation she essayed;
> But unsubstantial Form eludes her grasp
> As often as that eager grasp was made.
> The Phantom parts—but parts to re-unite,
> And re-assume his place before her sight.
>
> (25–30)

Aeneas's attempt at an embrace has the same anguish, but as part of a
movement toward acceptance it will allow him to assume his fated role
and achieve the internal control he needs to fulfill it. Laodamia's vain
embrace is an act of despair which shows her inability to accept the
laws of death and assume her role of surviving wife. This inability was
already foretold in her illicit conjuring of her dead husband and is
fixed by her final protest when, "all in vain exhorted and reproved"
(158), she dies into eternal separation, "Apart from happy Ghosts,
that gather flowers / Of blissful quiet 'mid unfading bowers" (162–
63).

The Virgilian details do not speak to this resolution. They merely
effect an atmospheric intensification of the unanswered passion of her
clasp. Complexity of intertextual reference in the poem's closure again
resides in a Miltonic echo—a glancing allusion to *Paradise Lost* (VI.330–
31), where Milton describes how Michael's sword passes through Satan
during the war in heaven, "but th'Ethereal substance clos'd / Not long
divisible." In its Wordsworthian repetition, the borrowed image encapsulates the main dramatic issue of "Laodamia": the dead are integrally
other for the living and cannot be parted either from their region or
from themselves, except momentarily and phantasmically by the thrust-
ing needs of the ego heedlessly seeking to satisfy itself alone. Indeed, it
is untutored and unrestrained desire which keeps the living and the
dead apart, because it suppresses those "best affections which proceed /
From [the] conjunction" of death and life. Only desire chastened by the
ego's submission to the structure of things can establish communion
with the dead—educated desire exemplified by the poet's tears in the
final stanza. They generate a natural image of wholeness emerging

from separation. So also does the poet's picture of the trees, growing and withering in a continuous cycle, which rise out of Agesilaus's tomb and, though the union is compromised, metaphorically unite husband and wife.

Separation at the level of ego consciousness is not just an emotional anguish caused by the brute facts of death but a psychological necessity. The sacrifice of the ego's cravings in the process of mourning entrains a deeper, and the only possible, union with the dead. Thus the ancient idea that the dead, if they are not ritually separated from the living, will haunt them or render them mad. To perceive this is to perceive a further inverting relevance in Wordsworth's Miltonic allusions, for the phantasm which Laodamia has conjured, though it speaks with the voice of the blessed ("my late espousèd Saint"), is in reality a devil—the objectification of the madness of unsubmissive human desire.

Concern over the limitations placed on human desire also evokes echoes of the ballads in Wordsworth's poetry. This is a frequent Wordsworthian technique, motivated by his feeling that ballads speak directly about the human condition.[25] He makes use several times of a later eighteenth-century poem in ballad form, Gottfried August Bürger's "Der wilde Jäger," most notably in "Hart-Leap Well" (PW2.249). Like Laodamia, though to different effect, the hunting knight of Wordsworth's poem, Sir Walter, has allowed the hunger of his ego to carry him beyond the proper limits of desire. Bürger's epiphany, in which all the objects and sounds of the hunt are swallowed up in a Todtenstille as the count passes into the blankness of unattached desire, thickens the atmosphere of "Hart-Leap Well." In Wordsworth's version, an act half of piety and half of pride saves Sir Walter from the fate of Bürger's count. It sets up a second part looking forward to an ultimate purgation by nature, so that the context of "Der wilde Jäger" continues to resonate as a subterranean comment on Wordsworth's naturalizing purpose.

The apparently glancing echo in "Strange fits of passion have I known" (PW2.29) of "Dulcina" from the Percy collection (3:153–55) seems on reflection to go beyond the level of merely assimilating atmosphere. It is hard on a first look to justify the assertion that such common coin as "Fresh as a rose in June" (line 6) is an echo at all, especially since Lucy is anything but what Dulcina is, an ordinary coquette (whose evident sexuality is expressed in line 17 of "Dulcina": "cheekes, as fresh as a rose in june"). But De Selincourt's notation (which relies on Arthur Beatty) that Wordsworth had just bought his copy of Percy's Reliques in Hamburg suggests there are factual grounds to support such an assertion. And there is a peculiar consonance in the situations of these disparate poems, the later one a meditative "crisis lyric," the earlier part of a section called *Loose and Humorous Songs*. Both deal with the untoward pressure of desire. Both avoid describing the action they lead us to expect (a concluding embrace) and end in a question: Wordsworth's mysterious supposition ("If Lucy should be dead!"), the balladeer's coy "Did shee consent, / Or he relent; / Accepts he night, or grants shee noone." And Wordsworth seems to play with the refrain of "Dulcina"— "Forgoe me now, come to me soone"—by displacing the setting from noon to night and describing the later moment when the woman is waiting for the man. The strongest consonance linking the poems is, however, their consistent opposition of circumstance. There is a contrast of scene and mood. "Dulcina" archly asserts that love springs eternal and youth will have its day:

> How, at last, agreed these lovers?
>   Shee was fayre, and he was young:
> The tongue may tell what th'eye discovers;
>   Joyes unseene are never sung.
>   (41–44)

We know what happened, though our eye never discovers it. But Wordsworth psychologizes and probes what impedes the joining of the lovers. In doing so he seems to reverse the sense of "Dulcina" 43–44: "Upon the moon I fixed my eye, / All over the wide lea," he says, and then tells us what happened. Only we are not sure what has happened; we know merely that sadness unseen is being sung. The fit of passion that is so familiar as it is expressed in "Dulcina" becomes strange indeed as the once-confident lover, proceeding automatically on the equine force of his instinct ("My horse moved on; hoof after hoof / He raised, and never stopped"), is brought face to face with human mortality. Love apparently does not spring eternal, and youth may not have its night.

"Strange fits of passion" is a large statement in the anthropologizing mood. The ballad source is echoed in a more-than-assimilative way that moves toward a confrontation of texts. Wordsworth's use of Burns in this mood is more typical. The echoes of "Man Was Made to Mourn" in the last two lines of "Simon Lee" (*PW*4.60) work to enforce the freshness of the poet's insight by simple reversal. "Man's inhumanity to Man / Makes countless thousands mourn!" ("Man Was Made to Mourn" 55–56) becomes:

> —I've heard of hearts unkind, kind deeds
> With coldness still returning;

Alas! the gratitude of men
Hath oftener left me mourning.
                    ("Simon Lee" 93–96)

The mood here borders on the stoical, and indeed Wordsworth was so deeply attached to Burns that he can use him across categories. A second echo of "Man Was Made to Mourn" in "Lines Written in Early Spring," accompanying echoes from Cowper and Coleridge, comes in support of a third major atmospheric category, the naturalizing mood.

THE NATURALIZING MOOD

The mood in which Wordsworth evokes or tests percepts linking man with nature calls up all those eighteenth-century contemporaries or successors of the Augustan Age who had made the concept of external nature a significant subject. It is the most populous of the assimilative groupings, including poets active in the early 1700s and ranging to late contemporaries of Wordsworth, but the majority are pre-Romantics. Some, like Gray and Collins, are still read by a small general audience; many, like Mark Akenside, John Dyer, and Samuel Rogers, are familiar only to students of the period; and some, like Moses Brown and Robert Greenwood, were obscure even in Wordsworth's day. Though he read them with attention, and clearly in some cases with avidity, Wordsworth by no means thought highly of them all. But he did find in all of them, whether generally or only in particular passages, hints and figurations, major and minor, of a sensitivity to the natural scene, a conceptualization of subject-object relations, or a style of poetic voice he was in the course of developing. He borrowed from them, consequently, to define or support his central enterprise—sometimes in a spirit of confrontation and revision, sometimes merely as a means of "spreading the tone" of a specific passage or piece.

The tonal use of them is my present concern. Among middle and earlier eighteenth-century voices we hear those of Young, Thomson, Blair, Gay, Collins, Gray, Akenside, Goldsmith, Macpherson, Langhorne, Thomas and Joseph Warton, and anonymous poets in various ballad collections; among near and actual contemporaries, Beattie, Bowles, Michael Bruce, Burns, Campbell, Coleridge, Cottle, John Dyer, James Hurdis, John Logan, Rogers, and Southey. Poets from before this era used sometimes in the same way include Virgil, Chaucer, Wyatt, Spenser, Shakespeare, George Wither, and Anne of Winchilsea. One way to give a classificatory shape to this mass of sources is to make a distinction based on Coleridge's famous description of the proposed division of labor between himself and Wordsworth in the creation of the *Lyrical Ballads:*

> The thought suggested itself (to which of us I do not recollect) that a series of poems might be composed of two sorts. In the one, the incidents and agents were to be, in part at least, supernatural; and the excellence aimed at was to consist in the interesting of the affections by the dramatic truth of such emotions, as would naturally accompany such situations, supposing them real. . . . For the second class, subjects were to be chosen from ordinary life; the characters and incidents were to be such, as will be found in every village and its vicinity, where there is a meditative and feeling mind to seek after them, or to notice them, when they present themselves. (*Biographia* 2: 5)

If we read this passage carefully, we can see that both poets took an interest in supernatural as well as homely natural materials and linked them even as they distinguished them. Thus when Wordsworth was in a naturalizing mood, his emphasis sometimes lay in demythologizing religious or philosophical conceptions of man's relation to the universe in order to dramatize a naturalized account of human experience, and sometimes in remythologizing that experience in order to express its numinous elements.

In his high style the two processes often seem to be going on at the same time, as when he describes in Book II of *The Prelude* how

> I would walk alone,
> In storm and tempest, or in star-light nights
> Beneath the quiet Heavens; and, at that time,
> Have felt whate'er there is of power in sound
> To breathe an elevated mood, by form
> Or image unprofaned; and I would stand,
> Beneath some rock, listening to sounds that are
> The ghostly language of the ancient earth,
> Or make their dim abode in distant winds.
> Thence did I drink the visionary power.
> (321–30)

The careful avoidance of obviously conventional religious terms, icons, or references, the deliberate lack of specificity and appropriated symbolism in the imagery, the links with elemental life in the nouns ("storm," "star-light nights," "rock," "winds") and verbals ("breathe," "make their abode," "drink") all act to prevent the reader from giving a Christian character to this spiritual night experience, a character poets like Young would give it and readers would expect. But the accumulating hints of numinosity, conveyed by the overall context, by charged terms ("Heavens," "power," "unprofaned," "ghostly"), and by direct suggestion ("elevated," "visionary power"), act in turn to supernaturalize the experience, making it an aspect of the myth of origins the poet develops in Book II of *The Prelude*.[26]

But in segments governed by the assimilative mode of echoing, the borrowed voice appears most often to support one or the other of these intentions. Thus an echo of Bowles is embedded in this passage in a way that thickens the atmosphere of numinosity. In the earlier poet's "St. Michael's Mount" we find these lines:

> Mountain! the curious Muse might love to gaze
> On the *dim* record of thy early days;
> Oft fancying that she *heard*, like the *low blast*,
> The *sounds of mighty generations past*.
> (124–27; italics mine)

Taken as a whole, the passage could not be more Bowlesian and un-Wordsworthian, yet the underlined words suggest that the passage was resident in Wordsworth's memory. The textual reworking in *The Prelude* shows a spirit not of confrontation but assimilation, and what Wordsworth has taken is not the stock naturalizing gestures Bowles has made (so tentatively, almost apologetically), but the hint of a *tremendum*. In borrowing from Bowles here, he has maneuvered the "mock-sublime" into true sublimity. Rather than a transumptive revision, the echo is a harmonic resetting that brings out something merely latent in Bowles's weak poeticizing. It is a good example of how Wordsworth could respond to and appropriate a poet whose inferiority he had already come to recognize. It is also a categorical example, since in this assimilative segment of a passage written in an exalted vein the demythologizing and remythologizing impulses are not concurrent.

DEMYTHOLOGIZING BORROWINGS: SUBSTANTIATING THE NATURAL STRUCTURE OF EXPERIENCE. Wordsworth's memory was stocked with phrases and images of poets who to him seemed to capture some element of the natural structure of experience. Out of the mass of now-obscure poems in which the subject matter had shifted away from

Augustan concerns to include or mainly feature nature description, certain lines or images became sufficiently charged with significance to remain in the penumbra of his naturalizing consciousness and to return upon him as emblems in the act of composition. One of the earliest examples is provided by his friend Robert Greenwood's "A Poem Written During a Shooting Excursion." An unremarkable-seeming phrase, "vivid rings of green," is reworded in *An Evening Walk* to help fix the image of a "lonely mountain horse . . . / Feeding 'mid purple heath, 'green rings,' and broom" ([1793], 113–14). Though Wordsworth soon moved away from this pastiche-like technique, with its pride in descriptive accuracy and meticulous footnoting of literary and scenic sources, he continued to accumulate and use such privately charged snatches as if they were touchstones of naturalistic vision.

Without producing isolable echoes, details of Michael Bruce's story of the peasant's fair daughter Levina in *Lochleven* (a rather crudely naturalized version of the central acts of *Paradise Lost* combining Miltonic phrases and folkloric motifs) are in play behind the peculiar twists of "Strange fits of passion" and "She dwelt among the untrodden ways"; and in the "Boy of Winander" segment of *The Prelude* (V.389–422), a line from the same part of *Lochleven* pushes to the surface. The locale for Levina's climactic act—her committing the mortal sin of uprooting for transplantation a small "Hesperian" apple tree through her lust to possess its fruit perpetually and so, she thinks, assure the continuous success of her coming marriage—is introduced in a verse paragraph beginning, "Fair in the bosom of the level lake / Rose a green island, cover'd with a spring / Of flow'rs perpetual" (*Lochleven* 326–28). Lashed to fury by a melodramatic tempest, the lake soon receives the body of the guilty Levina. In Wordsworth's much more subtle meditation on the costs of human development, the lake remains quiet as it closes the (tempestuous) scene of the hooting owls and, impassively maternal, preludes the death of the boy, who has also sought control over nature to secure its pleasurable response. We are left with the picture of an "uncertain Heaven, received / Into the bosom of the steady lake" (V.412–13).

The equally minor talents of John Logan provided a model for "To the Cuckoo" (*PW*2.207) and contributed to the image of Milton in *The Prelude* (III.287–93).[27] Similarly, John Langhorne and Samuel Rogers are echoed in the Lucy poems, and the obscure James Hurdis crops up in *The Excursion*.[28] These borrowings from relatively feeble poets usually have little functional weight in their new contexts and appear to feed into a private system of response, a silent encoding of naturalizing examples to which even readers familiar with the sources do not have a ready key. Assimilation here tends to fade into inaudible traces, which, if they have any poetic value at all, have it for the composing poet alone.

The echoes of poets whose vision of things, rather than just certain turns of phrase, was capable of engaging Wordsworth's thought often have more density. But this is not necessarily the case. It is hard to overemphasize the importance of Collins as a precursor and guide in Wordsworth's passage toward a naturalized understanding of his experience, yet many of the overt borrowings from Collins are found in *An Evening Walk* and *Descriptive Sketches*, where they often function in the code-like fashion of the "Spartan fife" from the first line of Collins's "Ode to Liberty." In its Wordsworthian context the phrase signals a set of eighteenth-century attitudes about the exemplary independence of mountain people who live in harsh natural conditions and thus complements Wordsworth's expostulation on the strong presence of freedom in the rough landscape he is describing (*Descriptive Sketches* [1793], 317–31).

On the other hand, in the second sonnet of "Personal Talk" (*PW*4.73), he trades on more than a coded concept when he echoes unchanged Collins's phrase about notes "by distance made more sweet," from "The Passions: An Ode for Music" (line 60). Here he sets aside the "Worldlings" view—of gibing social gossip as the necessary "bribe" that goads the "languid mind" into "Sound sense, and love itself, and mirth and glee"—by opposing it to the world of "blest, and powerful" children, which lies

> More justly balanced; partly at their feet,
> And part far from them:—sweetest melodies
> Are those that are by distance made more sweet;
> Whose mind is but the mind of his own eyes,
> He is a Slave; the meanest we can meet!

The effect of this quotation, set in the context of a group of poems defending the value of solitude and silence, is manifold. The image of distant melody recalls the close of the first sonnet in the sequence, which pictures the poet listening in solitary concentration to his "kettle whispering its faint undersong." When we realize that the image of distant melody in the second sonnet is taken from Melancholy's song in "The Passions," which in turn appropriates by echoic phrasing motifs from "Il Penseroso," we are brought to feel that the quotation is describing an inward mode of vision.

The turn by which it is associated with children in the happiness of their innocence seems to take us far from Collins, as well as from Milton's speaker, who is seeking to attain vision by that "old experience" the tutelage of melancholy affords. Yet this turn depends on an essential link, the ability of both the child and the melancholic to attune themselves to *distant*—invisible or imagined—realities. It is the world-lings who focus only on what is near and obvious to the eye: " 'Yet life,' you say, 'is life; we have seen and see, / And with a living pleasure we describe.' " As so often in Wordsworth, the implication is that the domi-nation of the eye leads to superficiality, and the ear is the better portal to the imagination, here opposed to "the mind of [one's] own eyes." The childlike combination of eye and ear, life at one's feet and distant melody, is "More justly balanced," and, developed through quiet thought, makes possible insightful transcendence of the busy, be-witched ego, to which gossip panders with the "bribe" of "sprightly malice."

The echo of Collins thus blends overtones into the overt assertions of the argument about insight, helping to give a subtle poetic concrete-ness to the poem's paraphrasable message about the importance of inwardness.[29] A similar distant music plays in the background of an echo of John Dyer's *Ruins of Rome*. The echo forms part of Words-worth's grandest statement of awakened inwardness dependent on a just balance of natural powers—the "spousal verse" of the "Prospec-tus" chanting the marriage of man's intellect to "this goodly universe," proclaiming how exquisitely the mind and the external world are fitted to each other, "And the creation (by no lower name / Can it be called) which they with blended might / Accomplish" (69–71). This blending gives the poet an essential force, such that by words

> Which speak of nothing more than what we are,
> Would I arouse the sensual from their sleep
> Of Death, and win the vacant and the vain
> To noble raptures.
>
> (59–62)

The phrase "sleep / Of Death" is a common expansion of 1 Corinthi-ans 15.51 ("We shall not all sleep, but we shall all be changed"), a subtext whose deep resonance in the demythologizing turn of Words-worth's "high argument" here has long been recognized; but "the vacant and the vain" has a relatively obscure origin. It is drawn from a passage in *The Ruins of Rome* whose relevance is much more tenuous. Wordsworth saw fit to ferret out this passage for his *Poems and Ex-tracts*, a private anthology he edited and presented in manuscript to Lady Mary Lowther. He admired the whole poem, in part because its manner of elaborating the fashionable ruin sentiment of the day con-tained hints of the kind of naturalizing turn he sought to master, just

as Dyer's "Grongar Hill" seemed to him to take the relation of mind
and nature a step further. And the most relevant part of the passage
bearing on the "Prospectus," containing a meditation on time's destructive power that through its "esemplastic" mood of melancholy
gives it a redemptive meaning, apparently imaged for Wordsworth
how—as with the "spots of time" in *The Prelude*—under bleak circumstances the mind and nature could be fitted to each other so as to free
the ego from blank submission to the law of time. Dyer ruminates
while gazing on the ruins of the Roman Forum, "Where Caesars,
heroes, peasants, hermits, lie / Blended in the dust together":

> There is a mood,
> (I sing not to the vacant and the young)
> There is a kindly mood of melancholy
> That wings the soul and points her to the skies;
> When tribulation clothes the child of man,
> When age descends with sorrow to the grave,
> 'Tis sweetly-soothing sympathy to pain,
> A gently-wak'ning call to health and ease.
> How musical, when all-composing Time
> Here sits upon his throne of ruins hoar,
> While winds and tempests sweep his various lyre,
> How sweet thy diapason, Melancholy!
>
> (344–55)

The substitution of "vain" for "young" may well be the result of his
calling to mind here another beloved minor poet. In Book I, stanza iv,
of Beattie's *Minstrel* we read how the Muses haunting the wild "sylvan
reign / . . . hate the sensual, and scorn the vain"—a phrase suggesting
also a literary source for the adjective "sensual" preceding "sleep / Of
Death" in the "Prospectus." Mary Moorman maintains that among
contemporary poets Beattie had the greatest effect on the young
Wordsworth. *The Minstrel*

> became and remained one of Wordsworth's favourite poems:
> its echoes are found even in the poetry of his maturity, and in
> the years of stress after his return from France, when he was
> struggling to prepare himself for his life's work as a poet, it was
> to Beattie that he turned for refreshment and inspiration.
> (Moorman 1: 60)

From Racedown, he wrote his friend Matthews to get him a copy, and in creating "Stanzas Written in My Pocket Copy of Thomson's 'Castle of Indolence' " (*PW*2.25), he pictured himself as Beattie's Edwin (Moorman 1:61, 287). Moorman gives a number of reasons why Beattie's outlook was so tunable to Wordsworth's, but does not mention the central one—Beattie's interest in combining an autobiographical impulse with a passion for the natural scene to compose a poem on the growth of a poet's mind. It is thus not surprising that Beattie is an important haunter of Wordsworth's naturalizing mood.[30]

Cowper, with his easy conversational style, the simplicity and unpretentiousness of his diction, the sincerity and intimacy of his poetic voice, the integrity of his outlook valuing, but not overrating, retirement and the country, and his lively descriptive powers—so keen in perception and so far from dependence on the mock-sublime—provided a strong model of naturalizing discourse for Wordsworth. This is reason enough for his being a submerged source in such important naturalizing documents as "Expostulation and Reply," "The Tables Turned," or "Lines Written in Early Spring."[31] The way in which Wordsworth at once relies on and revises his source is illustrated in "Gipsies" (*PW*2.226). The poem is a rewriting of a passage in *The Task* I.558–91, drawing particularly on lines 574–79. However, unlike Cowper, who castigates the gipsies for the sloth that leads them to steal and to "brutalize" their rational natures, Wordsworth expresses his shock that people living a natural life should have no regard for nature. He alters Cowper's conventional idea of the importance of industriousness to a more inward one of human energies finding their proper expression in interchanges with external nature, so that torpidity is seen as exile from being. In his original embodiment of this insight, he is not far from Blakean paradox:

> Behold the mighty Moon! this way
> She looks as if at them—but they
> Regard her not:—oh better wrong and strife
> Better vain deeds or evil than such life!
> The silent Heavens have goings-on;
> The stars have tasks—but these have none.
>   (1807 version, 19–24)

Though clearly a revision of the gipsy passage in *The Task*, Wordsworth's poem did not echo its source overtly until the poet devised a new ending to placate Coleridge's discomfort over the moral of the original version:

> Yet, witness all that stirs in heaven or earth!
> In scorn I speak not;—they are what their birth
> And breeding suffer them to be;
> Wild outcasts of society!
>
> (25–28; added 1820)

The final line recalls Cowper's statement that the gipsy is "self-banish't from society" (*The Task* I.578). In its pithy moralizing it is worthy of Cowper; but in terms of Wordsworth's main argument it is counter-productive, since the phrase "wild outcasts" seems to describe ener-getic figures who in their wildness and exile, like so many other Wordsworthian outcasts, are intimately connected with the "goings-on" of nature.[32]

Since Burns, as a contemporary of Cowper, shared the same sincer-ity and some of the same concerns, his persona and the tenor of his most famous pieces were sufficiently emblematic of naturalizing atti-tudes for Wordsworth to bring him to mind when he was inditing in this mood, though he is usually echoed in the context of the poet's moralizing mood. Some lines of "Tam o' Shanter" contributed to the "invention" by which Wordsworth tried to make a thorn tree he had seen "permanently an impressive object" (see the I.F. note, *PW*2.511). Tam passes

> thro' the whins, and by the cairn,
> Whare hunters fand the murder'd bairn;
> And near the thorn, aboon the well,
> Whare *Mungo*'s mither hang'd hersel.
>
> (93–96)

The elements persist in Wordsworth's "Thorn" (*PW*2.240), though their relationships are changed, and the way this poem plays with the supernatural and veers off from it, as well as the odd garrulity of the narrator, seems to derive in part from a peculiar twist given to the manner of Burns's tale.

Quite another aspect of the same tree, associated with young lovers in one another's arms " 'Beneath the milk-white thorn that scents the ev'ning gale,' " is invoked in stanza ix of Burns's "The Cotter's Satur-day Night." Wordsworth echoes the moralizing line that introduces this expostulation on youthful love when he says of the old man in "Resolution and Independence" that "In my mind's eye I seemed to see him pace / About the weary moors continually" (129–30). Burns had written in stanza ix, "I've paced much this weary, *mortal round*, / And sage EXPERIENCE bids me this declare . . ." ("this" is his encom-

ium on the *"cordial"* of modest love). The link between these poems of
wholly different character is tenuous, but Burns's celebration of rustic
life ("The short and simple annals of the Poor," as his epigraph from
Gray has it) emphasizes the kind of simplicity and ability to make do
that impress Wordsworth in the old man, and the purpose of the
Scot's poem is to admonish his friend Robert Aiken, a solicitor and
famous speaker:

> To you I sing, in simple Scottish lays,
>   The *lowly train* in life's sequester'd scene;
> The native feelings strong, the guileless ways,
>   What A**** in a *Cottage* would have been;
> Ah! tho' his worth unknown, far happier there I ween!
>   (5–9; the italics are Burns's)

Wordsworth's self-admonishment is more subtle and resonant, but the
representative of "grave Livers . . . in Scotland" who prompts it belongs
to the same social stratum, has the same set of mind and humble-
sublime capacity for endurance as Burns's "toil-worn," "priest-like"
cotter.

Pitched at a different literary level but similar in tone, Goldsmith's
partly nostalgic, partly Horatian celebrations of rural life also contributed images and phrases to Wordsworth's naturalistic store. There are
echoes of *The Deserted Village,* as one might expect; for instance, "sweet
was the sound" and "village murmur"—distant music again, from
lines 113–14—are imprecisely reproduced in *An Evening Walk*
([1793], 301, 323). But Wordsworth draws more often on *The Traveller.* In its Augustan way (it is an imitation of the Horatian verse-epistle
in the manner of Lyttleton's letters from abroad, with argumentation
about the true nature of freedom and the proper social bounds to set
to it), this poem evokes what would become the Romantic symbol of
the journey. The speaker, finding "no spot of all the world my own"
(30), searches for his true home, although he does so by assuming the
stance of the topographical observer and surveying in neoclassical
fashion the various locales of civilized life. He comes to see how "Vain,
very vain, my weary search to find / That bliss which only centres in
the mind" (423–24), arriving at an Augustan commonplace that nonetheless, granting the necessary changes, still operates in Wordsworthian contexts like *Home at Grasmere.* Wordsworth twice borrows
from the context of the lines quoted above in the course of his restless
journeying in *Descriptive Sketches;* uses "the philosophic mind" (39) in
the Immortality Ode (line 187, where he speaks of a compromised
bliss centered in the individual mind through meditation on experi-

ence); and plays off motifs from lines 1–62 of *The Traveller* in the
opening words of *The Prelude*.

In the last instance, the parallels are of a contrasting sort. Goldsmith's
uncertainty where to turn is oppressive, the concern of a weary man
who "drags at each remove a lengthening chain" (10); Wordsworth's
uncertainty is initially the expression of a joyous liberty felt by a freed
captive. "Creation's heir, the world, the world is mine" (*The Traveller* 50)
and "the earth is all before me" (*Prelude* I.15) both derive from *Paradise
Lost* XII.646–47, but the former is Goldsmith's deliberate attempt to
reconcile himself philosophically with his sense of homelessness, while
the latter is Wordsworth's spontaneous exultation over his expanding
opportunities. Both poets bless a "friend"—Goldsmith his domestically
settled brother, to whom he turns in thought with a "heart untrav-
elled," Wordsworth the traveling breeze.

This "corresponding mild creative breeze" (43) breaks up the frost
within him, promising fruitful days, though later it becomes "a redundant energy / Vexing its own creation" (46–47) by making it hard for
the poet to decide in what form he should couch his insights. By
contrast, Goldsmith stands over his hoard of percepts like a miser, his
heart filling "with alternate passions"—pleasure at all he has garnered
of good, pain at an irrepressible longing for more. He sits down,

> a pensive hour to spend;
> And, placed on high above the storm's career,
> Look[s] downward where an hundred realms appear,
>   (32–34)

but cannot decide in the following meditation where he belongs.
Wordsworth stretches on the level ground beneath a tree, makes "a
choice / Of one sweet Vale whither my steps should turn," and then
ceases to think at all,

>   sooth'd by a sense of touch
> From the warm ground, that balanced me, else lost
> Entirely, seeing nought, nought hearing, save
> When here and there, about the grove of Oaks
> Where was my bed, an acorn from the trees
> Fell audibly, and with a startling sound.
>   (I.89–94)

Some of these parallels might be explained as coincidences, since both
poets are making use—Wordsworth radically—of topographical conventions; but I think Wordsworth consciously looked on *The Traveller*

as an embodiment of traditions he had set himself to revise, and thus it helped shape his verse.

Though eighteenth-century sources dominate, naturalizing echoes occasionally come from earlier ones. Wordsworth transcribed parts of *The Shepherd's Hunting* by George Wither in *Poems and Extracts* and echoed it in a number of poems that express the naturalizing mood. Eclogue IV provides, in addition to the epigraph for "To the Daisy" (*PW*2.135), phrasing for some famous lines of "The Tables Turned" (*PW*4.57):

> One impulse from a vernal wood
> May teach you more of man,
> Of moral evil and of good,
> Than all the sages can.
>
> (21–24)

This is a bold re-turning of Wither's claim for his poetic muse, asserted in context by the fortune-oppressed Philarete:

> By the murmur of a spring,
> Or the least boughs rusteling;
> By a daisy whose leaves spread
> Shut when Titan goes to bed,
> Or a shady bush or tree,
> She could more infuse in me
> Than all Nature's beauties can
> In some other wiser man.[33]
>
> (371–78)

The last two lines of the Immortality Ode contain suggestions of Wither: "the meanest flower that blows" recalls "the meanest object's sight," which Philarete says his muse can employ to "raise pleasure to her height" (*Eclogue* IV, 369–70; curiously, omitted from *Poems and Extracts*), and the "thoughts that do often lie too deep for tears" recall the "thoughts too deep to be expressed / And too strong to be suppressed" of Wither's *Fair Virtue* (lines 1897–98, transcribed by Wordsworth in *Poems and Extracts* 41).[34]

Because they are minor talents, contributors to rather than fashioners of poetic traditions, whom Wordsworth could transcend or revise without an internal struggle, poets like Wither, Cotton, Anne of Winchilsea, and the host of later-eighteenth-century second fiddles could remain at the back of his poetic consciousness as a free field for casual, mood-inspired plunder. The case is different with Spenser,

Shakespeare, Milton, and, at key junctures, Coleridge. His relation to
these poets is most often front to front, for they were writers against
whom he was impelled to define himself.[35] Nonetheless, they were so
pervasive in his consciousness that they could be represented in any of
the categories of borrowing. "L'Allegro," "Il Penseroso," *Comus*, "Arcades," or the Nativity Ode, the major study-texts of the pre-
Romantics, may appear casually in some turn of Wordsworth's naturalizing mood, whether filtered through the Wartons, Collins, or Gray, or
transposed directly. In terms of referential weight, there is a range of
echoes, from blandly used allegrian details to rich entanglements with
Comus. In "Composed in the Valley near Dover" (*PW*3.114), the cock,
the smoke, the bells, the youth at play are details so ordinary and
conventional that we can suspect their literary source only through
their concatenation ("L'Allegro" 49ff., 81, 93, and 95–99, respectively).
On the other hand, "home-bred sense" in "To a Highland Girl"
(*PW*3.73, line 26), drawing on "home-felt delight," spoken by Comus to
the Lady (262), suggests by textual reference not only the girl's natural
bright innocence but the suppressed eros of Wordsworth's speaker that
underlies his visionary confrontation with her.

Wordsworth occasionally uses similar sorts of Chaucerian echoes.
Chaucer not only stands in the background of the companion poems
to the daisy ("In youth from rock to rock I went" and "With little here
to do or see," *PW*2.135 and 138) but enters into their details. In the
first, Wordsworth describes how,

> Fresh-smitten by the morning ray,
> When thou art up, alert and gay,
> Then, cheerful Flower! my spirits play
>   With kindred gladness:
> And when, at dusk, by dews opprest
> Thou sink'st, the image of thy rest
> Hath often eased my pensive breast
>   Of careful sadness.
>
>   (57–64)

The counterpart, from *The Legend of Good Women*, has Chaucer telling
us that, come May, he is always up betimes

> To sene this flour ayenst the sunne sprede
> Whan it upriseth erly by the morowe;
> That blisful sight softinith all my sorowe;
>   So glad am I when that I have presence

Of it, to doin it all reverence . . .
. . . .
And whan that it is eve I renne blithe,
As sone as evir the sonne ginnith to west,
To sene this flowre how it woll go to rest;
For fere of night, so hatith she derknesse,
Her chere is plainly spred in the brightnesse
Of the sunne, for ther it woll unclose.[36]

What does Wordsworth gain by this tenuous play on Chaucer? For one thing, the generic authentication provided by "imitation," the sense of a traditional genre or signal exemplar giving form and weight to his poem. For another, though the tonality is different, it helps mark and sustain the spirit of devoted whimsy in which both poets approach their ostensibly common subject. Finally, the appropriation of Chaucer's model permits Wordsworth to hold on in a subterranean way to the pretense of the courtly allegory which expounds a relationship between lover and beloved, and so to define as a kind of eros the interchange between himself and nature channeled through the daisy. At the same time, however, he naturalizes the allegory by using terms which speak of the daisy simply as a flower, a direct participant in the natural order.

There are more Spenserian than Chaucerian echoes by far that function as correlatives of the naturalizing mood, from the curious borrowing from line 213 of *Muiopotmos* in "Beggars" ("a weed of glorious feature," *PW*2.222, line 18), through the humorous pastiche of "A gentle knight was pricking on the plaine" in *The Waggoner* (*PW*2.176, Canto Fourth, 122–24), to the deep resonances of "Epithalamion" in the Immortality Ode (for instance, the idea of joyful holiday, the tabor, the boys shouting to fill the firmament, and Spenser's refrain in stanza III).

Shakespeare is a still-richer source. The "chartered wind" that blows the old Cumberland beggar's hair against his face (*PW*4.234, line 175) is borrowed from *As You Like It* (II.vii.47–48): Jacques' "I must have liberty / Withal, as large a charter as the wind." We have seen that in contexts bearing rich allusions, Shakespeare is often made a naturalistic foil to Milton, in order to support Wordsworth's radical "horizontalizing" of Milton's vertical order. For Wordsworth the sonnets, particularly, explore the world of human time, in which there is usually no sense of a divine presence ordering things from above, and ascendental and descendental impulses are blended to give moral authority to a sensitive stoic view of life, operating at the edge of despair but naturally resolved by a kind of centering. This perception of Shakespeare accords sufficiently with his own project to prevent

Wordsworth from reducing him, as Milton does, to an allegrian voice warbling "his native Wood-notes wild." He speaks in Wordsworth's assimilative echoes, though far less powerfully than in the comparative echoes, still as a sophisticated voice of natural perception. His voice is refined still further as he is further naturalized by the Wordsworthian context. Thus, in "To the Small Celandine" (*PW*2.142), the lines from *The Winter's Tale* that T. S. Eliot celebrated—"daffodils, / That come before the swallow dares, and take / The winds of March with beauty" (IV.iv.118–20)—appear to be embedded in Wordsworth's praise of the celandine's ratheness:

> Ere a leaf is on a bush,
> In the time before the thrush
> Has a thought about her nest,
> Thou wilt come with half a call,
> Spreading out thy glossy breast
> Like a careless Prodigal . . .
> (25–32)

Wordsworth occasionally tries to realize this demythologizing mood with generic echoing. In "The Contrast: The Parrot and the Wren" (*PW*2.155), the combination of terms in the second poem of the pair— "hermetess," "placid," "mossy shed"—and the idea of choosing a way of life ("Which would you be . . .") points to "Il Penseroso," lines 168– 69, for there the speaker tries to "find out the peaceful hermitage, / The Hairy Gown and Mossy Cell." However, noting suggestions of "L'Allegro" in the first poem, describing the parrot, "Arch, volatile, a sportive bird / By social glee inspired," one sees that not only Milton's companion poems are being invoked but also the tradition of "Come live with me" poems. In the emphasis on the parrot's glittering features there are, though no outright echoes, hints of the pleadings of Marlowe's "Passionate Shepherd" offering his love "buckles of the purest gold; / A belt of straw and ivy buds, / With coral clasps and amber studs." In the turns on the wren's ability to survive winter and sing upon bleak winds, there are hints of Raleigh's reply: "Time drives the flocks from field to fold, / When rivers rage and rocks grow cold, / And Philomel becometh dumb." The obvious comparison in these two poems also simplifies and further naturalizes the sort of contrast dear to the Miltonizing poets of the later eighteenth century, as in Joseph Warton's "Fashion: A Satire," "The Pleasures of Melancholy," or "The Approach of Summer," all variants on the choice-of-life motif.

More nakedly generic is the pastoral reference in the tenth stanza of "On the Power of Sound" (*PW*2.323):

The pipe of Pan, to shepherds
Couched in the shadow of Maenalian pines,
Was passing sweet; the eyeballs of the leopards,
That in high triumph drew the Lord of vines,
How did they sparkle to the cymbal's clang!
While Fauns and Satyrs beat the ground
In cadence,—and Silenus swang
This way and that, with wild-flowers crowned.
                              (146–52)

Something like the first three lines can be found in Virgil's eighth
Eclogue:

Maenalus argutumque nemus pinosque loquentis
semper habet, semper pastorum ille audit amores
Panaque, qui primus calamos non passus inertis.
                              (22–24)

Maenalus hath ever tuneful groves and speaking pines;
ever does he listen to the shepherd's loves and to Pan,
who first awoke the idle reeds.
                              (trans. Fairclough 1: 57)

But the passage in Wordsworth represents the whole pastoral tradition from Theocritus to Gray, whose "Progress of Poesy," line 34, is
echoed in "beat the ground / In cadence." In this case, the tradition is
invoked not to demythologize an old way of naturalizing but to
remythologize it—to assert against the heedlessly rationalizing energies of Enlightenment minds the necessity of fable, because it gives
access to life:

To life, to *life* give back thine ear:
Ye who are longing to be rid
Of fable, though to truth subservient, hear
The little sprinkling of cold earth that fell
Echoed from the coffin-lid.
                              (153–57)

Here the literary echo of pagan *religio* is meant to overwhelm the
wholly stripped natural one. It is this sort of refabulizing impulse
allied with Wordsworth's naturalism I want to consider next.

REMYTHOLOGIZING BORROWINGS: SUBSTANTIATING THE VISIONARY AS-
PECT OF NATURAL EXPERIENCE. English poets from the middle of the
eighteenth century onward attempted to embody the visionary aspect
of experience they conceived of as mediated by nature. Milton was the
unwitting progenitor of this attempt, and his voice (often fragmented,
altered by context or by lack of talent and insight, and too thinly
disguised) dominates the pre-Romantic period. Wordsworth and
Blake were the first poets with sufficient ability and spiritual penetration to turn this visionary purpose to account. Yet Blake did not
sustain in his poetic texts the impulse to look back allusively at the
poets intervening between him and Milton; after the *Songs of Innocence
and Experience,* his interest in his eighteenth-century heritage appears
mainly in his work as an illustrator. Wordsworth, on the other hand,
continued to draw heavily on eighteenth-century poetry. While Blake
breasted the tide of nature poetry, Wordsworth rode it.

Thus, although his work was revisionary and took him into new
territory, Wordsworth did not always proceed in a spirit of confrontation. He often blended the visionary notes of his eighteenth-century
predecessors into his radical compositions. When the echoes of these
assimilated notes are faint, it is often hard to assign a specific function
to them; but when they are sufficiently strong, Wordsworth uses them
to give the force of a myth or visionary structure to his naturalizing
perceptions. The sources he uses in a remythologizing way are frequently the same ones he uses in a demythologizing way. Indeed, the
two categories are hard to distinguish at times because of his poetic
restraint, born of the fear that (in Hartman's terms) by raising his
visionary insights to an apocalyptic pitch he would destroy the natural
basis on which they were raised. We thus find some passages where, as
the poet seems to be moving toward a visionary restructuring, he puts
in a disclaimer or a strongly naturalizing turn. For example, the "little
sprinkling of cold earth" in "On The Power of Sound" persists in the
mind as an image too powerfully naturalistic to be subsumed by the
mythic context about poetic voice. There is indeed more mixing of
effects in remythologizing contexts, so that categorizing echoes is
more problematical than in demythologizing contexts.

In a wide sense, all of Wordsworth's naturalizing echoes contribute
to the fashioning of a new myth. Some, however, can be seen as
remythologizing in a contextually specific way. Gray, the mediating
figure par excellence between Wordsworth and Milton, plays both
roles. Of nearly fifty echoes of Gray, about half are embedded in
three long early poems, "The Vale of Esthwaite," *An Evening Walk,*
and *Descriptive Sketches.* The mixture of naturalism and vision in these
poems is evident in its cruder pre-Romantic form, and Gray contrib-

utes on both sides. The "melancholy sound / Of drowsy bells for ever tinkling round," used to describe a remote spot in *Descriptive Sketches* (*PW*1.42ff. [1793], 434–35), like the "lowing herds" a few lines below (446), is a naturalistic detail from Gray's *Elegy* ("and drowsy tinklings lull the distant folds," line 8). Wordsworth likes it so well that he repeats it in line 508 of the *Sketches*.[37]

The function of these borrowings is on the face of it to spread the tone of rural atmosphere by calling up a voice traditionally associated with it through a famous poem. And yet the borrowed materials are displaced from the farming locale of the *Elegy* to "awful wilds," and through this displacement, with the assistance of key adjectives, Wordsworth invokes that aspect of Gray—and of the whole descriptive train of pre-Romantic poetry—which levies on the sense of vague *tremenda*. The adjectives belong to the stock of later-eighteenth-century terms which raise a dimly august presence, religious in the Latin sense of the word.[38] The passage is heavy with numinous terms of this sort and represents a visionary encounter with nature:

> —Is there who mid these awful wilds has seen
> The native Genii walk the mountain green?
> Or heard, while other worlds their charms reveal,
> Soft music from th'aereal summit steal?
> While o'er the desert, answering every close,
> Rich steam of sweetest perfume comes and goes.
> —And sure there is a secret Power that reigns
> Here, where no trace of man the spot profanes,
> Nought but the herds that pasturing upward creep,
> Hung dim-discover'd from the dangerous steep,
> Or summer hamlet, flat and bare, on high
> Suspended, mid the quiet of the sky.
> How still! no irreligious sound or sight
> Rouzes the soul from her severe delight.
> An idle voice the sabbath region fills
> Of Deep that calls to Deep across the hills,
> Broke only by the melancholy sound
> Of drowsy bells for ever tinkling round;
> Faint wail of eagle melting into blue
> Beneath the cliffs, and pine-woods steady sugh;
> The solitary heifer's deepen'd low;
> Or rumbling heard remote of falling snow.
> Save that, the stranger seen below, the boy
> Shouts from the echoing hills with savage joy.
>
> ([1793], 418–41)

This embodies the sort of association Wordsworth often makes with Gray in his naturalizing mood. And woven into the passage are other voices which he is likely to link to the "natural supernatural." *Paradise Lost* V.547–48 ("cherubic Songs by night from neighboring Hills / Aereal Music send") is the source of Wordsworth's "Soft music from th'aereal summit"; the Nativity Ode, line 100 ("with thousand echoes still prolongs each heav'nly close"), of "answering every close"; and, through homonymic contraction, *Comus* 556 (which describes a sound rising "like a stream of rich distill'd Perfumes") of "Rich steam of sweetest perfume comes and goes." The adjective "dim-discovered," popular among descriptive poets in the eighteenth century, probably originated with Thomson (*Summer* 946). A signal instance of its use that may be in Wordsworth's mind is found in Collins's "Ode to Evening" (37), where "dim-discovered spires" are linked to "hamlets brown," clusters of mountain dwellings that reappear in Wordsworth's "summer hamlets" and, according to Wordsworth's own note, are described by Virgil's phrase, *"castella in tumulis"* (*PW* 1.68, note 2). And, of course, "Deep that calls to Deep" is from Psalm 42. Virgil, Milton, Thomson, Gray, Collins: To these we need add only Young, Akenside, the Wartons, and Coleridge in order to pinpoint the main set of sources on which Wordsworth drew in a mythologizing spirit. Though the Bible in this instance contributes to the intermingling of "other worlds" to sustain a sense of the "awful," it rarely plays a role—for obvious reasons—in the mode of natural supernaturalism. It is of course a primary source for Milton, but the later-eighteenth-century poets, using Milton as a precursive voice of landscape numen, naturalized his biblical voice. Looking back from Wordsworth's early standpoint, therefore, one can see his remythologizing set of values as a nodal point in a direct line going from Virgil—especially the Virgil of the *Eclogues* and the *Georgics*—through Milton's minor poems to Young, Thomson, Gray, and the rest.

Virgil's blend of estheticized rural earthiness, melancholy animadversions on love and loss, and fictive restitution through song, prophecy, or myth resonates in the revaluations Milton pursued in his minor poems, which subvert pagan pastoral nature yet give it play. This complicated set of voicings shapes the variations of vocal standpoint that follow—Young's sky-born enthusiasm, Thomson's religiously philosophizing use of the natural sublime, Akenside's more Romanizing invocations of "powers" in the landscape, the Wartons' Allegro-Penseroso attitudinizings. It also shapes Gray's bardic tonalities combining scenic *religio*, psychological abstraction, nostalgic melancholy, and cultural vision, and Collins's more gently haunted naturalizing musings. Even Coleridge, partly as a revisionary inheritor of this kind of poeticizing, partly as a more supernaturally oriented alter ego, became a source for assimilative remythologizing when Wordsworth was not confronting him directly.

The two grand originals of this line, Milton and Virgil, come together in the 1802 sonnet, "Composed after a Journey across the Hambleton Hills, Yorkshire" (*PW*3.25). The first line, "Dark and more dark the shades of evening fell," is not a direct echo of Virgil, but it comes near the last line of his first *Eclogue*—*maioresque cadunt altis de montibus umbrae* ("and longer shadows fall from the tall hills")—and it involves the spirit of the Virgilian term *umbra*, thrice repeated in the closing lines of the final *Eclogue* in a modest affirmation of the Roman poet's effort to set his song against the perilous coming of the dark. Wordsworth's opening verse is at once natural description and prelude to a numinous moment, when "the glowing west with marvellous power" saluted him on his journey. The echo reinforces the evening atmosphere; but it is more than atmospheric in this case, for the imaginative pastoral world it looks back at is associated with the fabulous cloud-pageant the poet sees above the dark, a pageant where

> Many a tempting isle,
> With groves that never were imagined, lay
> 'Mid seas how steadfast! objects all for the eye
> Of silent rapture.

Yet this solacing vision is rejected in a naturalizing turn which closes the sonnet:

> but we felt the while
> We should forget them; they are of the sky,
> And from our earthly memory fade away.

These lines suggest a revisionary struggle with the Virgilian affirmation of imaginative play even as the poem maintains an earthbound view consonant with the close of the tenth *Eclogue*. Wordsworth's disappointment at not being able to see, in the dark, the magnificent landscape view "whereof many thousands tell" is met by the rapture of the imagination-stimulating sky view. But it is not enough, not permanently consoling like Virgil's backward glance at *his* "pageant," the achievement of his pastoral songs: *Haec sat erit, divae, vestrum cecinisse poetam* ("It will be enough, divine muses, for your poet to have sung these strains," *Eclogue* X.70). Wordsworth's vision, being too divorced from ordinary human reality, will fade from his memory.

Of course there is the sonnet itself to set against this assertion. Can one say that Wordsworth's song after all suffices? Wordsworth's intention is plainly to say that transcendental imagination does not suffice. His echo of Milton carries part of this intention. The echo—made precise in an 1815 revision—seems curiously wrenched out of context when we examine the original. Wordsworth's cloud-church, "with its tower / Substantially expressed" (the phrase had been "substantially distinct" before 1815) calls up words applied to Christ in Book III of *Paradise Lost:*

> Beyond compare the Son of God was seen
> Most glorious, in him all his Father shone
> Substantially express'd, and in his face
> Divine compassion visibly appear'd,
> Love without end, and without measure Grace.
>
> (138–42)

Milton's use of "substantially" has doctrinal force in regard to the Trinity, and it seems to prefigure the meaning of the Incarnation. In Wordsworth it figures a gentle self-mockery which preludes a rejection of descendental movement. The context of "substantially expressed" is so different in each case that one cannot speak of a transumption. But the transumptive impulse is there, and though it is muted by the sonnet's modest scope, it has enough force to turn aside both Virgilian and Miltonic consolations. What seemed to begin as a remythologizing vision has turned, by the poem's close, into its opposite.

The remythologizing mode predominates in a simpler and more direct use of Virgilian numinosity, the lines of "Yew Trees" (*PW*2.209) imitating Virgil's description of the forecourt of hell (*Aeneid* VI.273–81). The "ghostly shapes" in this poem ("Fear and trembling Hope, / Silence and Foresight; Death the Skeleton / And Time the Shadow" [26–28]) are similar to the living abstractions investing the entrance to Pluto's realm in Virgil, though they move about in a more naturalized scene, worshiping "As in a natural temple scattered o'er / With altars undisturbed of mossy stone" and listening "to the mountain flood / Murmuring from Glaramara's inmost caves" (29–30, 32–33).

These examples merely begin to sketch the variety of remythologizing uses of Virgilian and Miltonic echoes. Both poets are complex models who often push Wordsworth beyond assimilation. His simpler models limit his freedom less, and in assimilating them he can more easily take their dim hints in his own direction. Bowles is an example. Since he seemed to reveal to both Wordsworth and Coleridge, in their early careers, new possibilities in nature description, and for a time was a model of easy naturalism, it is curious that in the next stage of

Wordsworth's career he tends to come forward in association with more exalted feelings. Lines 25–26 of "Tintern Abbey," for example, appear to borrow from Bowles's Sonnet XIX.8–9 ("Nor, 'mid the busy scenes and 'hum of men' / Wilt thou my cares forget"), which in turn borrows from "L'Allegro" 118. In his sonnet "To the Torrent at the Devil's Bridge" (*PW*3.43), Wordsworth uses the phrase "As in life's morn." While this is undoubtedly part of the common language stock, in a river poem dealing with the emotions of recall and restoration, one has to suspect that Wordsworth has remembered Bowles's parallel poem on the River Itchin, especially "Is it—that many a summer's day has past / Since, in life's morn, I caroll'd on thy side?" In Wordsworth's "Torrent," the same phrase preludes the opening up of an "eternity feeling," suggesting a revision of Bowles's melancholy nostalgia while including him in the poetic brotherhood that responds to the might of waters: "Such power possess the family of floods / Over the minds of Poets, young or old!"

Akenside provides more teasing examples. His sophistication, in terms of restraint, subtlety, and penetration, is far greater than that of Bowles or the Wartons. His interest in and ways of thinking about the imagination, along with his refined evocations of the *genius loci*, make him more congenial to Wordsworth and more amenable to assimilation. Indeed, a careful study of *The Pleasures of the Imagination*, especially the earlier version, would undoubtedly show that Wordsworth owes him a debt both conceptual and metrical. He appears to stand in the background of the celebrated passage of *The Prelude* describing the Gorge of Gondo. Wordsworth has invented all those things which introduce tension, original insight, and visionary resolution, all those manipulations of detail which make the scene live as a vividly concrete, psychologically resonant natural description; but the black cliffs, dark ridge-borne woods, water-spouting sides, and hoarse torrent of Akenside's vision of "primeval joy" "spread around" by the "strong, creative mandate" of the "Sovereign Spirit of the world" ([1744], II.312, 315, 307) resonate with Wordsworth's "types and symbols of Eternity." Compare Akenside's lines with Wordsworth's:

>   'Twas a horrid pile
> Of hills with many a shaggy forest mix'd,
> With many a sable cliff and glittering stream.
> Aloft recumbent o'er the hanging ridge,
> The brown woods wav'd; while ever-trickling springs
> Wash'd from the naked roots of oak and pine
> The crumbling soil; and still at every fall
> Down the steep windings of the channel'd rock,

> Remurmuring rush'd the congregated floods
> With hoarser inundation . . .
>
> ([1744], II.274–83)

> The immeasurable height
> Of woods decaying, never to be decay'd,
> The stationary blasts of water-falls,
> And every where along the hollow rent
> Winds thwarting winds, bewilder'd and forlorn,
> The torrents shooting from the clear blue sky,
> The rocks that mutter'd close upon our ears,
> Black drizzling crags that spake by the way-side
> As if a voice were in them, the sick sight
> And giddy prospect of the raving stream . . .
>
> (*Prelude* VI.556–65)

The bright and plastic has become dark and bewildered, the bluntly rhetorical has gained immensely in power and subtlety through the creative energy of the unexpected and paradoxical details, and we are compelled to feel that the experience being transmitted is *sui generis*. Nonetheless, to be transmitted an experience must be shaped, and Akenside seems to have contributed to its shaping in the subtle fashion of the assimilative mode. The perceptible echoes Wordsworth draws from Akenside are not striking or numerous. He seems to use Akenside's text in the process of composing as one more link with an older vision, which Wordsworth's both entertains and overgoes.

Akenside also seems present in the surrounding context. Wordsworth's "light of sense," which "Goes out in flashes that have shewn to us / The invisible world" (*Prelude* [1805], VI.534–36), has connections with Akenside's "flame of passion," which, arising from a "meditated scene," "shows across that sudden blaze / The object of its rapture, vast of size, / With fiercer colours and a night of shade" (*Pleasures of Imagination* [1744], II.136–40). And the earlier poet appears to inform Wordsworth's reaction to the blind beggar in Book VII of *The Prelude*: Compare "My mind did at this spectacle turn round / As with the might of waters" (615–16) with Akenside's image of inner revelation, acting like stormy seas "when the might / Of these eruptions, working from the depth / Of man's strong apprehension, shakes his frame / Even to the base" ([1744], II.142–45). Neither is a close echo, and one can argue that the similarities are due to the incorporation of popular geological and meteorological imagery; but reading steadily in *The Pleasures of Imagination* suggests a rhetorical and ideological kinship between the two writers sufficient to give Akenside a privileged position as a poetic source for Wordsworth.

> Then Nature speaks
> Her genuine language, and the words of men,
> Big with the very motion of their souls,
> Declare with what accumulated force,
> The impetuous nerve of passion urges on
> The native weight and energy of things . . .
> (*Pleasures of Imagination* [1744], II.149–54)

The poet in such intensely emotional moments seems to be inditing in the spirit of Wordsworth as we know him from the prefaces and *The Prelude*.

Thomson, though in contrast he almost never sounds like Wordsworth, enjoys the same privileged position. Wordsworth uses him in many ways, but when his borrowing is determined by mood, it is generally in remythologizing contexts.[39] The "corresponding mild creative breeze" of *The Prelude* I.43 may have been shaped by Thomson. In *Autumn* Thomson wrote of his walks in a country estate:

> . . . I solitary court
> The inspiring breeze, and meditate the book
> Of Nature, ever open, aiming thence
> Warm from the heart to learn the moral song.
> (668–72)

The "inspiring breeze" is a commonplace, but the encompassing context in Wordsworth brings up the same idea of poetic dedication, of seeking to become an impassioned moral voice by responding to the "power" which comes from nature with the promise

> Of prowess in an honorable field,
> Pure passions, virtue, knowledge, and delight,
> Thy holy life of music and of verse.
> (I.52–54)

And in *Spring* Thomson speaks of "a thousand mixt emotions" which "vex the mind / With endless storm" (297, 299–300), reminding us verbally (though the contextual meaning is quite different) of Wordsworth's creative breeze "become / A tempest, a redundant energy / Vexing its own creation" (I.45–47).

Glossing another passage, De Selincourt notes that the combination of "changeful earth," "moving year," and "seasons" in I.586–88 of the 1805 *Prelude* recalls Thomson's *Winter* 105–6: "Nature! great parent! whose unceasing hand / Rolls round the Seasons of the changeful year."[40] On a grander rhetorical level, lines I.428–41 of the 1805 *Prelude* provide what might be called an imitation of Thomson's apostrophe to the "Universal Soul" in *Spring*. Characteristically, it transposes the Thomsonian celebration of the divine disposition of things in nature into praise for the natural providence which intertwines Wordsworth's inner life and the grand objects of the external universe. Thomson looks outward, while Wordsworth, beginning at a similar point, looks inward. Thomson has:

> Hail, Source of Being! Universal Soul
> Of heaven and earth! Essential Presence, hail!
> To thee I bend the knee; to thee my thoughts
> Continual climb, who with a master-hand
> Hast the great whole into perfection touched.
> By thee the various vegetative tribes,
> Wrapt in a filmy net and clad with leaves,
> Draw the live ether and imbibe the dew.
> By thee disposed into congenial soils,
> Stands each attractive plant, and sucks, and swells
> The juicy tide, a twining mass of tubes.
> At thy command the vernal sun awakes
> The torpid sap, detruded to the root
> By wintry winds, that now in fluent dance
> And lively fermentation mounting spreads
> All this innumerous-coloured scene of things.
>   (556–71)

Thomson's images jostle one another uncomfortably. The poet is not in full control of the movement between the general and the specific, and the sudden intrusion of exact detail pushes his straining rhetoric toward absurdity. Wordsworth takes only what he needs to reinvent the passage, disburdening the natural description of entangling minute particulars and manipulating the general to achieve a strong rhetorical unity. Yet he also manages through words mingling the organic and the spiritual to intimate the concrete basis of his vision:

> Wisdom and Spirit of the universe!
> Thou Soul that art the Eternity of Thought!
> That giv'st to forms and images a breath
> And everlasting motion! not in vain,

By day or star-light thus from my first dawn
Of Childhood didst Thou intertwine for me
The passions that build up our human Soul,
Not with the mean and vulgar works of Man,
But with high objects, with enduring things,
With life and nature, purifying thus
The elements of feeling and of thought,
And sanctifying, by such discipline,
Both pain and fear, until we recognize
A grandeur in the beatings of the heart.
                                    (I.428–41)

Thomson is redoing the passage on the Chain of Being in *Paradise Lost*
V.479–88 in terms of nature's spring awakening; Wordsworth, revising Thomson, is creating a new myth of equal interchange between
man and nature, inner life and outer life.

In the sources of Wordsworth's mood-borne echoes, as in the
Thomson quotation above, it is not necessarily the integral thought
or any sustained brilliance of insight in the original, or even a minor
rhetorical triumph, that catches the attention of the poet's composing mind. Often mere bits and pieces become settled in his poetic
memory by acts of inward recognition that are sometimes obvious to
a reader, sometimes obscure, and are stirred to life by the "corresponding mild creative breeze" of his mood. Despite his assertion
that he keeps his eye on the object, these fragments may surface
without reference to an external reality—a method that allows him a
great deal of freedom with his sources. If not all such manipulations
create effects readers find edifying or engaging, it is not in any
simple way due to the heterogeneousness of the borrowings or
Wordsworth's lack of concern with freshness of imagery. The following lines of juvenilia show that from early on the discovery of a fresh
image was a prized experience:

If, while I gaz'd to Nature blind,
In the calm Ocean of my mind
Some new-created image rose
In full-grown beauty at its birth
Lovely as Venus from the sea,
Then, while my glad hand sprung to thee [his dog],
We were the happiest pair on earth.
("The Dog—An Idyllium," *PW*1.264; see also *Prelude* IV.101–8)

Nor are any failures due to haphazardness. Wordsworth's echoes are governed by an underlying order acting at the local and particular surfaces from which imaginative constructs emerge. When his moralizing, anthropologizing, and naturalizing moods embed themselves purposively, his borrowings carry weight. It is when their purpose is weakly realized or is active only in the prelusive movements of the act of composition that they lack the power to engage us. This is what we find in the poeticizing mood.

THE POETICIZING MOOD

It is not surprising that Wordsworth's verse should contain diction common to his predecessors. Even though rejection of the "triviality and meanness, both of thought and language" and the "gaudiness and inane phraseology" of his contemporaries who were heirs to that diction was part of his revolutionary program, his commitment to the tradition was so instinctive that he never wholly divested himself even of the discourse of poets he considered second-rate.[41] The cento-making he indulged in as a form of play was only an extreme extension of an impulse constantly active in him and inherent in his idea of composing. Up to this point, I have been trying to demonstrate the various rationales for the different kinds of echoing. But I believe that there are borrowings for which no credible contextual motive can be found. Anterior voices seem to exert constant pressure on a certain type of poet whose consciousness is "throng'd with impregnations" (*Prelude* VIII.791), and they tend to break through to expression unless they are consciously contravened for reasons of principle or contextual coherence. In literary periods in which allusiveness is felt to be a natural device, the principle of originality is more active at other loci of poetic texture than sheer inventiveness of phrasing, and the poet's idea of contextual coherence accommodates echoes. When Wordsworth is most aggressively revolutionary—in the period from the *Lyrical Ballads* through the lyrics of 1802—he echoes least; but before and after this time, when he cares less about originality of phrasing, he echoes ad lib. And if among these ad-lib echoes the nonconfrontational ones often have a specific relevance ranging from the cunning to the bland, there are also echoes that seem to have no more point than to announce that Wordsworth is acting the role of the Bard.

Critics have always recognized this in his earliest poems, feeling more or less of the discomfort Legouis gave voice to in condemning

Descriptive Sketches as a literary pastiche. Since beginning poets naturally turn to naked imitation and borrowing, unless the literary code devalues them, readers looking at a poet's work over a lifetime can be indulgent of early efforts. No one bothers to condemn the purple Della Cruscan manner of Wordsworth's "Sonnet on Seeing Miss Helen Maria Williams Weep at a Tale of Distress" (*PW*1.269). But we expect more of *An Evening Walk* and *Descriptive Sketches*, written by a poet beginning to show a style marked by "impatient strength" (*Biographia* 1: 56); and despite my aim of making a general defense of the technique, I recognize that among the welter of borrowings crowding the lines of these poems many are merely "poeticizing" decorations. For example, Wordsworth communicates little more than the breadth of his reading and a private pleasure in Tasso's oxymoron, *"dolcemente feroci,"* by translating (and footnoting) it in the 1793 *Evening Walk:* "Sweetly ferocious round his native walks, / Gaz'd by his sister-wives, the monarch [rooster] stalks" (129–30).

Lines 13–14 of *Descriptive Sketches* ("But doubly pitying Nature loves to show'r / Soft on his wounded heart her healing pow'r") are also typical of the early verse in which echoes are guided mainly by a poeticizing mood. Wordsworth organizes the natural observations which are the poem's point by creating a dramatic perspective—that of a roamer who, by a conventional turn, is stereotypically melancholy. But no dramatic reason is given for this melancholy; it is simply an excuse to echo Gray. Line 15, which pictures the roamer as he "plods o'er hills and vales his road forlorn" and thus glances at the third line of Gray's *Elegy* ("the ploughman homeward plods his weary way"), has no function beyond constellating a "poetic" melancholy mood that communicates in easy, popular accents. The same can be said of "the meanest note that swells the gale" (line 20, adapted from the "Ode on the Pleasure Arising from Vicissitude" 45–46: "The meanest flowret of the vale, / The simplest note that swells the gale"). And the attempt to hint a motive for the roamer's melancholy in lines 43–44 seems feeble, emptily conventional: "Much wondering what sad stroke of crazing Care / Or desperate Love could lead a wanderer there" (compare Gray's *Elegy* 108: "Or crazed with care, or crossed in hopeless love").

With what is for modern readers a delicious irony, line 33 echoes a line of Gray's "Sonnet on the Death of Mr. Richard West" which Wordsworth was to denounce in the preface to *Lyrical Ballads* as mere "poetic diction" and so wholly without merit ("He views the Sun uprear his golden fire," picks up Gray's "And reddening Phoebus lifts his golden fire").[42] Other borrowings in this passage of *Descriptive Sketches* also sort with the poeticizing impulse: "velvet tread" (24), after *Comus* 898 ("Thus I set my printless feet / O'er the Cowslip's Velvet head"); "Upward he looks—and calls it luxury" (26), after Addison's *Cato*, I.i.71 ("Blesses his stars, and thinkst it luxury"); "moralize his pensive road" (30), a Wartonizing of *The Faerie Queene* I. Proem i.9 ("Fierce warres and faithfull loves shall moralize my song").

Although Wordsworth never again produced idle borrowings in such dense array, his later verse is not free from them, especially after 1804. A temporary change in the rhyme scheme of *The Waggoner* from couplets to varying interleaved quatrains (*PW*2.198, Canto Fourth, 11–23) helps mark a quotation from *Hamlet* I.v.58 (the ghost's "But soft, methinks I scent the morning air"):

> —Blithe spirits of her own impel
> The Muse, who scents the morning air,
> To take of this transported pair
> A brief and unreproved farewell.
>
> (11–14)

The poetry through line 56 of Wordsworth's fourth canto (describing the passage of the muse through a magically alive landscape) harks back to the mood of "L'Allegro," where ambulatory inspiration frees the authorial eye to take in a panorama of natural delight. Perhaps there is some wry humor in a fleeting contrast between Hamlet's supernatural binding to the violence of adult responsibility and the Waggoner's natural release into "freaks of proud delight" (Canto Fourth, line 1), but the enormous distance of *Hamlet* from this moment in *The Waggoner* makes the turn, if it is one, strained. On the other hand, there is a certain relevance in Wordsworth's obvious allusion to *Macbeth* V.iii.23 to express his awareness of aging in "Upon the Same Occasion [September, 1819]" (*PW*4.99), though here the fact that departing summer has taken on "The gentlest look of spring" (3) comes not to embitter but to cheer the poet "conscious that my leaf is sere, / And yellow on the bough" (14–15), and so inverts, without a specific confrontational purpose, the tonal force of the original. The lack of point or mood-matching relevance makes the allusion seem merely a reflex catching at a familiar voice.

Equally overt, and still more in the later-eighteenth-century patching manner, is the nod given to Horace in the same poem. Alcaeus's name comes up, and so we have a Horatian phrase ("fierce vindictive song") to honor him:

> Woe! woe to Tyrants! from the lyre
> Broke threateningly, in sparkles dire
> Of fierce vindictive song.[43]
>
> (40–42)

It is true that in this poem Wordsworth is asserting the "deathless powers" of verse, seeking in autumnal meditation to assure himself that despite feeling his poetic invention has worn thin, especially in response to nature, he can still find themes to produce "A genuine birth / Of Poesy" (25, 55–56). In such a context, a parade of older voices is appropriate; but the speaker does not seem able to rise much above posturing in calling these voices up. The poem's technique takes us back to the era of Gray. The final lines suggest an unintended negative answer to the central question of the piece:

> What Horace gloried to behold,
> What Maro loved, shall we enfold?
> Can haughty Time be just!

The idea of enfolding the essence of poetry comes up again in another poem written in a similar autumnal mood of assurance-seeking (though the time is spring). In "Musings near Aquapendente" (*PW*3.202), the poet asks,

> why should Poesy
> Yield to the lure of vain regret, and hover
> In gloom on wings with confidence outspread
> To move in sunshine?
>   (85–88)

He goes on to exhort:

> let me guard
> Those seeds of expectation which the fruit
> Already gathered in this favoured Land
> Enfolds within its core.
>   (103–6)

In the close, he shapes his victory over poetic despair through allusions to some favorite lines of Milton. Having not vainly "yielded up [his] soul / To transports from the secondary founts / Flowing of time and place," he will not

> fruitlessly have striven,
> By love of beauty moved, to enshrine in verse
> Accordant meditations, which in times
> Vexed and disordered, as our own, may shed
> Influence, at least among a scattered few,

> To soberness of mind and peace of heart
> Friendly; as here to my repose hath been
> This flowering broom's dear neighbourhood, the light
> And murmur issuing from yon pendent flood,
> And all the varied landscape. Let us now
> Rise, and to-morrow greet magnificent Rome.
>
> (362–72)

Though the theme is poesy, the use of Milton is not mere poeticizing. The poet is contemplating poetic genesis and its emblems in Milton's account of the Creation in *Paradise Lost*. He lights on an emblem he had used before in an entirely confident mood—in the "Prospectus," where he had asked that the "prophetic Spirit"

> upon me bestow
> A gift of genuine insight; that my Song
> With star-like virtue in its place may shine,
> Shedding benignant influence, and secure,
> Itself, from all malevolent effect
> Of those mutations that extend their sway
> Throughout the nether sphere!
>
> (87–93)

The reference is to the fourth day of creation, when God, separating night from day, fashions the sun, which then begins its celestial journey,

> Invested with bright Rays, jocund to run
> His Longitude through Heav'n's high road: the gray
> Dawn, and the *Pleiades* before him danc'd
> Shedding sweet influence.
>
> (*Paradise Lost* VII.372–75)

Involved in this emblem of poetic genesis is an image of the poet's earthly status provided earlier in Book VII by Milton's familiar lines describing his heroic self-assertion:

> Standing on Earth, not rapt above the Pole,
> More safe I Sing with mortal voice, unchang'd
> To hoarse or mute, though fall'n on evil days,
> On evil days though fall'n, and evil tongues;
> In darkness, and with dangers compast round,
> And solitude; yet not alone, while thou

Visit'st my slumbers Nightly, or when Morn
Purples the East: still govern thou my Song,
Urania, and fit audience find, though few.
(23–31)

The same fusion of images, compressed into a line and a half, is made
in "Musings near Aquapendente" when the poet asserts that his "Ac-
cordant meditations" will "shed / Influence, at least among a scattered
few." The compression is so great that unless the reader has some
familiarity with Wordsworth's methods the references will pass as poetic embroidery. But their thematic relevance to the sense of recovered poetic voice is fully dramatized by a further reference to Milton
in the final line. The exhortation to "Rise, and to-morrow greet magnificent Rome" recalls the close of "Lycidas": "At last he rose, and
twitch'd his Mantle blue: / Tomorrow to fresh Woods, and Pastures
new."

These considerations support Leslie Brisman's remark that "Wordsworth achieves some of his finest moments by turning to Milton"
(Brisman 215). Yet even Miltonic reference may at times add a merely
poeticizing flourish. In Book IX of *The Prelude*, describing his wanderings with Beaupuy in the Loire Valley, Wordsworth tells how they
came to a convent, "a roofless Pile, / And not by reverential touch of
Time / Dismantled, but by violence abrupt" (469–71). The phrase
depicting time's touch is a version of an adjective-noun pair used by
Milton in his essay "Of Education" to render the effect of an en-
semble, which may "with artful and unimaginable touches adorn and
grace the well-studied chords of some choice composer" (Hughes
638). Wordsworth twice applies the phrase "unimaginable touch" to
the hand of time. In his juvenile "Fragment of a Gothic Tale"
(*PW*1.287), he writes of towers split by "The unimaginable touch of
time / Or shouldering rend" (lines 66–67); and in the ecclesiastical
sonnet "Mutability" (*PW*3.401), he describes a "tower sublime" that
"could not even sustain / Some casual shout that broke the silent air, /
Or the unimaginable touch of Time." Not only has the meaning of
"touch," a musical term in Milton's text, been altered, but in none of
these places is there any link, even unimaginable, with the Miltonic
source beyond the striking adjective itself. In "Mutability" we can be
glad of this flourish for the sake of its sheer beauty. In *The Prelude*,
however, the substitution of "reverential" for "unimaginable" robs it
of all its magic, and the echo becomes idle.

Conclusion

If I have established that there is an art to Wordsworth's habit of borrowing, it remains to determine what its poetic value is. This question must finally be answered at two levels: its value to the poet and its value to the reader. These levels clearly coincide when a borrowing is at once the poet's means of structuring something integral that would otherwise be lost and an involving turn into new openings of meaning for the reader. This is the case in Wordsworth's comparative borrowings: The poet extends his reach in a stroke, and the reader pursues the confrontation of texts demanded by such an allusion in expectation of an enriched understanding. But with assimilative echoes, the value of recognizing and of pursuing the relevance of the markers is less certain. Is there any value in knowing that "The Sparrow's Nest" (*PW* 1.227) appropriates some no longer well-known phrases from a poem by Charles Churchill that is thematically quite unrelated to Wordsworth's poem?[1] Echoes like these may afford a mild gratification on construal, depending on the degree of meaningfulness in the echo and of responsive energy in the reader. But in many cases even the most well-disposed reader would wonder whether the construal was worth the effort.

For Wordsworth, echoing is one of the enabling acts of poetic composition. The writer who saw poetry as emotion recollected in tranquility, or the spontaneous overflow of powerful feelings which then had to be reworked, could not often complete the process of giving his experience a local habitation and a name without echoing at some level. In addition, echoing enacted and emblematized the process of interchange he believed took place between man and nature, thus prompting the myth of creativity he chose to advance and serve. The myth incorporated the three modes of envisioning on which he based his poetic approach—recalling past consciousness, responding to the natural landscape, and levying on predecessors. Each system involves a form of echoing. Thus the great poetic naturalizer, likewise reforming and didactic in his aims, started where Bacon did, with the marriage of Pan and Echo:

> It is an excellent invention that *Pan* or the world is said to make
> choise of *Echo* only, (above all other speeches or voices) for his
> wife; for that alone is true philosophy which doth faithfully

render the very words of the world, and is written no otherwise then the world doth dictate, it being nothing els but the image or reflection of it, not adding anything of its owne, but only iterates and resounds.[2]

But by "listening to sounds that are / The ghostly language of the ancient earth" and seeking to "make / Breathings for incommunicable powers," he came to deepen his sense of echo and radically alter Bacon's naturalizing enterprise. He extended the union of Pan and Echo to a *marriage à trois,* in which Echo becomes a mediator between the external world and the individual mind and helps the last two "with blended might" accomplish an exemplary creation. Iteration becomes exchange—"an ennobling interchange / Of action from within and from without"—so that the poet does not repeat the world but embodies it poetically by speaking "things oracular."[3] This rendering of the physical world into poetic voice becomes the process by which he draws childhood and books into his naturalizing myth: The "action from within" is principally the reincorporation of childhood vision into consciousness, and the "action from without" involves the intimate approximation of natural objects and words. We find all three—world, mind, and word—fused in a famous passage from Book V of *The Prelude:*

>   Visionary Power
>   Attends upon the motions of the winds
>   Embodied in the mystery of words.
>   There darkness makes abode, and all the host
>   Of shadowy things do work their changes there,
>   As in a mansion like their proper home:
>   Even forms and substances are circumfus'd
>   By that transparent veil with light divine;
>   And through the turnings intricate of Verse,
>   Present themselves as objects recognis'd,
>   In flashes, and with a glory scarce their own.
>   (V.619–29)

Words and their referential objects are seen as inextricable, so that we cannot be sure if by "shadowy things," "forms and substances," and "objects recognis'd" is meant natural things immediately grasped by sensation or verbalizings of thoughts sounded on the waters of memory. And the language, particularly the use of "abode," "mansion," "proper home," "recognis'd," "flashes," and "glory," suggests that the darkness which becomes a light-diffusing transparent veil represents the nurturing screen over buried childhood experience. The fusing energy here is echo, imagined as wind—a revivified conventional topos for spirit, the Romantic inspiratory breeze that evokes poetry. The wind is echo-like in function because it carries things to and fro, moving not only within the self and outside, but from outside in (as inspiration and as the ingress of other human voicings), and from inside out (as the observer's vocal response). It is, furthermore, itself a voice, repeating the spiritual language of the earth (which makes its "dim abode in distant winds") and representing the poet who stores up song by "rambling like the wind / As I had done in daily intercourse / With those delicious rivers, solemn heights, / And mountains."[4]

If echo is thus the mediator that helps Wordsworth bring together his three major sources of poetic power, it also functions as a screen which holds back or filters the influx threatening to inundate the poet in the act of composing. It provides room for creation (and, by the same action, evasion). For an echo, *pace* Bacon, is not a mere iteration or transfer, but an alteration: it produces, after a delay, something at once like and unlike the original, and this Derridean *différance* engenders creative acts in the poet attuned to tradition. Wordsworth's concept of himself as a didactic poet, much of his Enlightenment ideation, and many of his immediately definable poetic practices have precedents; but from this traditional base he evolved an original voice, and it led him into an unprecedented venture: the attempt to sustain human vision by naturalizing it. He tried to find in nature-molded feeling the ground of human redemption, not by abruptly casting out the old but by revaluing and reorienting it, giving it a new birth. Echo, in its capacity to defer and make different without dissolving the original, is a perfect instrumental metaphor for this process.[5]

In carrying forward into new mental space what has already been said, echo confers a kind of freedom, and Wordsworth—the borrower—is in this sense free. In "Imitation as Freedom: 1717–1798," W. K. Wimsatt makes a strong case for the liberating effect of imitation on the eighteenth-century poetic mind. A similar case, with certain cautions, can be made for the effect of echoic technique on Wordsworth's. It helped to root and substantiate his poetry and so, above all, to authenticate his original voice.

Though one can frequently trace elements of Milton, Thomson, Young, Akenside, Gray, Collins, Goldsmith, and Cowper in Wordsworth's verse—identical terms, blank-verse rhythms, rhetorical devices, the use of energetic image-generating verbs, didacticism, the avoidance of particular kinds of wit, a reliance on syntax in the sense proposed by Donald Davie (see especially 1–10)—these elements no longer function as they did in their original context. Davie shows that

Wordsworth's important nouns lie somewhere between the abstract
and the concrete, being used like "fiduciary" symbols as counters of
philosophical exchange, and that his syntax is operationally directive
yet "suggestive" in character, a "subjective syntax" for acting out the
drama of meditation in which he flees his personal feelings in such a
way as to ensure that he will be overtaken by them (106–7, 75–76).
R. A. Foakes has studied how the poet substitutes for witty or sharp
sensual images "images of impression" linked to assertive value terms.
These images of impression create a non-Augustan kind of generality
which, while stopping short of the explicitly mythical, has a mythic or
archetypal suggestiveness. The value of this suggestiveness is to enable
the images to figure forth large conceptions the poet cannot assume to
be established by religious, philosophical, or literary tradition (34–50,
69–79). The linguistic activity Davie and Foakes point to in their individual ways produces a characteristic feature of Wordsworth's style:
His poetic language does not appear to strain after special effects yet
has delaying complexities of syntax and image, complexities that force
one to ponder, to expand one's awareness of connotations.

    This poetic manner continually urges on the willing reader a kind
of double take. It might be called Wordsworth's natural wit, since it
does some of the work accomplished by Augustan wit but is different
in effect. It is active in a passage of *The Prelude* about the relation of
the ten-year-old observer to nature and to the future present in which
his adult successor is writing:

> Yes, I remember, when the changeful earth,
> And twice five seasons on my mind had stamp'd
> The faces of the moving year, even then,
> A Child, I held unconscious intercourse
> With the eternal Beauty, drinking in
> A pure organic pleasure from the lines
> Of curling mist, or from the level plain
> Of waters colour'd by the steady clouds.
>
> The Sands of Westmoreland, the Creeks and Bays
> Of Cumbria's rocky limits, they can tell
> How when the Sea threw off his evening shade
> And to the Shepherd's huts beneath the crags
> Did send sweet notice of the rising moon,
> How I have stood, to fancies such as these,
> Engrafted in the tenderness of thought,
> A stranger, linking with the spectacle
> No conscious memory of a kindred sight,

And bringing with me no peculiar sense
Of quietness or peace, yet I have stood,
Even while mine eye has mov'd o'er three long leagues
Of shining water, gathering, as it seem'd,
Through every hair-breadth of that field of light,
New pleasure, like a bee among the flowers.

   Thus, often in those fits of vulgar joy
Which through all seasons, on a child's pursuits
Are prompt attendants, 'mid that giddy bliss
Which, like a tempest, works along the blood
And is forgotten; even then I felt
Gleams like the flashing of a shield; the earth
And common face of Nature spake to me
Remembereable things; sometimes, 'tis true,
By chance collisions and quaint accidents
Like those ill-sorted unions, work suppos'd
Of evil-minded fairies, yet not vain
Nor profitless, if haply they impress'd
Collateral objects and appearances,
Albeit lifeless then, and doom'd to sleep
Until maturer seasons call'd them forth
To impregnate and to elevate the mind.

                            (I.586–624)

The passage consists of three long, complex sentences, and as we read
we are dependent on the syntax to sort out and coerce into meaning a
host of imaged statements. Thus, as Davie maintains, syntax carries a
significant burden of the poetic argument. Yet the syntax is not
smoothly continuous: The clausal logic is constantly interrupted by
new starts which, to keep us from losing our way, entrain repetitions
of terms that force us to hold harder to the thread to which qualifications are being attached. The movement from "Yes, I remember,
when" to "even then, / A Child, I held" involves a doubling of adverbial conjunctions *(when, then)*; the passage from "The Sands of Westmoreland" through "they can tell / How when" and "How I have
stood" to "yet I have stood" is negotiated through doublings of subjects *(Sands, they; I, I)*, a verb *(stood, stood)*, and adverbial clauses ("How
when," "How I"). The complete clause, "the earth / And common face
of Nature spake to me / Remembereable things," is joined to the complex unwinding of the two preceding clauses (heavily linked with ad-
verbs: "thus, often" . . . "even then") so abruptly that Wordsworth has
inserted a helping dash by 1850. And the long concluding clause

(beginning "sometimes, 'tis true"), acting as an immense adverbial modification of "spake" (in "Nature spake to me"), in fact has no main verb and no logical connector linking it to the preceding clause. In reading one's way through this sort of construction, one feels that the syntax, though still occupying the foreground, has joined itself to a new principle of organization—an echoic mode of dovetailing and multiplying conceptions. These "windings intricate" are on one hand the language of plenitude, of experience so full that it cannot be smoothly parsed, and on the other what Davie asserts Wordsworth's syntax to be, an enactment of the poet's thought in the course of struggling to find what will suffice.

Crabb Robinson recorded that Wordsworth, "Speaking of his own poems, . . . said he principally valued them as being a *new power* in the literary world, [looking] to the powers of mind his poems call forth, as the standard by which they are to be judged" (1: 89). The style amounts to what has been called "process mimesis," which, as opposed to "product mimesis," embodies the creative mind representing itself on the way to discovery rather than embodying the discovery itself.[6] It proceeds not by compression, as eighteenth-century wit does, but by moving through a broad mental territory, collecting bits and pieces of a totality. Yet the common function of syntax is not really abrupted; it is at work bringing the bits and pieces into conjunction. Wordsworth's poetry is still to an important degree a poetry of argument.

If we turn to the imagery of the *Prelude* passage, we find only a few sharply descriptive images, like "the lines / Of curling mist" or "every hair-breadth of that field of light." In both, the concrete image seems the sharper for being held beside a more general or abstract one—the curling mist against "pure organic pleasure," the hair-breadth measuring a "field" of light. The scenic description is sensuously concrete yet dominated by the more generalized "images of impression." Since these pictorialize broadly assertive value terms or terms designating fundamental phenomena in human experience—"the tenderness of thought," "fits of vulgar joy," "giddy bliss / Which, like a tempest, works along the blood"—the scene is not finally delineated by the hard, precise data we get in either Jacobean or Augustan poetry of wit but experienced as a medium of philosophical and psychological exploration.

Most of the imagetic energy is pent in the verbs ("drinking in," "threw off," "engrafted," "gathering," "works along"). That much of the concrete imagery is contained in such verbs enforces a sense of movement, of localization by process rather than crystallization; and this process allows the verbs to mediate between the psyche and external nature, fitting nature to the mind and the mind to nature. The nouns, on the other hand, are largely of Davies's "fiduciary-symbol" sort ("intercourse," "Beauty," "fancies," "thought," "spectacle," "joy," "bliss," "tempest," "Nature," "objects," "appearances," "mind"—favorite Wordsworthian terms all), standing for still-unfixed philosophical, psychological, or moral complexes of ideas made relatively concrete by context. In all these ways, the poet is using process mimesis to develop material similar to that of his predecessors in a manner distinct from theirs, which normally works toward product mimesis.

A large element of process mimesis is generated by internal echoing. "The changeful earth," the "faces of the moving year," the "unconscious intercourse / With . . . eternal Beauty," the "drinking in" of pleasure, the "lines / Of curling mist," and the "level plain / Of Waters" are each iterated in "the earth / And common face of Nature" (which takes in the first two phrases above), "the tenderness of thought" (which takes in "unconscious intercourse"), "gathering . . . New pleasure" (equivalent to "drinking in / A pure organic pleasure"), "every hairbreadth of that field of light" (combining the lines of mist and the plain of waters). Syntax, rhythm, and phrasing are also repeated: "I remember when" / "even then . . . I held" is done again by "How when" (596) / "even then I felt"; "How I have stood" by "Yet I have stood"; "Which, through all seasons, on a child's pursuits / Are prompt attendants" by "Which, like a tempest, works along the blood / And is forgotten." There is yet another form of iteration using rhetorical figures—hendiadys ("the earth / And common face of Nature") or simple doubling ("twice five seasons"). Internal echoes like these have often been noted, particularly in Wordsworth's blank verse. Their net effect is to intensify the feeling of a weaving movement, of a texture being made up as one goes along.

My main reason for giving this concrete demonstration of Wordsworth's manipulation of familiar material is to emphasize his freedom. The reliance on tradition generated by his echoic predilections bound him in one sense to his predecessors but at the same time gave him room to transform what he received. His predilection for echoes loosened from strict contextual ties also helped free him in a more direct way from genre constraints; for since his echoing methods often led him to seize on words, phrases, short passages, or localized constructions, he silently weaned himself of generic imitation, the main method of the eighteenth century. The general and rapid abandonment by the main poets of the Romantic period of imitation and the construction of wholes was noteworthy, though certainly the process was already underway in the fragmenting of imitation among the pre-Romantic poets. Wordsworth did of course write odes and sonnets, and one can trace the effect of genres in the depths of his major works, but it is clear that once his juvenilia and the special case of *Lyrical Ballads* were behind him, he seldom approached composition in the traditional spirit of imitation (the Miltonic sonnets are the main exception), and as a result he helped mightily to transform the shape of English poetry. Even the poems of *Lyrical Ballads* stretch the ballad so far that they constitute something new.

If Wordsworth was bound in a constraining way to anyone, it was to Milton. He modeled his idea of the poet's career after Milton's. Miltonic rhythms exert themselves in his blank verse, though often filtered through Akenside and Cowper, and of course Miltonic phrases and conceptions press upon him strongly in the act of composing. It was because of this that his echoes of Milton, bulking so much larger than his echoes of anyone else, were often confrontations, tending to rich comparative allusion. He was always struggling to free himself of this giant—often fruitfully, so far as individual pieces go. Shakespeare, the next most compelling voice for Wordsworth, rarely exerted the same degree of domination, though he often enlisted Shakespeare as an ally in the poetic psychomachia between himself and Milton (the first verse paragraph of Book V of *The Prelude* is a wonderful illustration of this). Of his remaining major sources, Spenser, Thomson, Gray, Collins, Burns, and Cowper were colleagues to emulate rather than adversaries to overcome. Only Coleridge among the later poets laid constraining bands on Wordsworth of a sort that invited a creative struggle like that with Milton.

But whether it required creative struggle or simply completed a method of invention that came naturally, the literary echo freed Wordsworth by giving him an important means of authenticating his voice. Authentication involved more than marshaling to his aid the voices of his literary past, however. The "audible seclusion" (*Prelude* VIII.794) was a hiding place of his power because it was at once the transmutable matter of poiesis and an emblem of the vision in whose service he wrote. Its privileged role in poiesis is granted by the fact that for this poet, whose rise to command of his medium was fostered by drawing closer to oral traditions and whose method of composition from the start involved intoning, launching phrases on the air while pacing a landscape, the world of poetry was the world of sound. A command to the ear of chaos stood at the origin of things: "A Voice to Light gave Being"; "By one pervading spirit / Of tones and numbers all things are controlled" ("On the Power of Sound," *PW*2.323, lines 209, 177–78). Furthermore, if the ear of man is most closely in touch with the origin of things and, by the Romantic association of origin and essence, with the sublime, it is also deeply attuned to earthly existence, especially to the human core of living experience. And finally it is involved in ultimate events, as in "On the Power of Sound," where the poet imagines voice as heralding the end of things: "A Voice shall finish doubt and dim foreseeing, / And sweep away life's visionary stir" (211–12).

It is characteristic of Wordsworth's vision, however, that he does not allow apocalypse to annihilate the human:

> O Silence! are Man's noisy years
> No more than moments of thy life?
> Is Harmony, blest queen of smiles and tears,
> With her smooth tones and discords just,
> Tempered into rapturous strife,
> Thy destined bond-slave? No! though earth be dust
> And vanish, though the heavens dissolve, her stay
> Is in the WORD, that shall not pass away.
>
> (217–24)

This harmonious word, the bond-work of the poet, is the final link between subjective and objective reality. The timely utterance of the Intimations Ode is ambiguously internal and external because it mediates human existence in the world. And the voice that carries it is an echo: It is the internal echo of the poet's joys and despairs over the process of maturation and a response to the external world; it perceives yet half-creates the mountain echoes, registers and also evokes the winds that come from the fields of sleep. But the poet's voice is necessarily an echo above all because the original voice, the voice that gave being to light, was the voice of the Other, and all subsequent voices are responses to the existence created by that voice.

The echo is also, as I have argued, an emblem of Wordsworth's particular poetic purpose—to renew the grounds of hope by showing that man had simple access to spiritual reality and that the poet could open it for him by "speak[ing] of nothing more than what we are." Wordsworth's perception that the imagination too easily led its pursuer beyond the bounds of the human into spiritual annihilation was a complication of his vision that led him to restrain his imaginative flight in poem after poem. Since it is the eye of imagination that presses it so swiftly beyond the bourne of human existence, he tries to redress the balance by emphasizing the ear, which stays attuned to the "still, sad music of humanity" and "the ghostly language of the ancient earth" while responding to the imageless deep truth. In "On the Power of Sound," the final voice sweeps away not the eternal word poets have affirmed but "life's visionary stir," the confused yearnings of insatiable human desire projected by the inner eye. The human echo of original voice remains.

There is one last way in which the echo is emblematic of Wordsworth's poetic concerns. One of Echo's ur-texts for the Renaissance consciousness is in Wordsworth's beloved Ovid. In the *Metamorphoses* Echo achieves her Aristotelian actuality through a divine intervention, the revenge of Juno for Echo's boasting about her love affair with the god-principle, Jupiter. In the Ovidian account she fades to a mere mechanism of voice, her bones becoming the stony cavity that harbors this limited responsiveness in the earth. Because she wastes away in hopeless love for the all-too-human Narcissus, her transformation is the image of a self-forgetting, an annihilation opposed to the Narcissan extreme of self-obliteration by excessive concentration on self. Both figures can be interpreted from a Wordsworthian point of view as representing a divorce between man and nature and the dehumanization it entrains (for each is disconnected from the sources of life and so no longer human). It is precisely this divorce which Wordsworth wants to redress by chanting the spousal verse of man's intellect wedded to "this goodly universe."

The pattern of that spousal verse is represented by Ovid in the story of Deucalion and Pyrrha. This pair exemplifies not only blissful human marriage but a deep connectedness with the natural world, imaged in their final transformation into the coupled oaks that survive the divine flood. As oaks, they are Jupiter's votive presences; their piety has permitted them to become emblems of *religio* made concretely actual in this world. But the pious act by which they have proved themselves worthy of Jupiter's redemptive intervention is simple hospitality—no more than the natural expression of what they are. So Wordsworth, by speaking of "nothing more than what we are," attempts to give man a natural access to the ear of the divine.

Through his spousal verse, Wordsworth will rehumanize Echo—give her back her full fleshly life through the sensuous and passionate medium of verse. In her resurrected life she becomes the mediator between the poet and the world, between his philosophic mind and its childhood base, between his new voice and the old prophetic voices of the past, between the parts of his textural poetic weave in the process of making itself up. If when we read this poet without special training many of his intertextual echoes, except for the stronger comparative allusions, slide by unnoticed, it does not finally matter. Wordsworth could not have proceeded in his enterprise without pursuing his need to embody them. But we need only attend to the substantial realizations of his vision fostered by his humanizing echoic techniques, and to the borrowings which help us grasp these realizations, in order to read him as he wanted to be read—as a man speaking to men.

Notes

INTRODUCTION

1. Though I agree with this statement, qualifications are needed. Pope was the first major poet to see English poetry steadily and whole. He read every poet of importance in English; he experimented early, if not very profoundly, with imitations of Chaucer, Spenser, Waller, Cowley, Rochester, Charles Sackville, and Dryden (before he had clearly settled on Dryden as his master); he wrote his own version of *The Shepheardes Calender* in his *Pastorals* and assimilated to them other elements of English as well as classical pastoral; he edited Shakespeare, "translated" Chaucer and Donne, and deeply imitated Denham; he continued the seventeenth-century practice of versifying psalms and other texts of the King James Bible; and, finally, he was obviously steeped in Milton, alluding to his works, internalizing a sense of the Miltonic sublime, and in common with other poets of his age confronting the impulse to write an epic, with an eye, inevitably, on *Paradise Lost*. On the other hand, classical literature clearly had priority for him, directly or indirectly inspiring most of his best pieces. Furthermore, his style, the urban social character of his subject matter and themes, and his role as a satirical moralist in exile prevented him from employing the full scale of his assimilated music.

Both Wordsworth and Pope felt that in English literature things were going downhill to an end; but Pope's doomsday feelings discouraged him more than Wordsworth's did Wordsworth from experimenting with England's poetic tradition as if it were a still-unsubdued Pegasus. Blake, on the other hand, began his career with an unparalleled romp through English literary history. *Poetical Sketches*, as W. K. Wimsatt reminds us, "is a volume saturated with the English poetic tradition from the Elizabethan age through the mid-eighteenth century, brimming with imitative exuberance, and thus wildly and torrentially free" (137). Blake is freer than Wordsworth, in part because his mastery of the tradition at this early point in his career is superior to Wordsworth's in 1787–94, but in still greater part because, however important as a formative influence his imitations may have been, what he imitated was not as deeply bound up with his vision of things, nor was echoing a fundamental element in his conception of poiesis—quite the contrary. The things rough-sketched in his "volume of sub-cultural expressions" (Wimsatt 136)—Ossian, for instance, or the King James Bible, Percy's *Reliques* (ballads, mad songs), a Shakespearean history play, a Miltonic Prologue, apostrophes to the four seasons drawing on Thomson and Collins—were all, with the exception of Milton and the Bible, dispensable as his vision and his technique developed. Wordsworth's case was not the same: Many voices, not just the biblical and the Miltonic, were important in his writing throughout his career.

2. "With tow'rs and woods a 'prospect all on fire'" (line 158 [1793]). I quote from the de Selincourt–Darbishire *Poetical Works*. I have checked quotations wherever possible against the Cornell edition of Wordsworth's poetry but continue to use the flawed de Selincourt edition because it is still the most easily accessible. (Where significant revisions have been made by the Cornell editors, I have substituted them in the de Selincourt text, using square brackets. I have not changed de Selincourt's punctuation, as a rule, except where the more recent editors' punctuation added clarity.) This edition will hereafter be cited as *PW*, followed by volume and page number. Thus the above quotation would be cited as *PW*1.18, line 158 (1793). For quotations from *The Prelude* I have used Helen Darbishire's revision of de Selincourt's edition, again cross-checking with more recent editions. *Unless otherwise noted, all quotations and citations are of the 1805 version.*

3. Though I sometimes recognize likenesses of tone, manner, situation, or structure not signaled by parallelisms, I have generally subscribed to the limits for adducing borrowings used by Roger Lonsdale in his superb redaction, *The Poems of Thomas Gray, William Collins, Oliver Goldsmith* (hereafter cited as "Lonsdale"). Lonsdale (xvi–xvii) has examined all parallels adduced in the past, has omitted the seemingly coincidental (often classical parallels cited by nineteenth-century commentators), and in adding his own has "concentrated . . . on the debts to earlier English verse." He criticizes those who in discussing the significance of supposed borrowings have lacked caution in failing to take coincidence into account, and he notes that he has not recorded "mere isolated parallels" unless they are striking. In the matter of isolated parallels, I have not followed him, because I want to account for them whether striking or not—indeed, especially when not.

I also take exception to one of Lonsdale's statements—in the second sentence below—because I feel it is based on a false theory of allusion:

> Some parallels verge upon "imitation," in the sense acceptable to the eighteenth century, where the reader was expected to cooperate by appreciating the parallel as a virtual allusion to another poet. . . . To a separate category belong such conscious borrowings as those which Gray was himself prepared to acknowledge in public (although he admitted that there were many others he was not owning): these, and others which, though genuine echoes, need not have been conscious, cannot be supposed to count as effective allusions affecting the meaning of the poem in which they occur in a precise way. (xvi–xvii)

Although I emphatically agree in recognizing echoes which cannot be said to act allusively and here distinguish them from both "virtual" allusions and indubitable allusions, I do not think Lonsdale's designation of this nonallusive group is properly formulated. Why can Gray's conscious borrowings not act allusively? Lonsdale's reason is not explicitly stated, but it seems to be that they are not tacit or indirect references. His view is traditional, if I am right; but the falsity of this traditional formulation—that allusions are tacit references—is convincingly exposed by Carmela Perri. Perri shows that in true allusions the reference is explicit or directive enough to lead us clearly to the source, while the alluding passage is inevitably indirect about the *relevance* of the source:

> For allusion is a way of referring that takes into account and circumvents the problem of what we mean when we refer: allusion-markers act like proper names in that they denote unique individuals (source texts), but they also tacitly specify the property(ies) belonging to the source text's connotation relevant to the allusion's meaning. . . . in allusion, the referent must be recognized and the relevant aspects of its connotation determined and applied. (291–92)

Gray's unconscious borrowings, though by definition not allusions, may also act *like* allusions. In *The Figure of Echo*, Hollander, while recognizing that "an inadvertent allusion is a kind of solecism" (64), points out that "echo, allusion, and quotation . . . are forms of citation that are clearly related and clearly distinct. We generally bracket them under the heading of allusiveness" (72). Making the distinctions clear, Hollander shows how quotation and particularly echo can act with allusive force. Thus the key to allusive*ness* is not the nature of the marker (though the nature of the marker *is* the differentia of the kind of device termed in the strict sense "an allusion"), but the fact that something in a text which we immediately or later recognize to have been shaped by a prior text *invites construing* by intertextual comparison. It seems to me also necessary to require that the truly allusive marker, in inviting construal, entrain a manifest enrichment of connotation in the alluding text. The reason for this qualification will become clear when I deal with Wordsworth's nonalluding echoes.

4. In other words, he prays that he may be a tragic poet, which is to say, a great poet. It is possible to interpret Collins to be offering his mind as her whole temple, since "temple's pride" could be a periphrasis for "temple" rather than meaning "chief adornment of your temple." This would make Collins the perfecter of her already-established but unfinished temple, the fashioner of "Its southern site, its truth complete" (28).

5. The cataracts blowing their trumpets may be a visual rather than an aural image. A loco-descriptive "tradition" begins in and runs forward from a fragmentary mid-eighteenth century poem of John Brown, suggesting that in a prospect one cannot hear the mountain waters until nightfall. Wordsworth, who knew this fragment, imitates the idea in *An Evening Walk* (1793), 433–34 (see Legouis 147).

On the other hand, if Wordsworth is ignoring this tradition here, the cataracts may be themselves the "timely utterance"—a possibility because of the odd insertion in the next line of a discursive comment into this series of images: "No more shall grief of mine the season wrong." This suggests that the series might be temporal—progressive in time through linked, dependent states of consciousness—so that what happens in each line is a result of what happened in the line before. From this point of view, the sounding of the cataracts becomes the force that removes the grief. Many more likely referents for the "timely utterance" have been suggested—indeed, too many for the matter to be resolved.

6. Only in Stanza IV do the external sounds come clearly into focus for the speaker, though, strangely, their expression is capped, in line 41, by the phrase, "I *feel*—I *feel* it all" (italics mine). It is not until line 50, following a series of visual and tactile images, that the speaker at last says, "I hear, I hear, with joy I hear!"

7. One might even say that they are in three places at once: in the poet's mind, in external nature, and in the traditions of Western culture (thus the suggestion that they may mean the Elysian fields, among other things). The possibility of this triple reference supports the idea of echo as mediating at once nature, psyche, and the poetic past.

8. To pretend to an exact count of Wordsworth's echoes would be misleading, partly because some can be disputed, and partly because some no doubt have been overlooked. I have studied the de Selincourt–Darbishire edition of the 1805 and 1850 versions of *The Prelude* and the Norton edition of the 1799, 1805, and 1850 texts; 277 separately entered poems and fragments in the de Selincourt–Darbishire *Poetical Works;* and "The Barberry Tree," a poem not included in that edition—about 280 pieces in all. These pieces (all of the longer ones of whatever date, most of the verse written before 1807, and upward of 30 poems written in 1807 and after), along with the nearly 1,000 unique lines included in the notes and apparatus criticus of the *Poetical Works*, account for some 39,000 lines out of about 63,000 original lines in the total corpus of approximately 980 pieces. Although I have not fully encompassed the later Wordsworth, I believe my sampling is representative of his allusive practice.

9. This conclusion is predicated in large measure on the scholarship of others. I am not sufficiently familiar with Landor's *Imaginary Conversations* or Scott's novels to confirm the complete absence of these texts from Wordsworth's poetry.

10. It seems odd that Wordsworth should echo Mandeville but not Shaftesbury, for Shaftesbury's system of thought in some ways resembles Wordsworthian attitudes, whereas Mandeville's thought turns on opposite premises. As far as I am aware, however, there is no proof that Wordsworth deeply engaged himself with Shaftesbury. Chester L. and Alice C. Shaver show that he owned a copy of the *Characteristics;* but as he did not annotate it, the volume gives no clue to how he reacted to it, or whether he even read it. There is no simple relation between a plausible influence on Wordsworth and his impulse to echo it.

11. In a note recorded by Isabella Fenwick and appended to the "Ode to Lycoris" (see *PW* 4.422–23; the poem's date is 1817), Wordsworth defends his classicizing: "But surely one who has written so much verse as I have done may be allowed to retrace his steps in the regions of fancy which delighted

him in his boyhood, when he first became acquainted with the Greek and
Roman poets." In this note he attests his early passion for Ovid's *Metamorphoses* and his love of Homer; but he also says that the great degree of "importance and . . . sanctity . . . attached to classical literature" in the Renaissance
can no longer be maintained, and he observes that he had "abstained in my
earlier writings from all introduction of pagan fable" (he forgets certain exceptions, such as "The world is too much with us") through sharing the general
reader's disgust at the "hackneyed and lifeless use" of mythology during the
neoclassical period and on through the eighteenth century.

  12. See Curtis, *Wordsworth's Experiments with Tradition* 61–70. He describes
in Wordsworth's lyric poetry of 1802 a new movement

> from the bare elements of meter and concrete image to a chaste deploy-
> ment of metaphor and symbol. And the concrete image itself begins to
> serve a wider, more "variegated" purpose. This "new" language, by no
> means a full return to the poets of the sixteenth and seventeenth centu-
> ries, is modern in its apparent privateness. But, somewhat in the man-
> ner of Robert Herrick, George Herbert, and [Henry] Vaughan, Words-
> worth permits the lightest elements of nature, phrased in the simplest
> elements of language, to disguise the meditating mind, but fulfilling
> that mind's buried intent nevertheless. Especially in the matter of syn-
> tax does Wordsworth recall Herbert or Drayton, George Wither or
> William Browne: it is utterly simple and paratactic in most of the lyrics.
> (62–63)

Interestingly, though, Curtis does not find many borrowed or even reminiscent
phrases; the resemblance of Wordsworth's lyrics to sixteenth- and seventeenth-
century poems lies in subtle features like those pointed out in the quotation
and, above all, in their playful manner and metrical variety. Even then, Curtis
does not think the language and meter of Wordsworth's lyrics are as closely
indebted as some critics have thought, and he shows that Wordsworth's manner is more wayward, privately personal, and sportive than that of the earlier
poets, who are toughly witty and surround the personal with an ambiance of
amused detachment (78–81). This is a typical and instructive case of a significant influence on the poet which led him to attune his verse in response to his
sources but not to use textual interplay or rich allusion.

  13. See Robert Anderson, ed., *The Works of the British Poets.* Of this thirteen-
volume work, the first five volumes, which Wordsworth got from his brother
John in 1800, contain poetry of Chaucer (some of it pseudonymous and the
text frequently corrupt), Wyatt, Surrey, Sackville, Spenser, Shakespeare, Sir
John Davies, Joseph Hall, Drayton, Daniel, Carew, Suckling, Donne, William
Browne, Phineas and Giles Fletcher, Jonson, Drummond, Crashaw, Davenant, Milton, Cowley, Waller, Butler, and Denham. These 25 poets are
matched in the next six volumes (volumes 12 and 13 present neoclassical
translations of various classical works) with about 100 poets representing the
period from the Restoration to the 1770s. Wordsworth echoes about 25 Renaissance and 90 neoclassical-and-after poets, a proportion of earlier to later

poets similar to Anderson's, though somewhat more favorable to the Renaissance. He favors the Renaissance even more, quantitatively, in terms of echoes as against poets, because of his attachment to Milton and Shakespeare.

Among the anthologies and critical collections listed by the Shavers in their catalogue of Wordsworth's library are, by short titles: Winstanley, *England's Worthies* (1684); Johnson, *The Lives of the Poets* (1779–81); Bell, *The Poets of Great Britain* (1776–83); Anderson, *The Works of the British Poets* (1792–95); Harrison, *Poetical Recreations* (1806); Southey, *Specimens of the Later English Poets* (1807); Dyce, *Specimens of British Poetesses* (1825) and *Specimens of English Sonnets* (1833); D'Israeli, *Curiosities of Literature* (1838). Kurt Lienemann, in *Die Belesenheit von William Wordsworth,* a useful but not always reliable work, also lists two collections edited by Anthony Harrison, *Ancient British Drama* (1810) and *Modern British Drama* (1811). Wordsworth helped Dyce prepare the anthology of poetesses.

14. Wordsworth asserted in selective hindsight (for he did often and importantly think of the rest):

> When I began to give myself up to the profession of a poet for life, I was impressed with a conviction, that there were four English poets whom I must have continually before me as examples—Chaucer, Shakespeare, Spenser, and Milton. These I must study, and equal *if I could;* and I need not think of the rest. (Quoted in Smith 256, from remarks Wordsworth addressed to his nephew, Christopher Wordsworth.)

CHAPTER 1

1. See the note to "Lines Written While Sailing in a Boat at Evening," *PW*1.324 (the poem is at *PW*1.40). The five-stanza form was printed in the first edition of *Lyrical Ballads* (1798).

2. Compare, for example, A. Reeve Parker's judgment on a highly allusive passage at the end of Book X of the 1805 *Prelude.* Parker's sensitive analysis shows how Wordsworth evokes texts of both Milton and Coleridge. His discussion is suggestive and interesting, but he concludes that the passage is " 'un-Wordsworthian' in style and digressive from the poem's central concerns. Agile as imitation and resourceful in analogy, it nevertheless does not go beyond deft literary pastiche, and in its failure of coalescence between playful tribute and the investment of moral power it falls short of Wordsworth's great poetic achievements in *The Prelude*" (227). Other recent critics avoid assessing the allusive techniques of passages in which borrowings other than echoes of Milton occur. De Selincourt conveys indirectly his estimation of *An Evening Walk* and *Descriptive Sketches* in his introductory note to the former, where he clearly depreciates the borrowings and makes Wordsworth himself seem to pass negative judgment on them (*PW*1.320). In fact, Wordsworth

does not. He faults the obscurity and inflation of style, while emphasizing the novelty of the imagery and the general vigor which the inflated style could not suppress; but echoes are neither specifically mentioned nor marked indirectly as faults. Legouis carries Wordsworth's estimate of the style in *An Evening Walk* and *Descriptive Sketches* to an extreme, fashioning his own schizophrenic judgment by splitting style and substance completely apart. Arthur Beatty, who has a much more catholic taste than Legouis, is more responsive to *Descriptive Sketches* than these other critics. He ascribes part of the fascination of the poem to the inherent interest of one of Wordsworth's sources, Ramond de Carbonnières, and the skillful use Wordsworth made of him. Yet, while Beatty says that de Carbonnières gave Wordsworth "his first effective lessons in self-expression and in language," he deprecates the style and the willingness of the poet to imitate. See Beatty xxx for the strictures on style, xxii–xliii and 31–35 for discussions of the poet's sources and his use of them, including, on xliii, the quotation above about "effective lessons."

3. The controversy was over the appropriateness of so pagan a term. The pious Mrs. Barbauld thought it lacking in respect and propriety, foreign to Thomson's Christian outlook, while the tolerant Langhorne, thinking it expressed a poetic sensitivity to nature, found it happily characteristic (see Lonsdale 486–87). It is in the latter sense that Thomson applied the term to himself in *The Castle of Indolence*. His tone is slyly humorous: "He came, the bard, a little Druid wight, / Of wither'd aspect; but his eye was keen, / With sweetness mix'd" (II.xxxiii.1–3). But the term's connotations are conflicting, and the resulting ambiguity is active in Collins's poem, giving added energy to his daring naturalization of Thomson (see also note 4).

4. See Lonsdale 487. Lonsdale is summarizing an article by J. M. S. Tompkins, "In Yonder Grave a Druid Lies," which applies to Collins's poem the picture of the druid presented by eighteenth-century antiquarians like Stukeley, Carte, and Toland. In a variant of MS. A of the 1805 *Prelude*, Wordsworth speaks of himself as, in his early years, "A youthful Druid taught in shady groves / Primaeval mysteries," using "druid" in much the same sense (see page 75 of *The Prelude*).

5. Lonsdale does not mention the "Ode to Evening" in annotating the image of the "sedge-crowned Sisters." But Wordsworth apparently caught its presence here, because he makes a thematically important reference to the ode in lines 13–16 of his poem.

6. For the continuity persisting through the changes undergone by the eighteenth-century art of imitation (defined as creating "free-running parallels"), see Wimsatt.

7. The dullest echoes are generally those that have no allusive force. Yet even these may constellate an intertext of sorts, in the sense of the term found in Michael Riffaterre (e.g., "Intertextual Scrambling"). A single word in a minor poem in the penseroso mode may connect its reader with practically the entire roster of post-Augustan poets. For instance, what eighteenth-century poet active later than Pope and Swift has not, somewhere, used the adjective "tufted" from line 78 of "L'Allegro" ("tufted Trees")? William

Crowe's apparently novel descriptive phrase in his *Lewesdon Hill*, 30–31, "the nesh tops / Of the young hazel" merely substitutes "nesh" for "tufted" because Crowe has already used "tufted orchards" and "tufted woods" in his opening lines 10 and 28. Typically, this and other single-word echoes are passive and ornamental; they are not genuine allusions because they do not require construing. Though later-eighteenth-century poetry is steeped in Miltonic and Augustan voices, it does not have the intensive character of, say, Japanese court poetry, in which we can feel assured that every echo has allusive energy.

Nonetheless, one should always prick up one's ears on recognizing such echoes, for there may be some yield in a confrontation of texts. The more significant the word or phrase is in its original context, the more likely this is. Hollander gives subtle yet brilliantly convincing examples (see, for example, his discussion of Keats's "Ode to Psyche," *The Figure of Echo* 67–68). He shows, too, that in the English literary tradition echoes range from nonreverberant uses to the most powerfully troping forms of allusiveness. Discussing the subtle ways in which echoes may bring two texts into confrontation, he strikingly demonstrates how what seem at first sight accidental or dead echoes are in fact alive with allusive or allusion-like connotations (see chapters 4 and 5 of *The Figure of Echo*, especially 92–100). He is careful, however, to distinguish between allusion per se and echo:

> Intention to allude recognizably is essential to the concept, I think, and that concept is circumscribed genetically by earlier sixteenth-century uses of the word *alluding* that are closer to the etymon *ludus*—the senses of "punning" and "troping." Again it should be stated that one cannot in this sense allude unintentionally—an inadvertent allusion is a kind of solecism.
>
> But then there is echo, which represents or substitutes for allusion as allusion does for quotation. There seems to be a transitive figurational connection among them; it points to what we generally mean by *echo*, in intertextual terms. In contrast with literary allusion, echo is a metaphor of, and for, alluding, and does not depend on conscious intention. The referential nature of poetic echo, as of dreaming (or Coleridgean "symbol" as opposed to conscious "allegory"), may be unconscious or inadvertent, but is no less qualified thereby. In either case, a pointing to, or figuration of, a text recognized by the audience is not the point. (64)

I cannot hear any reverberations coming from the "cave of the prior text" in Crowe's case; but Hollander's work makes one more cautious about dismissing what seem to be unconscious minor echoes as intertextually trivial.

I have thus tried to be sensitive to the subtlest forms of allusion-like intertextuality; but I have also tried to show that echoing and paralleling can fulfill an important nonallusive or nontroping function which has a long literary history and was often used by Wordsworth. While Hollander does not explore this aspect of echoing, his book provides one basis for it. Support can also be found in the work of Michael Riffaterre *(Essais de stylistique structurale, Semiotics of Poetry)* and Julia Kristeva *(Semiotiké: Recherches pour une sémanalyse, La Révolution du langage poétique)*, as well as in chapter 5 of Jonathan Culler's *The Pursuit of Signs.*

8. Letter to R. P. Gillies, 15 April 1816, *The Middle Years, Part II: 1812–1820* 301. (This is vol. 3 of *The Letters of William and Dorothy Wordsworth,* hereafter cited as *MY2*; vol. 2, *The Middle Years, Part I: 1806–1811,* is hereafter cited as *MY1*.)

9. Lindenberger has noted that "the possibility of disaster is a central element in Wordsworth's vision" (221). He shows that because bleakness, terror, and other negative-seeming experiences are associated with religious awe, Wordsworth's practice of brinkmanship provokes his rescue by "a spirit hallowing what I saw / With decoration and ideal grace" (*Prelude* V.478–79). "The 'internal Being' by its very nature will perform its task of conciliation and renewal" (224), so that nothing will be lost:

> Of foes
> To wrestle with and victory to complete,
> Bounds to be leapt, darkness to be explored,
> All that inflamed thy infant heart, the love,
> The longing, the contempt, the undaunting quest,
> All shall survive—though changed their office, all
> Shall live,—it is not in their power to die.
> *(Home at Grasmere* 738–44)

This tendency to seek a dimension beyond the tragic is an important element not only in Wordsworth's poetry but in high Romanticism generally (though often counterpoised by a self-reflexive skepticism, especially in Byron, Shelley, and Keats).

10. De Selincourt dates "Remembrance of Collins" 1789 *(PW1.41)*. Mark L. Reed (22, item 33) and Mary Moorman (1: 124–25) agree that Wordsworth read Bowles's first publication, *Fourteen Sonnets, Written Chiefly on Picturesque Spots During a Tour,* around Christmas of 1789, when he was in London to visit his brother John. (This was just before John was to sail again on the *Earl of Abergavenny;* he had returned from a West Indian voyage in the spring of 1789.) Yet this chapbook must have been published early enough in 1789 to permit Bowles to revise and add to the sonnets in time for the second edition, also published in 1789. (The success of the sonnets "was extraordinary, the first small edition being speedily exhausted" [*Dictionary of National Biography* 2: 977–78].) And since Reed cannot date the five-stanza original of "Remembrance of Collins" more precisely than 1788–91, and allows the possibility of a date as late as 1797, the walk could have taken place earlier in the year, during a part of the long vacation from Cambridge. Comparing "The Vale of Esthwaite" (which Reed thinks produces Bowles-like tonalities and diction long before Wordsworth could have read Bowles) with poems written soon but certainly after Wordsworth had read Bowles lends internal support. To me, the tone of "The Vale of Esthwaite" is quite un-Bowles-like. Close attention to

diction, rhythm, and meter shows that the "Vale" is dominated by starched and stretched Augustanisms, while the post-Bowles early poems are far more limber and easy in manner.

11. See, for instance, W. J. B. Owen. Carmela Perri makes it clear, however, that all allusions tacitly stake out and limit the qualities of the source text they engage (291–92).

12. This humanizing turn is set up by the personal matter at the opening of the poem (which draws on medieval dream-vision tradition but has an original directness) and culminates one of the movements in it. Both etymology and word-play at the end help effect the shift downward from the cosmic to the human level: The future bridegrooms are compared to Castor and Pollux, human in form though (by one account) born from the egg Leda produced after being raped by Zeus-as-swan; their future wives, imaged to this point as swans, are here given human shape by their description as "faire brides." The closeness in form of the two words "birdes"/"brides"—emphasized by the use of *i* rather than *y* in the latter term (it is spelled with a *y* in lines 178 and 179 and throughout the refrain)—is an example of Spenser's "secret wit," through which he uses orthographic and other manipulations of words to bring out idiosyncratically conceptualized "etymologies" that develop his thematic meaning. Here this wit helps fuse the mythicizing and the humanizing elements. The technique was first expounded in Martha A. Craig, "The Secret Wit of Spenser's Language."

13. R. A. Aubin traces the history of the topographical poem, briefly from classical times to the English Renaissance and then in detail from Drayton's *Polyolbion* (1622) to George James's *Novum Iter ad Brundisium* (1879). According to Aubin, Denham was the first to provide a shapely and malleable vehicle for local description by inventing the "hill" or "prospect" poem, in which the reader is made to look down or out on a scene through the poet's eyes. With this imaginative vantage, he could combine "incidental meditation" (the phrase is Dr. Johnson's), a review of history, and the description of a place into a dramatic whole. Although earlier topographical poets, like Drayton in *Polyolbion*, "attest a lively interest in the works of nature and man, they lack a convenient mould for its presentation. The supplying of this urgent need was the great contribution of John Denham. . . . Denham is the father of prospect poets . . . [and] may be credited with the invention of the true local poem" (32–35). He established the popularity of the genre as well: According to Aubin, more than 200 verse and prose works borrowed from him between 1650 and 1840; "only Milton, Pope, and Thomson were more powerful influences on eighteenth-century topographical verse" (36).

14. Wordsworth's fear of discontinuities seems overdetermined by his experiences: the early deaths of his parents, the course of the French Revolution, with its violent development in Paris and England's declaration of war against it (the famous alienating "stride at once / Into another region" of *Prelude* X.241–42), the adolescent polarities of the affair with Annette (as expressed in *Vaudracour and Julia*), the negative events of his relationship with Coleridge, to mention only the best-known ones.

CHAPTER 2

1. The lines of Wordsworth are from MS.Y, as given in the de Selincourt–Darbishire *Prelude*, p. 572, lines 32–33 and 29–30.

2. "To the Cuckoo," *PW*2.207. The doubleness is seen not only in the twofold shout but in the uncertainty whether the creature is a bird or a voice; in its babbling "only to the Vale / Of sunshine and of flowers," yet bringing the poet "a tale / Of visionary hours"; in its being at once the voice of "schoolboy days" and of the present, or a physical "Cry" and "a hope, a love"; in its power to restore a vivid past reality that is yet "unsubstantial"; and so on. Even the rhetoric has a variety of iterative components, as in "I have heard, / I hear thee" and "thrice welcome, darling of the Spring!"

3. See Moorman 1: 319–20, 556–57, and *PW*2.466 and 531–32.

4. Moorman quotes Dorothy's words from Christopher Wordsworth (94).

5. Contrast Thomson's "charmingly dreary" natural scenes, where "the desolated prospect thrills the soul" (*Autumn*, 1003), with Wordsworth's ambiguous disclosure of "visionary dreariness" as an originating experience of consciousness (*The Prelude* XI.285–343). Thomson finds the sublime an exalting and joyous experience; Wordsworth finds it often oppressive, puzzling, a moment when something promising is involved with something wounding. Wordsworth's doubleness must be resolved by unconscious ripening and conscious meditating; only by this equally double process can a dubious insight become a healing truth.

6. In what follows, I draw substantially on Hollander's *Images of Voice: Music and Sound in Romantic Poetry*.

7. They cannot produce music in any traditional sense. Fear lays a "bewildered" hand on his instrument and recoils; Anger strikes the lyre "in one rude clash"; Revenge blows his trumpet too loud and beats his drum too furiously; Jealousy's song is "veering" and confused in its multiplicity of themes, as Despair's is "sullen," "strange," and "mingled"—sad and wild by fits. All this suggests disordered noise more than music.

8. See his *Wordsworth's "Natural Methodism,"* especially chapter 4. Brantley argues against the interpretation of the Wordsworthian worldview I am making, attempting to show that Wordsworth's standpoint can be better understood if it is seen to be founded on a version of Christian orthodoxy rather than on semiphilosophic explorations of the nature of being. Brantley views Wordsworth as "a definably moral and religious poet," "an unproblematical (though not unprofound) figure whose complexity was more the result of deeply informed convictions than of the unresolved inner conflicts and the propensity for paradox characteristic of epistemological sophistication" (x).

9. To take the "living Presence" here as simply God the Creator seems to me a weak reading that undermines the force of the passage. True, the poet tells us at line 222 of Book V that "Nature's self . . . is the breath of God." And one readily interprets "sovereign Intellect" in line 14 (the language is typical of eighteenth-century poets) as God in the ordinary sense. It, or He, it is "who

through that bodily Image ["the speaking face of earth and heaven . . . his soul's / prime Teacher"] hath diffus'd / A soul divine which we participate, / A deathless spirit" (V.15–17). But It or He as a character is rather perfunctory. What is important is the "soul divine"—the "breath" or power of articulation—which through its continually renewed action permits uninterrupted participation in the life of nature, assuring, because it is bound to incarnate itself, that even the "bodily Image" will always be reconstituted after a cataclysm. How reconstituted? How was the physical universe originally constituted? This of course is a concern of the biblical account, and because he loathed the idea of the watchmaker God, Wordsworth simply elided such issues. The fundamental aspect of genesis for him was the originary activity of the diffuse deathless spirit of articulation.

Participation in the life of nature, not turning toward the God beyond nature, is the essential step in spiritual development. Nature is the durable medium for the questing soul. The poet complains that the things "worthy of unconquerable life" wrought by man can find no vessel to contain them as imperishable as animated nature; and the prospect of orthodox heavenly immortality—of soul-life divorced from its bodily vessel—depresses the poet in Book V of *The Prelude*. What will never happen to the physical universe as a whole, "sure . . . of a returning day," will happen to man (the echo of *Paradise Lost*, III.40–42, "Thus with the Year / Seasons return, but not to me returns / Day, or the sweet approach of Ev'n or Morn," enforces the contrast):

> Tremblings of the heart
> It gives, to think that the immortal being
> No more shall need such garments; and yet Man,
> As long as he shall be the Child of Earth,
> Might almost "weep to have" what he may lose,
> Nor be himself extinguish'd; but survive
> Abject, depress'd, forlorn, disconsolate.
> (V.21–27)

This extraordinary reaction is hard to explain if one takes "the living Presence" as just a fancy title for the mercifully designing spiritual Father of Evangelical Christianity.

10. The quotations are from *The Prelude* I.55–67, where Wordsworth describes how "to the open fields I told / A prophecy."

11. Wordsworth's rejection of Deism is expressed in many different ways in his writings. An explicit statement of rejection appears in a letter to Catherine Clarkson, in which the poet is meeting objections to *The Excursion* made by a friend of Mrs. Clarkson:

> [I do] not indeed consider the Supreme Being as bearing the same relation to the Universe as a watch-maker bears to a watch. In fact, there is nothing in the course of religious education in this country and in the use made by us of the holy scriptures, that appears to me so injurious as perpetually talking about *making* by God. (*MY2* 189)

His relation to the idea of original sin is perhaps best expressed in his curious remark, recorded by Crabb Robinson, that "I have no need of a Redeemer" (1: 158). About thirty years later he "declared in strong terms his disbelief of eternal punishment" (2: 628), so his earlier thoughts seem to have in some manner resisted his increasing orthodoxy.

12. The quotations of Milton are from the same passage, given in the Hughes edition, p. 989; the final quotation is from Hartman, *The Fate of Reading* 292.

13. On five other occasions Wordsworth used a variant of this passage: "The Vale of Esthwaite" 506–13 (*PW*1.281); "Dear native regions" (*PW*1.2); *An Evening Walk* [1793], 185–90 (*PW*1.22); Descriptive Sketches (1793), 108–9 and 338–47 (*PW*1.48 and 62).

CHAPTER 3

1. Through the *Canzoniere* he developed a publicly shared relationship with Laura that was in one sense actual, and he got a friend to act the role of Homer and write him a letter so that he could answer it directly, as if he were literally corresponding with Homer. For this fact and its interpretation, and in much of what follows, I am indebted to Thomas M. Greene's *The Light in Troy: Imitation and Discovery in Renaissance Poetry,* and to an unpublished lecture by Greene on the same subject.

2. See *PW*4.396–97 for the text of this cento yoking together Akenside, Thomson, and Beattie, and for Wordsworth's comment.

3. The phrase "conscious step of purity and pride" may be drawn from Bowles's sonnets "On the Busts of Milton in Youth and Age, at Stourhead," where a similar phrase is applied to Milton—Milton in his later years, however, when "the conscious pride / Of wisdom, patient and content to brook / All ills" showed his "unalter'd mind" ("Milton in Age," 10–12, 13). But the combining of "conscious" and "pride" was a linguistic commonplace in this period.

4. Petrarch's attempt to "correspond" with Homer has been noted above. Milton's creative ambivalences about his Greek and Roman literary-mythological inheritances have been the subject of much critical annotation; they are clearly seen (for example) in "On the Morning of Christ's Nativity."

5. I do not mean to overstate the case. While Wordsworth has subverted traditional Christian hierarchy in envisioning the 1805 passage, he has not necessarily dropped out the living core along with the architecture. He is still in touch with—or preempts—religious terms and conceptions. The "invisible world" (line 105), vague as it is, contains the conception important to St. Paul and other early Christians that "Eye hath not seen, nor ear heard, neither have entered into the heart of man, the things which God hath prepared for

them that love him" (1 Corinthians 2.9); and the conquerable impercipience
of Wordsworth's "grossest minds" (83) recalls Acts 28.27 (where the impercipience is, however, not to be redeemed):

> For the heart of this people is waxed gross, and their ears are dull of
> hearing, and their eyes have they closed; lest they should see with their
> eyes, and hear with their ears, and understand with their heart, and
> should be converted, and I should heal them.

6. The phrase is applied to the way in which Nature exerts her domination in special moments. I take "interchangeable" to mean "communicable" or
"able to be reflected by the observer's consciousness." Both nature and mind,
through natural mediation, can participate in the divine presence; but that
presence, in the 1850 passage, stands over and above the created order.

7. My distinction between assimilative and comparative echoes, worked
out before the appearance of Greene's *Light in Troy*, is similar to his distinction
between "simple imitation, where history, time, and intertextuality are not
thematized, and complex imitation, where they are" (52). In simple imitation,

> the diachronic interplay [is] altogether distinct from the synchronic
> meaning. The interplay supplies a kind of frame within which the
> synchronic poem is experienced. Or perhaps better than *frame* is the
> Renaissance term *surround*, a design with a life of its own that presses in
> upon the picture it contains without destroying the picture's integrity.
> (ibid.)

In complex imitation, "one has to account for the *impingement* of the dia-
chronic on the synchronic and the counter reflection in the other direction"
(53). This is very much the kind of distinction I am trying to make, though my
viewing it from the standpoint of allusion and echoing rather than "imitation"
in the strict sense defined by Greene entails some important differences in
exposition (related to differences in period) and allows me to give a value or
function to echoic modes which Greene rightly, from the Renaissance viewpoint, demotes *en bloc*.

8. See Frye's "Nature and Homer," Riffaterre's "Intertextual Scrambling," and Harold Bloom's *A Map of Misreading*.

9. Of course Virgil's *Aeneid* was a model often as important as the Bible. It
was transmitted to Wordsworth through Italian Renaissance epics, Spenser,
Milton, and many Restoration and Augustan writings, as well as by his direct
reading of the Latin.

CHAPTER 4

1. See Perri 300 (item 9) and 301 (item 3).
2. The quotations, in order, are from: Hartman, *Beyond Formalism* 39;

Prelude III.188; "Address to Kilchurn Castle" 7–9 (*PW*3.78); "It was an April morning" 18–19 (*PW*2.111); *Prelude* II.324–26; Wordsworth, letter to Coleridge [5 May 1809], *MY*1: 336 (noted in *PW*3.448); Coleridge, *Biographia* 1: 59; Hartman, *Wordsworth's Poetry* 252; "It was an April morning" 29; *Prelude* II.331–32; and Hartman, *Fate of Reading* 163.

3. Another borrowing from the same source is a direct quotation used in *An Evening Walk* (1793), *PW*1.18, line 158. The image of the sun sinking to rest and making objects incandesce with its final rays was early on something of a picturesque obsession with Wordsworth. See chap. 2, n. 13.

4. In this technique, according to Hartman, Wordsworth embodies something basic to the Britannic mind,

> a peculiarly English relation of new to old. The internal structure of [the *Lyrical Ballads* piece, 'Hart-Leap Well'] reflects a historical principle of canon formation. Even when, as in *The White Doe of Rylstone*, he begins with personal speculation rather than with an impersonally narrated ballad, the essential structure remains that of the reflective encirclement and progressive purification of symbols from Romance. (*Beyond Formalism* 297)

This supports the underlying idea that Wordsworth, even in revolt, is culminating while renewing and varying a traditional set of poetic strategies.

CHAPTER 5

1. See chap. 2, n. 11, for the source of his statement about not needing a redeemer. On Wordsworth's heterodox and sometimes self-contradictory religious views, see Raymond Dexter Havens, *The Mind of a Poet: A Study of Wordsworth's Thought*.

2. Akenside may have provided something toward the striking imagery of the "blue chasm; . . . / A deep and gloomy breathing-place through which / Mounted the roar of waters" (*Prelude* XIII.56–58). Cf. *The Pleasures of Imagination* (1744), III.387–90: "From the womb of earth, / From ocean's bed they come; the eternal heavens / Disclose their splendours, and the dark abyss / Pours out her births unknown."

CHAPTER 6

1. This can be confirmed by studying the passages from female poets Wordsworth gathered in *Poems and Extracts* and his marginal glosses in a copy of *Paradise Lost*, commented by Bishop C. Hunt, Jr., in "Wordsworth's Margi-

nalia on *Paradise Lost.*" But on another level Wordsworth did respond to the subtler aspects of texts, too, and his deeper responses vitally informed his vision; indeed, his comparative and assimilative echoes often embody such responses. Nonetheless, at the rational-discursive level of his thinking he did not often attempt inclusive and complex formulations of them. This is one of the reasons he was so unsatisfactory as an interpreter of particular poems and could suggest as a guide to recognizing a good poem little more than an instinctive sense that the writer has sincerely expressed genuine feelings. He is more interesting when he is writing as a poetic theorist and is forced to clarify assumptions that depend on deeper responses (see Wellek on Wordsworth's critical position in *The Romantic Age* 130–50).

2. Interestingly, all these poets appear in the sonnet "It is not to be thought of that the flood." Milton and Shakespeare are merely named. The direct quotation, "with pomp of waters, unwithstood," is from Daniel's *Civil Wars* 2.7. Denham seems to supply the idea informing the whole sonnet—that of analogizing British freedom to the Thames, which flows out to the world via the sea, bearing British products (see *Cooper's Hill* 179–88, 353–58). Indeed, Wordsworth's 1827 variant makes a more explicit echo: "Road by which all might come and go that would, / And bear out freights of worth to foreign Lands" (*PW*3.117, *app. crit.*); cf. *Cooper's Hill* 181–88. It appears that Wordsworth is also echoing Patrick Henry's famous cry in "We must be free or die."

3. That these lines of "Personal Talk" (*PW*4.74) constitute an echo is perhaps dubious; however, the lines to which they seem to refer are from one of Wordsworth's favorite passages in Daniel, and he quotes them directly in *The Excursion* IV.324–31, italicizing them and placing them in their full context. Daniel's stanza represents the essence of his stoicism:

> Knowing the heart of man is set to be
> The centre of this world, about the which
> These revolutions of disturbances
> Still roll; where all th'aspects of misery
> Predominate; whose strong effects are such
> As he must bear, being pow'rless to redress:
> And that unless above himself he can
> Erect himself, how poor a thing is man.
> ("To the Lady Margaret, Countess of
> Cumberland" 89–96)

Wordsworth's lines in "Personal Talk" change the image but keep the main sense of the final couplet: "Whose mind is but the mind of his own eyes, / He is a Slave; the meanest we can meet!"

4. See de Selincourt's text and notes (*PW*3.281 ff. and *PW*3.535 ff.). The first quotation, dealing with *The White Doe of Rylstone* as "the Apotheosis of the Animal," is from a letter to Francis Wrangham, dated 18 January 1816 (*MY*2 276; *PW*3.547); the second is from *The White Doe* 1070–72 (these lines recall the last three verses of *Samson Agonistes*, and line 1069 is a near-quotation from Milton's sonnet on his blindness—both references apposite and inapposite in

ways that are discussed below); the third is from a remark of Wordsworth to John Taylor Coleridge (see *PW*3.548); the fourth is from the I. F. note to the poem (*PW*3.543); and the final quotation is from the "Dedication" 17–18.

5. Because of the unplucked-rose tradition, this echo has a certain generic force. I have found only a few generic references in the stoic moralizing mode, and these are more imitations than echoes—at least they pretend to imitation, though they are very unlike in effect. They refer the reader to various forms of discourse—the Elizabethan or the seventeenth-century sonnet, the allegorical poem or moral debate, the dramatic soliloquy or set piece, or the pastoral elegy. The pastoral elegy is "imitated" in "Address to the Scholars of the Village of——," in the "Elegiac Stanzas" on Peele Castle, and other poems in the section Wordsworth titled *Epitaphs and Elegiac Pieces* (*PW*4.248–78). "Captivity. —Mary Queen of Scots" (*PW*3.33) is a stoic soliloquy curiously confined to the space of a strict Italian sonnet. In *The Excursion*, shortly after the Solitary is described as having the "look, gesture, tone of voice" of a "proficient of the tragic scene / Standing before the multitude" (III.463, 466–67), he is heard speaking in accents of the Elizabethan stage, especially at III.488–97. The whole of *The Excursion*, though leaning more on *Night Thoughts* as a model, echoes throughout some of the tone and organizing method of philosophical-debate poems, particularly Daniel's *Musophilus*. In "Nuns fret not at their narrow room" (*PW*3.1), Wordsworth sets resonating in our ears the Elizabethan and early seventeenth-century image of the sonnet or short stanzaic piece as a narrow room of large dimensions which endures forever, immortalizing its subject:

> in how small a room doe lie,
> And yet lie safe, as fresh as if aliue,
> All those great worthies of antiquitie,
> Which long foreliu'd thee, and shall long suruiue
> Who stronger tombes found for Eternitie,
> Then could the powres of all the earth contriue.
> (Daniel, *Musophilus* 391–96)

Wordsworth gives the paradox a twist by reversing it, asserting that the narrowness is liberating precisely because it binds, confinement being a natural recourse for those who find too much liberty a weight. His version of the traditional view thus verges on heuristic allusion; but by undermining his claim in the last line—the solace he found there was "brief," a "pastime"—he sidesteps a full confrontation with the tradition (that the constriction of verse is an intensification making "one little room, an every where," in the words of Donne's "The Good-Morrow") and renders it only a background echo, contributory to the theme of absence as presence (freedom surrendered is freedom gained).

6. Yet Wordsworth, who hotly maintained that he knew most of Pope and Dryden by heart, does echo them. I have found nearly twenty borrowings from Pope and possibly seven from Dryden—relatively high frequencies. Many of these echoes are clustered in the early poems and in the few later poems in which Wordsworth is working in something like an imitative mode.

Pope crops up in "Lines, Written as a School Exercise," "The Vale of Esthwaite," *Descriptive Sketches*, "A Poet's Epitaph," "Hart-Leap Well," "Written in London, September 1802," "The Character of the Happy Warrior," "Musings near Aquapendente," and on five occasions in *The Prelude*. Dryden is echoed in the school exercise, in "Glen Almain," in "Dion" (expressly modeled on Dryden's translation of Plutarch's "Life of Dion"), in "On the Power of Sound" (which turns to the "Song for St. Cecilia's Day" as one model), and a few times in *The Prelude*.

7. Reversal of Milton is frequent in passages in which Wordsworth is attempting to assert an earthly plenitude. This notably alters the Wartonian habit of using the allegrian/penserosan Milton to directly support plenitude.

8. The phrase "strange discipline" is found in the *ejecta* of "The Ruined Cottage," *PW*5.400 (var. 1, line 11).

9. See Jonathan Carver, *Travels* 132.

10. The pronoun "it" in verse 16 seems to refer to "their heart" in verse 15. *The New English Bible* translates in a way that makes Moses the referent: "However, as Scripture says of Moses, 'whenever he turns to the Lord the veil is removed' " (2 Corinthians 3.6, p. 220).

11. Jane Worthington [Smyser] states from evidence in the early letters and other sources that the poet read studiously and with "usual regularity" at Racedown, and at one point was devoting "twelve hours of thought to society to every one to poetry" (11–12).

12. See *The Ruined Cottage, ejecta* (*PW*5.401), addendum to MS B, line 36. See also Cooper 129.

13. Matthew Hodgart, *The Ballads* 33. I have relied here on Hodgart's excellent brief account of the ballad.

14. Wordsworth's remark was penciled in the margin of Barron Field's manuscript "[Critical] Memoirs of the Life and Poetry of William Wordsworth" ("Critical" is lined out). See William A. Knight.

15. These writers include Greeks who dealt importantly with Roman matters, such as Plutarch and Polybius. Wordsworth read Latin with ease, but probably not Greek—or at least his Greek was too weak for him to read extensively in the original. See Worthington, chap. 1. In developing her thesis that Wordsworth's wide reading "had an appreciable effect upon his thought and work" (vii), Worthington shows that his interest in the Roman prose writers was not principally the result of his classical training at St. John's but was fired by the revolutionary fervor he encountered in France (the Republicanism of the Girondists, with whom he allied himself, was permeated by enthusiasm for the historians of the Roman Republic). She also shows that Wordsworth's stoicism was developed by his reading of Roman stoic philosophers; yet I have found his echoes of these authors more in social and political than in straightforwardly stoic contexts. In any case, everything that in Worthington's view attracted Wordsworth to the Roman writers was in tune with the attitudes of the Augustans toward their classical heritage.

16. De Selincourt's note (*PW*2.506), which has the quotation but not the location in Bartram (159), gives no essential reason for its assertion that

Wordsworth's echo is a "subconscious recollection." The echo is embedded by a typical Wordsworthian technique, and I see it as conscious.

17. Cf. *PL* IV.153–71 and 248 with *The Prelude* III.448–55:

> A habitation sober and demure
> For ruminating creatures, a domain
> For quiet things to wander in, a haunt
> In which the Heron might delight to feed
> By the shy rivers, and the Pelican
> Upon the cypress spire in lonely thought
> Might sit and sun himself. Alas! alas!
> In vain for such solemnity we look.

18. Lane Cooper suggested that the *Prelude* passage had an echo of the *Travels* but did not cite an exact source (Cooper 114).

19. "Lines, Written as a School Exercise at Hawkshead, Anno Aetatis 14" 85–86 (*PW*1.259). The lines turn of course on Epistle II, 1–2.

20. An echo of the *Essay on Man* II.118 in line 2 of *Descriptive Sketches* (1793) belongs to the "anthropologizing" assimilative mood; but other echoes of Pope—at lines 66, 563, and 697—allude to *Windsor Forest* and the *Essay on Criticism* and belong rather to the naturalizing and poeticizing moods. Several of the few remaining echoes of Pope, in *The Prelude,* are of the moralizing sort (e.g., XIII.384–85, recalling *Essay on Man* I.191–92).

21. He was apparently well read in Tacitus and owned copies of Cassius Dio, Florus, Herodian, Valerius Maximus, Suetonius, Sallust, Cornelius Nepos, and Velleius Paterculus (see Worthington 15).

22. This echo of Plutarch's "Life of Agesilaus" appears in De Selincourt's *app. crit.* to lines 598–99 of *The Excursion* III (*PW*5.96).

23. The referenced passages are Virgil's *Georgics* IV.126 and Horace's *Odes* II.6.10 for the Galesus, and *Georgics* II.146 for the Clitumnus. Though the demythologizing-remythologizing passage (beginning "Yet hail to You, / Your rocks and precipices, Ye that seize / The heart with firmer grasp!" [lines 353–55]) treats the pastoral mode transumptively, it is not specifically a transumption of the passages in Virgil and Horace. They are used assimilatively to build toward the overgoing insight.

24. Cf. Aeneas's meeting with Anchises in *Aeneid* VI.700–703:

> ter conatus ibi collo dare bracchia circum,
> ter frustra comprensa manus effugit imago,
> par levibus ventis volucrique simillima somno.

> [Thrice there he strove to throw his arms about his neck;
> thrice the form, vainly clasped, fled from his hands, even
> as light winds, and most like a winged dream.]
>   (Trans. H. Rushton Fairclough, *Virgil* I.555)

25. This feeling led the poet to base whole poems on a ballad, the most extended being *The White Doe of Rylstone.* On the other hand, there are poems containing no more than tame glances at a ballad, as if he were merely parad-

ing the influences that he had declared were a revolutionary basis of his poetic stance—for example, the reference to "The Children of the Wood" 125–28 in "The Redbreast Chasing a Butterfly" (*PW*2.149), lines 20–23 (see Percy's *Reliques of Ancient English Poetry* 3: 175). This relatively inert echo reminds us that Wordsworth included in the category of the ballad not just the classical folk piece but, following Percy, street ballads, Elizabethan lyrics, contemporary poems pretending to ballad status (e.g., Chatterton's), and even prose tales and nursery rhymes.

26. M. H. Abrams deals with this doubleness of ideational purpose in *Natural Supernaturalism;* R. A. Foakes studies a corresponding doubleness in the use of language in *The Romantic Assertion.*

27. Cf. Logan's "Ode to a Young Lady." The imagery here also borrows, as already noted, from Bowles's "On the Busts of Milton in Youth and Age."

28. Langhorne's "Owen of Carron" is echoed in a 1799 ms. version of "She dwelt among the untrodden ways" (see *PW*2.30, *app. crit.*); Rogers's "And Lucy, at her wheel, shall sing" (from "A Wish") is echoed in "I travelled among unknown men" (*PW*2.30). Hurdis is quoted directly in *Excursion* VI.387 (the redbreast imaged as a " 'feathery bunch,' " from *The Favourite Village;* Hurdis has in turn borrowed from Thomson's *Winter*).

29. The echo may also enforce the idea of inwardness by contrast. Collins's "fable" about the passions expressing themselves directly as instruments is a call for deep inspiration, in an uninspired age, through the naturalizing of poetic voice. "Where is thy native simple heart?" he cries to Music, bidding it "Arise as in that elder time, / Warm, energic, chaste, sublime!" and "Revive the just designs of Greece, / Return in all thy simple state! / Confirm the tales her sons relate!" (103, 105–6, 116–18). His setting Greece as his model ties his outlook to neoclassical canons, and his use of allegorical devices and declamatory poetic conventions invokes some discordance with his aim. Wordsworth's conversational tone, his drawing of the echoed line into the context of the child's view of things, and his setting the idea of "undersong" (heard as he sits "without emotion, hope, or aim") against Collins's oversong of loud impassioned music form a contrast that makes his voice seem more, and more naturally, inward.

30. And yet the importance to Wordsworth of his source does not guarantee a substantial assimilative use of it. Beattie and Dyer surface together again in "The Old Cumberland Beggar" (*PW*4.234), lines 59–66:

> His staff trails with him; scarcely do his feet
> Disturb the summer dust; he is so still
> In look and motion, that the cottage curs,
> Ere he has passed the door, will turn away,
> Weary of barking at him. Boys and girls,
> The vacant and the busy, maids and youths,
> The urchins newly breeched—all pass him by:
> Him even the slow-paced waggon leaves behind.

The echoes draw from their source only a few descriptive details: Wordsworth's "cottage curs" reproduces exactly Beattie's phrase in the first line of

The Minstrel I.xxxix ("the cottage curs at early pilgrim bark"), his "slow-paced waggon" slightly alters Beattie's "ponderous waggon" in line 4 of the same stanza, and Dyer's line discussed above comes out once more, a bit changed, in "the vacant and the busy."

31. *PW*4.50, 57, and 58, respectively. Cowper's presence in these poems is hard to establish convincingly, because the templates in Cowper are diffuse and Wordsworth's details are different. Both poets are recommending the idleness of retirement that leads to deeper knowledge through a leisurely study of rural nature,

> Scenes form'd for contemplation, and to nurse
> The growing seeds of wisdom; that suggest,
> By ev'ry pleasing image they present,
> Reflections such as meliorate the heart,
> Compose the passions, and exalt the mind.
> (*The Task* III.301–5)

Cowper's picture of "Domestic life in rural leisure pass'd" (III.292) provides a neat, orderly, active kind of retirement, "studious of laborious ease" (361) and consciously aimed at "the service of mankind" (372); and his presentation of the healing influences of such a country life derives from eighteenth-century versions of Virgil's *Georgics*. A sentiment like that in stanza five of "The Tables Turned"—"[Nature] has a world of ready wealth, / Our minds and hearts to bless— / Spontaneous wisdom breathed by health, / Truth breathed by cheerfulness"—agrees in spirit with Cowper's outlook in *The Task*. But the idea of spontaneity, allied to the "wise passiveness" of "Expostulation and Reply" and to the view that the independent life of nature shares a common being with man (see "Lines Written in Early Spring"), goes beyond anything Cowper could have imagined. Wordsworth's idleness is more inwardly active, and his sense of nature is quite ungeorgic. On the other hand, when Wordsworth says, "And much it grieved my heart to think / What man has made of man" ("Lines Written in Early Spring" 7–8), he is summarizing a persistent theme of *The Task*. Sentiment about man's inhumanity to, and dehumanization of, man was common in his day, and he could have drawn it from the air around him; however, the study of his assimilative habits shows that he rarely formulated poetic ideas based on moods without drawing on prior formulations. One cannot read *The Task* without feeling that it is full of things that stocked his imagination. The lines from "Written in Early Spring" may echo Burns's "Man's inhumanity to man / Makes countless thousands mourn" ("Man Was Made to Mourn" 55–56), but in the context of the poem, which deals with man's essential brotherhood with nature, he could easily be thinking of Cowper's indictment of social relations in the antislavery expostulation beginning *Task* II:

> My ear is pain'd,
> My soul is sick, with ev'ry day's report
> Of wrong and outrage with which earth is fill'd.
> There is no flesh in man's obdurate heart,

> It does not feel for man; the nat'ral bond
> Of brotherhood is sever'd as the flax
> That falls asunder at the touch of fire.
>
> (5–11)

32. A strong version of Cowperian moralizing is seen in Wordsworth's satirical picture of the modern preacher in *The Prelude* VII.546–65, where he indulges in a freshly phrased but genuine imitation of the mocking of the same figure in *The Task* II.351–71.

33. The same passage and its surrounding context, with minor alterations and omissions, is reproduced in *Poems and Extracts* 33–37. I have previously noted in the epigraph of "To the Daisy" a characteristic Wordsworthian mis-quotation, substituting "instruction" for "invention" in echoing Wither's "Her [the Muse's] divine skill taught me this, / That from every thing I saw / I could some invention draw." This substitution contains in a nutshell the naturalizing of Wither's idea, originally expressed as a complete faith in poetry, or the muse who "hath taught me by her might / To draw comfort and delight" in the darkest circumstance, and re-presented by Wordsworth as the growth of his ability to find meaning in the humblest manifestation of nature:

> In youth from rock to rock I went,
> From hill to hill in discontent
> Of pleasure high and turbulent,
>   Most pleased when most uneasy;
> But now my own delights I make,—
> My thirst at every rill can slake,
> And gladly Nature's love partake
>   Of Thee, sweet Daisy!
>
> (1–8)

34. But Wither's words express commonplaces. Wordsworth's celebrated lines are intertextually the most overdetermined of any I have found in the canon. As a result, it is impossible to point to any single source as the determining one. Thomson (*Spring* 473) has "in every bud that blows"; Cowper (*Task* VI.584), "the meanest things that are"; Gray ("Ode on the Pleasure Arising from Vicissitude" 45), "the meanest flowret of the vale." In the background is Shakespeare's Sonnet 65, with its meditation on "sad mortality": "How with this rage shall beauty hold a plea, / Whose action is no stronger than a flower?" In the foreground is Anne of Winchilsea: "But silent musings urge the mind to seek / Something too high for syllables to speak" ("A Nocturnal Reverie" 41–42; quoted in *Poems and Extracts* 11). And though its sense is opposite, the phrase "Too foolish for a tear" at the end of Coleridge's "Ode to Tranquillity" (first published in *The Morning Post*, 4 December 1801) is echoically suggestive (the poem has motifs in common with the Intimations Ode, especially in its third stanza).

35. Although he appreciated the size of Chaucer's genius and took the trouble of putting some of his pieces into modern English, Wordsworth never seems to have felt threatened by him or to have engaged his poetic voice at the

level of confrontation. On the other hand, Wordsworth's relationship with Coleridge was complex. Various uses of *The Seasons* and *The Castle of Indolence* suggest that to some extent Wordsworth approached Thomson in a spirit of confrontation. This is also true of Gray, on whom Wordsworth sometimes passes oddly harsh judgments.

36. I have given these lines in the form Wordsworth most likely knew them, as they are printed in Anderson 1: 38 (*The Legend of Good Women* 48–52 and 60–65). They are reasonably close to the modern Text F 48–52 and 60–65 (see, for example, Chaucer, ed. Robinson 568–69).

37. The phrase in line 508 is "drowsy tinkling bell." Wordsworth also repeats "lowing herds" in the singular at line 469. By the time of the 1849 version, he has altered both references. His rewording of Gray's "lull the distant folds" to "for ever tinkling round" may owe something to "L'Allegro" 92–93: "The upland Hamlets will invite, / When the merry Bells ring round." The hamlets also appear in line 428 of *Descriptive Sketches* (1793), just above Wordsworth's borrowing from Gray. The hamlet is changed to "*chalets*" in the 1849 version of *Descriptive Sketches*.

38. Cf. Gray's alcaic ode (Lonsdale 317):

O Tu, severi religio loci,
Quocumque gaudes nomine (non leve
    Nativa nam certe fluenta
        Numen habet, veteresque silvas;

Praesentiorem et conspicimus Deum
Per invias rupes, fera per iuga,
    Clivosque praeruptos, sonantes
        Inter aquas, nemorumque noctem; . . .

(1–8)

[O Thou, divine spirit of this forbidding place, by whatever title pleases Thee (for certainly no mean power rules over these native streams and ancient forests; and we perceive God closer to us among the pathless rocks, wild ridges and precipitous ravines, and in the thundering of waters and the darkness of the woods . . .]

39. Exceptions may be quickly found, such as the echo of *The Castle of Indolence* (II.xxxiii.3) in the phrase "clad in homely russet brown" in "A Poet's Epitaph" (*PW*2.65), or the contribution to "lovely as a Lapland night" by *Winter* (859–65). Thomson's passage is based on Johannes Scheffer's *History of Lapland*, which Wordsworth may have been stimulated to read by Lapland imagery in Beattie's *Minstrel* (I.lix).

40. De Selincourt is responding to the evanescent connections of the assimilative mode of borrowing. The atmosphere of the *Prelude* segment is, as so often in this mode, quite different: "when the changeful earth, / And twice five seasons on my mind had stamp'd / The faces of the moving year" suggests a different kind of relation between the observer and nature. To concentrate on the image is to be reminded of the disparity in the outlook of the two poets:

the contrast between Thomson's patriarchal hand rolling round the seasons and the maternal "spirit" of "Tintern Abbey," which "rolls *through* all things" (emphasis mine).

41. The quotations are from the Preface to the second edition of *Lyrical Ballads* (*PW*2.387 and 386, respectively).

42. See *PW*2.391 for Wordsworth's comment on Gray's poem.

43. "Fierce vindictive song" is a translation of *Odes* IV.9.7–8: "[et Alcaei] minaces / stesichorive graves camenae."

CONCLUSION

1. The speaker in "The Sparrow's Nest" says of Dorothy ("Emmeline") as a tender, nature-loving girl:

> She gave me eyes, she gave me ears;
> And humble cares, and delicate fears;
> A heart, the fountain of sweet tears;
>   And love, and thought, and joy.
>   (17–20)

The first line of this passage picks up the phrasings Churchill used in lines 142–43 of "Independence" to describe a catatonic and artificial aristocracy:

>   —'twas Nature's first intent
> Before their rank became their punishment,
> They should have pass'd for men, nor blush'd to prize
> The blessing she bestow'd—she gave them eyes,
> And they could see; she gave them ears—they heard;
> The instruments of stirring, and they stirr'd.
>   (39–44)

I feel confident that this echo is either coincidental or unconscious (the urtext for both poets is Acts 28.27). Awareness of Churchill's context is counterproductive for the reader, and it would have proved counterproductive for Wordsworth in the act of composing had he brought it into focus. It is not simply that Churchill's satirical tone is so opposite to the homely mystique of Wordsworth's lines, but that the reversal of satire can have no functional meaning in the borrowing poet's piece. The same is true of the implied ideation: For Churchill, nature's original gift of eyes, ears, and heart is primal and automatic; for Wordsworth it is won through increase of consciousness and must be mediated.

2. From "Pan, or Nature," in Arthur Gorges's translation of Bacon, *The Wisedom of the Ancients* (1619) 37. The Latin is in *De dignitate et augmentis scientiarum* II.xiii (see *The Works of Francis Bacon*, ed. Spedding, Ellis, and Heath 1: 530, and these editors' translation, 4: 327).

3. The preceding quotations, in order of appearance, are from: *Prelude* II.327–28, III.187–88; "Prospectus" 70; *Prelude* XII.376–77, XII.252.

4. *Prelude* II.359, I.277–78. Among the "delicious rivers" is the Derwent, whose "voice / That flowed along my dreams" is wind-harp-like in its blending with his nurse's song and its echoic ability to convey "a dim earnest of the calm / That Nature *breathes* among the hills and groves" (see I.269–85; italics mine).

5. Of course, for the reader at the point of Derridean awareness, it is also the perfect instrument for undermining Wordsworth's project.

6. Montaigne is an exemplary Renaissance practitioner of process mimesis, and the way in which he uses it has a structural resemblance to Wordsworth's general approach to poetic composition and to his assimilative treatment of his sources. In discussing the revisions Montaigne made silently in the successive editions of his *Essais,* Patrick Henry notes that the master who said, "Je ne peints pas l'estre. Je peints le passage," is "constantly self-referential and . . . is so at the levels of both product and process mimesis" (181, 180). Despite Montaigne's disguising pretense of presenting his persona as a habitual self, his continual revisions suggest an implicit avowal of an evolving self, and this in turn entrains, as Henry shows, an effort to close the gap between his present self and former selves embodied in earlier versions of the *Essais.* This effort, never made openly, is nonetheless persistent, and it is carried on in part through process mimesis, the natural language of the evolving "I." It involves in both Montaigne and Wordsworth the manipulation of subtexts initially representing the other. Henry writes of the subtexts in Montaigne:

> The author of the *Essais* frequently defends his right to use other texts as his own, and claims more generally in *De l'institution des enfans* that if one embraces Xenophon's and Plato's opinions by his own reasoning: "ce ne seront plus les leurs, ce seront les siennes" (I.26. 151.a). There is, therefore, a conscious effort on the part of the author to convert the intertext into the intratext, to appropriate it, to make it his own, to transform it from other to self. (182)

Though, unlike Montaigne, Wordsworth did not make an explicit defense of his procedure, this conversion of intertext to intratext as a means of including the other, or authenticating one's proper voice, is *mutatis mutandis* the essential activity of his assimilative mode of borrowing.

Works Cited

Abrams, M. H. *Natural Supernaturalism: Tradition and Revolution in Romantic Literature.* New York: Norton, 1971.

Akenside, Mark. *The Poems of Mark Akenside and John Dyer.* Ed. Robert A. Willmott. London: George Routledge, 1855.

Anderson, Robert, ed. *The Works of the British Poets: With Prefaces Biographical and Critical.* 13 vols. London: John and Arthur Arch; Edinburgh: Bell and Bradfute, and J. Mundell, 1792–95.

Arnold, Matthew. *The Complete Prose Works.* Ed. R. H. Super. Vol. 3. Ann Arbor: University of Michigan Press, 1962. 11 vols. 1960–77.

Aubin, Robert A. *Topographical Poetry in the Eighteenth Century.* Modern Language Revolving Fund Series 6. New York: MLA, 1936.

Bacon, Sir Francis. *The Wisedom of the Ancients: Written in Latine by the Right Honorable Sir Francis Bacon, Knight, Baron of Verulam, and Lord Chancelor of England.* Trans. Arthur Gorges. London: John Bill, 1619.

——. *The Works of Francis Bacon, Baron of Verulam, Viscount St. Albans, and Lord High Chancelor of England.* Ed. James Spedding, Robert L. Ellis, and D. D. Heath. 15 vols. London: Longmans, 1860–64.

Bartram, William. *Travels of William Bartram.* Ed. Mark Van Doren. 1928. New York: Dover, 1955.

Beattie, James. *The Poetical Works of Beattie, Blair and Falconer.* Ed. George Gilfillan. Edinburgh: James Nichol, 1854.

Beatty, Arthur. See, under Wordsworth, *Wordsworth: Representative Poems.*

Beers, Henry A. *A History of English Romanticism in the Eighteenth Century.* New York: Holt, 1899.

Blair, Robert. See Beattie.

Blake, William. *The Poetry and Prose of William Blake.* Ed. David V. Erdman. Comm. Harold Bloom. Rev. ed. Garden City, NY: Doubleday, 1970.

Bloom, Harold. *A Map of Misreading.* New York: Oxford University Press, 1975.

Bowles, William Lisle. *Fourteen Sonnets, Elegiac and Descriptive: Written During a Tour.* Bath: printed by R. Cruttwell, 1789.

——. *The Poetical Works of William Lisle Bowles.* Ed. George Gilfillan. 2 vols. Edinburgh: W. P. Nimmo, 1868.

Brantley, Richard E. *Wordsworth's "Natural Methodism."* New Haven: Yale University Press, 1975.

Brisman, Leslie. *Milton's Poetry of Choice and Its Romantic Heirs.* Ithaca: Cornell University Press, 1973.

Brower, Reuben A., ed. *Forms of Lyric.* Selected Papers from the English Institute. New York: Columbia University Press, 1970.

Bruce, Michael. *The Poetical Works of Michael Bruce.* In vol. 9 of Anderson.

Bürger, Gottfried August. *The Wild Hurtsman's Chase. . . .* [Trans. ?H. J. Pye.] London: Sampson Low et al., 1798.

Burns, Robert. *Poems and Songs.* Ed. James Kinsley. London: Oxford University Press, 1969.

Carver, Jonathan. *Three Years Travels through the Interior Parts of North America . . . Containing an Account of the Great Lakes.* Philadelphia: printed by J. Crukshank, 1789.

Chalmers, Alexander, and Samuel Johnson, eds. *The Works of the English Poets, from Chaucer to Cowper.* 21 vols. London: J. Johnson et al., 1810.

Chaucer, Geoffrey. *The Poetical Works of Geoffrey Chaucer.* In vol. 1 of Anderson.

———. *The Poetical Works of Chaucer.* Cambridge Edition. Ed. F. N. Robinson. Boston: Houghton Mifflin, 1933.

Churchill, Charles. *The Poetical Works of Charles Churchill.* Ed. Douglas Grant. Oxford: Clarendon, 1956.

Colcridge, Samuel Taylor. *Biographia Literaria: With His Aesthetical Essays.* Ed. John Shawcross. 2 vols. Corrected ed. Oxford: Clarendon, 1954.

———. *The Poems of Samuel Taylor Coleridge.* Ed. Ernest Hartley Coleridge. London: Oxford University Press, 1912.

Collins, William. *The Poems of Gray, Collins, and Goldsmith.* Ed. Roger Lonsdale. London: Longman 1969; New York: Norton, 1972.

Cooper, Lane. "A Glance at Wordsworth's Reading." *Methods and Aims in the Study of Literature: A Series of Extracts and Illustrations.* Cornell Studies in English 31. Ed. Lane Cooper. 1915. London: H. Milford, Oxford University Press; Ithaca: Cornell University Press, 1940. Pp. 96–132.

Cowper, William. *The Poetical Works.* Rev. 4th ed., with corrections and additions by Norma Russell. London: Oxford University Press, 1969.

Craig, Martha A. "The Secret Wit of Spenser's Language." *Elizabethan Poetry: Modern Essays in Criticism.* Ed. Paul J. Alpers. London: Oxford University Press, 1967. Pp. 447–72.

Crowe, William. *Lewesdon Hill.* Oxford: Clarendon, 1788.

Culler, Jonathan. *The Pursuit of Signs: Semiotics, Literature, Deconstruction.* Ithaca: Cornell University Press, 1981.

Curtis, Jared R. *Wordsworth's Experiments with Tradition: The Lyric Poems of 1802.* Ithaca: Cornell University Press, 1971.

Daniel, Samuel. *Complete Works in Verse and Prose of Samuel Daniel.* Ed. Alexander B. Grosart. 5 vols. London: Hazell, Watson and Viney, 1885–96.

———. *The Civil Wars.* Ed. Laurence Michel. New Haven: Yale University Press, 1958.

———. *Musophilus: Containing a General Defense of All Learning.* Ed. Raymond Himelick. Purdue University Studies. West Lafayette: Pauley, 1965.

Davie, Donald. *Articulate Energy: An Inquiry into the Syntax of English Verse.* London: Routledge, 1955.

Davies, Sir John. *The Complete Poems.* Ed. Alexander B. Grosart. 2 vols. London: Chatto and Windus, 1876.

Denham, Sir John. *The Poetical Works.* Ed. T. H. Banks. New Haven: Yale University Press, 1928.

Drayton, Michael. *Works*. Ed. J. William Hebel, Katherine Tillotson, and Bernard H. Newdigate. 5 vols. Oxford: Blackwell, 1931–41.

Durling, Dwight L. *Georgic Tradition in English Poetry*. Columbia University Studies in English and Comparative Literature 121. New York: Columbia University Press, 1935.

Dyer, John. See Akenside.

Field, Barron. *Barron Field's Memoirs of William Wordsworth*. Australian Academy of the Humanities 3. Ed. Geoffrey Little. Sydney: Sydney University Press, 1975.

———. "[Critical] Memoirs of the Life and Poetry of William Wordsworth, with Extracts from His Letters to the Author." Ms. Add. 41325–7. British Museum, London.

Foakes, R. A. *The Romantic Assertion: A Study in the Language of Nineteenth-Century Poetry*. London: Methuen, 1958.

Frye, Northrop. "Nature and Homer." *Fables of Identity: Studies in Poetic Mythology*. New York: Harcourt, 1963. Pp. 39–51.

Goldsmith, Oliver. See Collins.

Gray, Thomas. See Collins.

Greene, Thomas M. *The Light in Troy: Imitation and Discovery in Renaissance Poetry*. New Haven: Yale University Press, 1982.

Habington, William. *The Poems*. Ed. Kenneth Allott. Liverpool: Liverpool University Press, 1948.

Hartman, Geoffrey H. *Beyond Formalism: Literary Essays 1958–1970*. New Haven: Yale University Press, 1970.

———. "Blessing the Torrent: On Wordsworth's Later Style." *PMLA* 93 (1978): 196–204.

———. *The Fate of Reading and Other Essays*. Chicago: University of Chicago Press, 1975.

———. *Wordsworth's Poetry 1787–1814*. Newly added introduction. New Haven: Yale University Press, 1970.

———, ed. *New Perspectives on Coleridge and Wordsworth*. Selected Papers from the English Institute. New York: Columbia University Press, 1972.

Havens, Raymond Dexter. *The Mind of a Poet: A Study of Wordsworth's Thought, with Particular Reference to* The Prelude. 2 vols. Baltimore: Johns Hopkins University Press, 1941.

Henry, Patrick. "Recognition of the Other and Avoidance of the Double: The Self and the Other in the *Essais* of Montaigne." *Stanford French Review* 6 (1982): 175–87.

Hodgart, M. J. C. *The Ballads*. New York: Norton, 1962.

Hollander, John. *The Figure of Echo: A Mode of Allusion in Milton and After*. Berkeley: University of California Press, 1981.

———. *Images of Voice: Music and Sound in Romantic Poetry*. Churchill College Overseas Fellowship Lectures 5. Cambridge: Heffer, 1970.

———. *The Untuning of the Sky: Ideas of Music in English Poetry, 1500–1700*. With new preface. New York: Norton, 1970.

———. "Wordsworth and the Music of Sound." See Hartman, ed. Pp. 41–84.

Horace. *The Odes of Horace*. Trans. James Michie. 1963. New York: Washington Square Press, 1965.

Hughes, Merritt Y. See Milton.

Hunt, Bishop C., Jr. "Wordsworth's Marginalia on *Paradise Lost.*" *BNYPL* 73 (1969): 167–83.

Hurdis, James. *Poems.* Oxford: Oxford University Press, 1808.

Knight, William A. "Wordsworth and Barron Field—I." *The Academy* 69 (1905): 1332–35.

Kristeva, Julia. *La Révolution du langage poétique.* Paris: Seuil, 1974.

———. *Semiotiké: Recherches pour une sémanalyse.* Paris: Seuil, 1969.

Langhorne, John. *Owen of Carron: A Poem.* London: Dilly, 1778.

Legouis, Emile. *The Early Life of William Wordsworth, 1770–1798: A Study of The Prelude.* Trans. J. W. Matthews. With additional appendix. London: Dent, 1921.

Lienemann, Kurt. *Die Belesenheit von William Wordsworth.* Berlin: Mayer and Müller, 1908.

Lindenberger, Herbert. *On Wordsworth's* Prelude. Princeton: Princeton University Press, 1963.

Logan, John. *The Poetical Works of John Logan.* In vol. 9 of Anderson.

Lonsdale, Roger, ed. See Collins.

Macpherson, James. *The Poems of Ossian: Translated by James Macpherson.* Ed. William Sharp. Edinburgh: J. Grant, 1926.

Marvell, Andrew. *Poems and Letters.* Ed. H. M. Margoliouth. 2 vols. Oxford: Clarendon, 1952.

Mayo, Robert. "The Contemporaneity of the *Lyrical Ballads.*" *PMLA* 69 (1954): 486–522.

Mill, John Stuart. *The Earlier Letters, 1812–1848.* Ed. Francis E. Mineka. Toronto: University of Toronto Press, 1963. Vol. 12 of *The Collected Works.* 21 vols. to date. 1963–.

Milton, John. *Complete Poems and Major Prose.* Ed. Merritt Y. Hughes. Indianapolis: Odyssey Press, 1957.

Moorman, Mary. *William Wordsworth: A Biography.* 2 vols. 1957, 1965. Oxford: Oxford University Press, 1968.

The New English Bible, with the Apocrypha: Oxford Study Edition. Ed. Samuel Sandmel et al. New York: Oxford University Press, 1976.

Ovid. *Metamorphoses.* Trans. Rolphe Humphries. Bloomington: Indiana University Press, 1963.

Owen, W. J. B. "Literary Echoes in *The Prelude.*" *Wordsworth Circle* 3 (1972): 3–16.

Parker, A. Reeve. *Coleridge's Meditative Art.* Ithaca: Cornell University Press, 1975.

Percy, Thomas, ed. *Reliques of Ancient English Poetry . . .* 4th ed. Rev. Henry B. Wheatley. 3 vols. 1885. London: Allen and Unwin, 1927.

Perri, Carmela. "On Alluding." *Poetics* 7 (1978): 289–307.

Philips, John. *The Poems.* Ed. M. G. Lloyd Thomas. Oxford: Blackwell, 1927.

Plutarch. *The Lives of the Noble Grecians and Romans.* Modern Library Edition. Trans. John Dryden et al. Rev. Arthur Hugh Clough. 1864. New York: Random, n.d.

Pope, Alexander. *The Poems of Alexander Pope: A One-Volume Edition of the Twickenham Text with Selected Annotations*. Ed. John Butt. New Haven: Yale University Press, 1963.

Potts, Abbie F. "The Spenserian and Miltonic Influences in Wordsworth's *Ode* and *Rainbow*." *SP* 29 (1932): 607–16.

Price, Martin. *To the Palace of Wisdom: Studies in Order and Energy from Dryden to Blake*. 1964. Carbondale: Southern Illinois University Press, 1970.

Raleigh, Walter. *Wordsworth*. London: Arnold, 1903.

Reed, Mark L. *Wordsworth: The Chronology of the Early Years, 1770–1799*. Cambridge: Harvard University Press, 1967.

Riffaterre, Michael. *Essais de stylistique structurale*. Paris: Flammarion, 1971.

———. "Intertextual Scrambling." *Romanic Review* 68 (1977): 197–206.

———. *Semiotics of Poetry*. Bloomington: Indiana University Press, 1978.

Robinson, Henry Crabb. *Henry Crabb Robinson on Books and Their Writers*. Ed. Edith J. Morley. 2 vols. London: Dent, 1938.

Rogers, Samuel. *Poems*. London: Cadell, and Moxon, 1834.

Scheffer, Johannes. *The History of Lapland: Shewing the Origin, Manners, Habits, Religion, and Trade of That People*. London: R. Griffith, 1751.

Scott, John. *The Poetical Works*. In vol. 9 of Anderson.

———. *Critical Essays on Some of the Poems of Several English Poets*. London: J. Phillips, 1785. Facsimile. New York: Garland, 1970.

Shakespeare, William. *The Complete Works*. Ed. Alfred Harbage et al. 1956–57. Baltimore: Penguin, 1969.

Shaver, Chester L., and Alice C. Shaver. *Wordsworth's Library: A Catalogue*. New York: Garland, 1979.

Sidney, Sir Phillip. *The Poems of Sir Phillip Sidney*. Ed. W. A. Ringler, Jr. Oxford: Clarendon, 1962.

Spacks, Patricia Meyer. *The Poetry of Vision: Five Eighteenth-Century Poets*. Cambridge: Harvard University Press, 1967.

Spenser, Edmund. *The Poetical Works of Spenser*. Cambridge Edition. Ed. R. E. Neil Dodge. 1908. Boston: Houghton, 1936.

Stahmer, Harold. *"Speak That I May See Thee!": The Religious Significance of Language*. New York: Macmillan, 1968.

Sylvester, Richard S., ed. *The Anchor Anthology of Seventeenth-Century Verse*. Vol. 2. Garden City, NY: Doubleday, 1969.

Taylor, Jeremy. *The Rule and Exercises of Holy Dying . . . Together with Prayers and Acts of Virtue . . .* Philadelphia: Willis P. Hazard, 1857.

Thomson, James. *The Complete Poetical Works of James Thomson*. Ed. J. Logie Robertson. London: Henry Frowde, 1908.

Tompkins, J. M. S. "In Yonder Grave a Druid Lies." *RES* 22 (1946): 1–16.

Virgil. *Virgil*. Loeb Classical Library. Ed. and trans. H. Rushton Fairclough. Rev. ed. 2 vols. Cambridge: Harvard University Press; London: Heinemann, 1934–35.

Warton, Joseph. *Poems*. In vol. 18 of Chalmers.

Warton, Thomas. *Poems*. In vol. 11 of Anderson.

Weiskel, Thomas F. *The Romantic Sublime: Studies in the Structure and Psychology of Transcendence*. Baltimore: Johns Hopkins University Press, 1976.

Wellek, René. *The Romantic Age*. New Haven: Yale University Press, 1955. Vol. 2 of *A History of Modern Criticism: 1750–1950*.

Wilkie, Brian F. *Romantic Poets and Epic Tradition*. Madison: University of Wisconsin Press, 1965.

Wimsatt, W. K. "Imitation as Freedom—1717–1798." *Day of the Leopards: Essays in Defense of Poems*. New Haven: Yale University Press, 1976. Pp. 117–39.

Winchilsea, Anne, Countess of. *The Poems*. Ed. Myra Reynolds. Chicago: University of Chicago Press, 1903.

Wither, George. *The Poetry of George Wither*. Ed. Frank Sidgwick. 2 vols. London: A. H. Bullen, 1902.

Wittreich, Joseph A., Jr., ed. *The Romantics on Milton: Formal Essays and Critical Asides*. Cleveland: Press of Case Western Reserve University, 1970.

Wlecke, Albert O. *Wordsworth and the Sublime*. Berkeley: University of California Press, 1973.

Wordsworth, Christopher. *Memoirs of William Wordsworth, Poet Laureate, D.C.L.* 2 vols. London: Moxon, 1851.

Wordsworth, Dorothy. *The Journals of Dorothy Wordsworth*. Ed. Ernest de Selincourt. 2 vols. London: Macmillan, 1941.

Wordsworth, William. *Benjamin the Waggoner*. Ed. Paul F. Betz. Ithaca: Cornell University Press, 1981.

———. *Descriptive Sketches*. Ed. Eric Birdsall. Ithaca: Cornell University Press, 1984.

———. *An Evening Walk*. Ed. James Averill. Ithaca: Cornell University Press, 1984.

———. *Home at Grasmere: Part First, Book First of* The Recluse. Ed. Beth Darlington. Ithaca: Cornell University Press, 1977.

———. *The Letters of William and Dorothy Wordsworth*. Vol. 1., *The Early Years, 1787–1805*. Ed. Ernest de Selincourt. Rev. Chester L. Shaver. 2d ed. Oxford: Clarendon, 1967.

———. *The Letters of William and Dorothy Wordsworth*. Vols. 2 and 3. *The Middle Years, 1806–1820*. Ed. Ernest de Selincourt. 2d. ed. Part I. *1806–1811*, rev. Mary Moorman, Oxford: Clarendon, 1969; Part II. *1812–1820*, rev. Mary Moorman and Alan G. Hill, Oxford: Clarendon, 1970.

———. Poems, in Two Volumes *and Other Poems*. Ed. Jared Curtis. Ithaca: Cornell University Press, 1983.

———. *The Poetical Works of William Wordsworth*. Ed. Ernest de Selincourt and Helen Darbishire. Rev. Helen Darbishire. 5 vols. Oxford: Clarendon, 1952–59. The individual volumes: vol. 1, corrected, with additions, 1952; vol. 2, 2d ed., 1952; vol. 3, 2d ed., 1959; vol. 4, corrected first ed., 1958; vol. 5, corrected first ed., 1959.

———. *The Prelude: 1799, 1805, 1850*. Norton Critical Edition. Ed. Jonathan Wordsworth, M. H. Abrams, and Stephen Gill. Toronto: George J. McLeod; New York: Norton, 1979.

———. *The Prelude: Or Growth of a Poet's Mind*. Ed. Ernest de Selincourt. Rev. Helen Darbishire. 2d ed. Oxford: Clarendon, 1959.

———. *The Prose Works of William Wordsworth.* Ed. W. J. B. Owen and Jane Worthington Smyser. 3 vols. Oxford: Clarendon, 1974.

———. *The Ruined Cottage and The Pedlar.* Ed. James Butler. Ithaca: Cornell University Press, 1979.

———. *Wordsworth: Representative Poems.* Ed. Arthur Beatty. New York: Doubleday, Doran, 1937.

———. *Wordsworth's Literary Criticism.* Ed. Nowell C. Smith. London: Henry Frowde, 1905.

———, ed. *Poems and Extracts: Chosen by William Wordsworth for an Album Presented to Lady Mary Lowther. Christmas, 1819.* London: Henry Frowde, 1905.

Worthington [Smyser], Jane. *Wordsworth's Reading of Roman Prose.* Yale Studies in English 102. New Haven: Yale University Press, 1946.

Young, Edward. *The Complaint: Or, Night Thoughts.* Ed. George Gilfillan. Edinburgh: James Nichol, 1853.

INDEX

Abrams, M. H., 108, 158–59, 240
Addison, Joseph, 11
    Cato, 205
Akenside, Mark, 3, 10, 30, 46, 48, 51, 62, 86, 91, 137, 138, 178, 196, 199, 213, 218, 233
    The Pleasures of Imagination, 48, 88, 99, 123, 131, 135, 136, 137, 199–201, 235
Alcaeus, 206
allusion, vii, 1, 2, 3, 14, 15, 20, 22, 24, 41, 71, 86, 107, 108, 222, 223, 234
    assimilative vs. comparative, 26, 30, 34, 37, 83–110, 114, 115, 121, 122–41, 142–209, 234
    generic, 130–41, 150, 235
    tradition and, 1–9, 25, 108
    virtual, 3, 87, 222
    See also echo, Frye, Greene, imitation, intertextuality, Renaissance, Restoration, Wordsworth
Anacreon, 21
Anderson, Robert, ed., *The Works of the British Poets*, 14, 225–26
Archimedes, 12
Aristotle, 12
Arnold, Matthew, 130–31
auditory, the, in poetry: mediating divine and natural order, 45, 50–52, 53–54, 55, 57–63, 70
    music and echo, 42, 49, 60, 68
    music as manipulator of passions, 52, 57, 59–60
    natural poiesis and, 45, 54
    originary voice, 66–72
    recovery of voice in Enlightenment, 117
    shift in relation to nature, 52, 53, 55, 57, 58, 59–61
    sound vs. sight, 65–69, 71
    split between music and words, 52, 53, 68–69
    transcendentalizing term not available, 53–54, 57
    voice at sources of literature, 72
    See also Wordsworth, Hollander
Augustan Age. *See* Restoration

Bacon, Francis, 13, 45
    Novum Organum, 45

Wisdom of the Ancients, 211–12, 244–45
Ballads, 10, 11, 12, 13, 73, 82, 89, 149, 164, 165, 167, 176–77, 178, 221, 239–40
    "Balowe," 13
    "Children of the Wood," 13, 240
    "Dulcina," 13, 176–77
    "Rising of the North," 13
Barbauld, Anna Letitia, 227
Barrow, John, 11
Bartram, William, 11, 164, 167
    Travels, 166, 167, 168, 238–39
Beattie, James, 10, 47, 178, 233
    The Minstrel, 123, 184–85, 240–41, 243
Beaumont, Francis, 13
Beaumont, John, 13
Bede, 13
Beers, Henry A., 46
Bell, George, 10, 226
Bible, 10, 13, 55, 67, 70, 104, 107, 123, 127, 128, 152, 158, 159, 196, 221
    Acts, 234
    1 Corinthians, 106, 160, 183, 234
    2 Corinthians, 159, 160, 162, 238
    Daniel, 163
    early Christian discourse, 106, 107
    Ecclesiastes, 159
    Exodus, 160, 161, 162
    Genesis, 159
    Luke, 159
    Matthew, 159
    Philippians, 159
    Psalms, 159, 160, 196, 221
    Revelation, 159, 160, 162–63
    St. Paul, 233
    2 Samuel, 163
    Song of Solomon, 160
Blair, Robert, 11, 178
    The Grave, 84
Blake, William, 10, 40, 52, 87, 99, 185, 193–94, 221
    Poetical Sketches, 221
    Songs of Innocence and Experience, 194
Bloom, Harold, 2, 97, 107, 108, 234
borrowing. *See* allusion, echo, Greene, imitation, intertextuality, Renaissance, Restoration, Wordsworth
Bourne, Vincent, 11
Bowles, William Lisle, 10, 30, 31, 32, 33, 35, 87, 178, 180, 198, 199, 229–30
    Fourteen Sonnets, 30, 31, 229

"On the Busts of Milton in Youth and Age," 233, 240
"St. Michael's Mount," 180
Sonnet XIX, 198
Sonnets, 2d ed., 32
"To the River Itchin," 199
Brantley, Richard, 69, 158–59, 231
Bridges, Sir Edgerton, 26
Brisman, Leslie, 74–75, 126–28, 209
Brown, John, 11, 223
Browne, Moses, 2, 11, 178
    "Sunday Thoughts," 118
Browne, William, 225
Bruce, James, 11
Bruce, Michael, 10, 47, 178
    Lochleven, 10, 123, 181
Bruce, Peter Henry, 11
Brun, Frederika, 11
Bunyan, John, 10
Bürger, Gottfried August, 11, 165
    The Wild Huntsman's Chase ("Der wilde Jäger"), 176
Burnet, Thomas, 13
Burns, Robert, 10, 11, 87, 146, 165, 178, 186, 218
    "A Bard's Epitaph," 146–47
    "Man Was Made to Mourn," 177–78, 241
    "Tam o' Shanter," 186
    "The Cotter's Saturday Night," 186–87
    "The Vision," 147
    "To J. S. ****," 147
Butler, Samuel (1610–85), 11, 13, 225
Byron, Lord (George Gordon), 130, 229

Campbell, Thomas, 10, 178
Carew, Thomas, 225
Carter, Elizabeth, 11, 21
Carver, Jonathan, 11
    Travels, 156, 238
Cassius Dio, 239
Catullus, 21
Cervantes, Miguel de, 12
Chain of Being, 25, 40, 99, 101, 103, 104, 131, 133, 134, 137, 139, 203
Chatterton, Thomas, 11, 87, 165
Chaucer, Geoffrey, 1, 10, 13, 14, 108, 122, 150, 178–79, 190, 221, 225, 226, 242–43
    Legend of Good Women, 150–51, 190–91, 243
Chiabrera, Gabriello, 10
Churchill, Charles, 11
    "Independence," 211, 244
Churchyard, Thomas, 13, 147
Cicero, 12, 172
    De re publica, 84
Coleridge, E. H., 166
Coleridge, Hartley, 155–58

Coleridge, Samuel Taylor, 10, 14, 32, 43, 46, 47, 52, 72, 80, 81, 87, 106, 109, 118, 123, 163, 171, 178, 185, 189, 196–97, 218, 226, 228, 230, 243
    Biographia Literaria, 32, 80, 116, 179, 204, 235–36
    "Frost at Midnight," 145, 155–56, 158
    "Ode to Tranquillity," 242
Collins, William, 3, 5, 8, 10, 14, 19–41, 46, 51, 59, 61, 86, 120, 145, 178, 182, 190, 213, 218, 221
    "Ode Occasioned by the Death of Mr. Thomson," 20, 22, 23, 24, 25, 27, 28, 29, 227
    "Ode to Evening," 24, 29–30, 33, 61–63, 86, 87, 88, 89, 152, 196, 227
    "Ode to Liberty," 182
    "Ode to Peace," 92–93
    "Ode to Pity," 4, 5, 9, 223
    personification in, 4, 5, 30, 59
    poetic voice and, 5, 22, 25, 33, 61–63
    "The Passions," 59–60, 182–83, 240
Columbus, Ferdinand, 12
Constable, Henry, 147
contaminatio. See Renaissance, imitation in
Cooper, Lane, 164, 238, 239
Corbet, Richard, 13, 147
Cornelius Nepos, 239
Cottle, Joseph, 10, 178
Cotton, Charles, 13, 147, 189
Cowley, Abraham, 221, 225
Cowper, William, 10, 32, 51, 185, 213, 218
    The Task, 185–86, 241–42
Crabbe, George, 10
Crashaw, Richard, 225
Crowe, William, 10
    Lewesdon Hill, 46–49, 228
Cunningham, John, 10
Curtis, Jared, 13, 151, 225
Curtius Rufus, Quintus, 12, 172

Dampier, William, 11
Daniel, Samuel, 10, 13, 143, 145, 147, 225
    Civil Wars, 236
    "Funerall Poem upon the Earl of Devonshire," 143–44
    Musophilus, 143, 237
    "To the Lady Margaret," 236
Dante, *Paradiso*, 12
Darwin, Erasmus, 10
Davenant, Sir William, 225
Davie, Donald, 119, 213–17
Davies, Sir John, 13, 147, 225
    "In Philoneum," 149–50
De Carbonnières, Ramond, 11, 227
Delille, Jacques, 11
Della Cruscans, the, 21, 204

Denham, John, 36, 37, 38, 143, 221, 225, 230
  Cooper's Hill, 36, 37, 38, 39, 236
Descartes, 12
De Selincourt, Ernest, 143, 166, 167, 176, 201, 221, 226, 229, 236, 238, 243
Donne, John, 36, 37, 221, 225
  "The Good Morrow," 237
Drayton, Michael, 10, 13, 147, 225
  Nymphidia, 147, 150
  Polyolbion, 147, 148, 151, 230
  The Muses' Elysium, 147
Drummond, William, of Hawthornden, 225
Dryden, John, 10, 59, 86, 89, 91, 113, 221, 237
  "A Song for Saint Cecilia's Day," 59, 238
  "Alexander's Feast," 59
  Palamon and Arcite, 93
  Plutarch's *Lives*, translation of, 172
Dyer, John, 10, 46, 178
  "Grongar Hill," 184
  Ruins of Rome, 123, 183–84, 240–41

echo, vii, viii, 1, 2, 3, 4, 13, 14, 15, 26, 39, 41, 61, 66, 71, 73, 74, 86, 90, 95–96, 105, 108, 113, 114, 115–16, 117, 138, 142–209, 218, 222, 223, 227–29, 234
  as metaphor for allusion, 115
  as metaphor for or action of poetic voice, 5–6, 44–72, 75, 213
  as model of continuity in change, 75
  as naturalizing and humanizing voice, 4, 6, 7, 8, 50, 64–66, 75, 78–79, 213, 240
  as poetic image, 42–44, 51
  as re-creation, 79
  as verbal or structural iteration, 42–44, 64–65, 78–79, 214–17
  conscious intention and, 115, 223, 228
  in assimilative mode, 26, 41, 105, 109–10, 113, 115–16, 118, 119, 121, 142–209, 211, 218, 234
  in comparative mode, 105, 108–9, 113, 115–16, 119, 121, 122–41, 211, 218, 234
  marriage with Pan, 45, 211–12
  mediating between man, nature, and God, 4, 5, 6, 7, 44–72 passim, 80, 90, 103, 211, 213, 218, 224
  mediating tradition, 9, 24, 25, 26, 39, 90, 107, 108, 211, 224
  nonallusive, 3, 71, 87–89, 106–10, 114–16, 121, 142–209 passim, 211, 222, 223, 227–29
  ontological role, viii, 63–72, 218–19
  personification of, 4, 5, 45, 55, 58, 60, 70, 76, 211–12, 220

role in poetic genesis, viii, 6, 9, 41, 63–72, 75–82, 208, 213, 218
  See also allusion, Hollander, imitation, intertextuality, Renaissance, Restoration, Wordsworth
Erasmus, *Praise of Folly*, 98, 99
Euripides, *Iphigenia*, 174
Eusebius, 12

Fielding, Henry, 11
Fletcher, Giles, 225
Fletcher, Phineas, 225
Florus, 239
Foakes, R. A., 214, 216, 240
Forsyth, Joseph, 11
Frye, Northrop, 1, 107, 234

Garth, Samuel, 11
Gay, John, 11, 86, 178
Gilbert, William, 11
Gilpin, William, 11
Godwin, William, 11
Goethe, Johann Wolfgang von, 130
Golding, Arthur, 13
Goldsmith, Oliver, 3, 11, 86, 178, 187, 213
  The Deserted Village, 187
  The Traveller, 187–88
Grahame, James, 164
Gray, Thomas, 1, 10, 14, 21, 25, 26, 27, 28, 30, 39, 46, 51, 62, 86, 159, 178, 186, 190, 193, 195, 196, 206, 213, 218, 222, 243
  "Alcaic Ode," 243
  "Alliance of Education and Government," 137–38
  Elegy Written in a Country Churchyard, 194, 195, 205, 243
  Guide to the Lakes, 11
  "Ode on a Distant Prospect of Eton College," 28
  "Ode on the Pleasures Arising from Vicissitude," 205, 242
  "Sonnet on the Death of Mr. Richard West," 205, 244
  "The Progress of Poesy," 123, 193
Greene, Thomas M., viii, 83, 84, 91, 93, 94–98, 105, 122, 123, 126, 141, 233, 234
Greenwood, Robert, 10, 178
  "A Poem Written During a Shooting Excursion," 181
Greville, Fulke, 13

Habington, William, 152
  "Description of Castara," 154–55
Haie, Edward, 13
Hakluyt, Richard, *Voyages*, 13
Hall, Joseph, 225
Hamilton, William, of Bangour, 11

Hartman, Geoffrey, viii, 10, 28, 45, 62–63, 72, 76, 108, 109, 113, 114, 116, 117, 118, 120, 233, 234, 235
Hearne, Samuel, 11
   Journey from Fort Prince Wales, 168
Henry, Patrick (1736–99), 236
Henry, Patrick (1940–   ), 245
Herbert, George, 225
   "Sunday," 158
   "The Temper, I," 123
   "Virtue," 158
Herd, David, ed., *Ancient Scottish Ballads*, 11
Herodian, 239
Herodotus, 12, 172
Heron, Robert, 11
Herrick, Robert, 147, 225
Hogg, James, 10
Hölderlin, Friedrich, 76
Hollander, John, viii, 3, 45, 51–54, 57, 60, 61, 64–65, 115, 223, 228, 231
Home, John, 11
Homer, 12, 21, 83, 86, 87, 89, 131, 224, 233
   Iliad, 95–96
Horace, 12, 21, 86, 89, 187
   Odes, 86, 174, 206, 239, 244
Hurdis, James, 10, 85, 178, 181
   The Favourite Village, 240
   The Village Curate, 85
Hutchinson, William, 11

imitation, 21, 71, 73, 83–110, 120, 149, 191, 201, 205, 218, 221, 222, 234, 238
   eighteenth-century, 86–90, 91–96, 120, 150, 217, 227
   generic, 150, 214
   See also allusion, echo, Greene, Renaissance, Sensibility (Age of), Wordsworth
influence, poetic, 2. *See also* poetic influence *under* Wordsworth
intertextuality, vii, viii, 2, 3, 15, 107, 113, 120, 223. *See also* allusion, Bloom, echo, Frye, Greene, Hollander, imitation, Renaissance, Restoration, Riffaterre, Sensibility (Age of), Wordsworth
Isola, Agostino, 12

Johnson, James, ed., *The Scots Musical Museum*, 11
Johnson, Samuel, 10, 11, 12, 226, 230
Jonson, Ben, 13, 56, 147, 225
   "On Inviting a Friend to Supper," 94
Juvenal, 21, 86

Keats, George, 11
Keats, John, 11, 118, 229
   "Ode to Psyche," 228

Lamb, Charles, 11, 69
Landor, Walter Savage, 11
   Imaginary Conversations, 11, 224
Langhorne, John, 11, 178, 181, 227
   Owen of Carron, 240
Legouis, Emile, 204, 223, 226, 227
Lindenberger, Herbert, 1, 47, 120, 229
Livy, 12, 172
Logan, John, 11, 47, 178, 181
   "Ode to a Young Lady," 240
Longinus, 98
Lonsdale, Roger, 3, 20, 88, 93, 222, 227
Lovelace, Richard, 147
Lucian, 98
Lyttleton, George, 187

Macpherson, James 11, 178
   Ossian poems, 87, 221
Macrobius, 45
Mandeville, Bernard, 11, 224
Marlowe, Christopher, "The Passionate Shepherd to His Mistress," 192
Martial, 94
Marvell, Andrew, 13
   "On a Drop of Dew," 157–58
   "The Garden," 166
Mayo, Robert, 21
melancholy: school of, 3, 21
   as tone-sound blending, 60–61
   in landscape, 87
   white (leucocholy), 46
Michelangelo, *Sonnets*, 12
Mill, John Stuart, 172
Milton, John, vii, 3, 4, 10, 12, 13, 14, 21, 22, 23, 25, 26, 27, 30, 32, 34, 35, 39, 40, 51, 52, 54, 55, 57, 62, 75, 81, 84, 85, 86, 87, 88, 89, 90, 91, 97, 98, 102, 103, 104, 105, 106, 108, 109, 113, 116, 117, 122, 123, 125, 126, 127, 128, 130, 131, 132, 143, 152, 159, 171, 174, 181, 189, 191, 193, 196, 197, 198, 207, 213, 218, 221, 225, 226, 228, 230, 233, 234, 236, 238
   "L'Allegro," 5, 6, 21, 23, 26, 44, 51, 55–57, 84, 91, 114, 117, 189, 190, 191, 192, 198, 206, 227, 238, 243
   "Arcades," 189
   "At a Solemn Music," 51, 55, 123
   "At a Vacation Exercise," 24
   Christian Doctrine, 69–70, 81, 233
   Comus, 51, 52, 55, 87, 88, 123, 146, 189, 190, 195, 205
   Doctrine and Discipline of Divorce, 118
   Elegy V, 123
   Italian Sonnets, 26
   "Lycidas," 23–24, 46, 51, 208, 209
   music in, 51, 54, 55–57
   Nativity Ode, 88, 92, 93, 152, 153, 189, 195, 233

"Of Education," 209
Paradise Lost, 22, 32, 52, 84, 85, 87, 88, 89, 93, 97, 99–105, 118–19, 123, 125, 126, 127, 128, 134, 135, 139, 148, 166, 175, 181, 188, 195, 197, 198, 203, 207, 208, 221, 232, 236
Paradise Regained, 126, 127, 153
"Il Penseroso," 5, 21, 22, 23, 25–26, 51, 56–57, 58, 84, 87, 91, 114–15, 116–17, 126, 152, 153, 182–83, 189, 192, 238
Samson Agonistes, 74, 126, 127, 128, 129, 236
Sonnet XV, 171
Sonnet XIX, 145, 236
Sonnet XXIII, 174–76
Mimesis, process and product types of, 216–17, 245
Montaigne, Michel de, 245
Montesquieu, 11
Montgomery, James, 11
Moorman, Mary, 42, 43, 184–85, 229, 231
Moschus, 12, 21

Narcissus, 4, 37, 45, 55, 70, 220
Neoclassical period, poets, practices. *See* Restoration
Newton, John, 11

Oldham, John, 11
Otway, Thomas, 5
Ovid, 4, 10, 12, 89
Heroides, 174
Metamorphoses, 4, 220, 224
personification in, 4

Pan, 4, 45, 211–12, 244–45
Parallels. *See* allusion, echo, Greene, Hollander, imitation, intertextuality, Pope, Renaissance, Restoration, Wordsworth
Park, Mungo, 11
Parnell, Thomas, 11, 21
Pennant, Thomas, 11
Percy, Bishop Thomas, 10, 11, 13
Reliques of Ancient English Poetry, 13, 176–77, 221, 240
Perri, Carmela, 115, 121, 223, 230, 234
Petrarch, 12, 83, 86, 91, 98
Africa, 84
Canzoniere, 233
"Letter to Posterity," 83
"Triumph of Eternity," 89–90
Philips, Ambrose, 46
Philips, John, 22, 30, 46, 86
Cider, 86, 88
"Splendid Shilling," 86
picturesque, the, 10, 32, 37, 44, 53, 65, 90, 147, 164, 235
Pindar, 86

Plato, 12
Pliny, 12, 172
Plutarch, 12, 172, 238
Lives, 172, 238, 239
Politian, 91
Polybius, 12, 172, 238
Pope, Alexander, 10, 54, 62, 86, 88, 89, 90, 91, 98, 116, 120, 135, 165, 171, 221, 227, 230, 237, 238
"Eloisa to Abelard," 93
Essay on Criticism, 239
Essay on Man, 131, 135, 169–70, 239
Imitations of Horace, 94
Moral Essays, 171
Pastorals, 221
The Dunciad, 168–69
The Rape of the Lock, 95–96, 169, 170
Windsor Forest, 24, 90, 239
post-Augustan poetry. *See* Sensibility (Age of)
pre-Romantic period, poets, practices. *See* Sensibility (Age of)
Price, Martin, 62
Price, Uvedale, 11
Prior, Matthew, 11

Quotation. *See* allusion, echo, Hollander, imitation, intertextuality, Restoration, Wordsworth

Raleigh, Sir Walter (1552?–1618), "The Nymph's Reply," 192
Raleigh, Walter Alexander (1861–1922), vii
Ramsay, Allan, 11
Renaissance and seventeenth century, 4, 12–13, 14, 23, 55, 60, 107, 125, 146, 151, 152, 164, 221, 224, 225, 226, 230, 234, 237, 245
Elizabethan and 17th-century English poets, 13–14, 143–63, 178
English metaphysical style, 77, 151, 157
historicity in, 83, 84, 86, 93–95, 96, 98–99, 122
imitation in, viii, 14, 83–110 passim, 123, 140, 150; types of imitation: (1) dialectical, 98–105, 109, 126, 130, 140, 141, 216, 217; (2) eclectic (*contaminatio*), 85–94, 97, 98, 99, 105; (3) heuristic, 91, 93–98, 105, 109; (4) sacramental (liturgical), 84–85, 90, 105
music and voice in, 44–45, 51, 52, 53, 57, 59
Restoration and Augustan Age, 4, 7, 11, 13, 14, 21, 23, 30, 32, 36, 37, 38, 40, 44, 51, 52, 73, 77, 84, 89, 90, 91, 94, 98, 120, 124, 146, 165, 178, 180, 187, 213, 214, 216, 217, 225, 228, 230, 234, 238, 240

allusion and imitation in, 25, 86, 91–96, 120, 150, 227, 230, 241
neoclassical discourse, 106
Riffaterre, Michael, 107, 227, 229, 234
Robinson, Henry Crabb, 130, 216, 233
Rochester, John Wilmot, Earl of, 221
Rogers, Samuel, 11, 178, 181
"Lucy, at her wheel, shall sing" (from "A Wish"), 240
Roman prose writers, 165, 171, 172
Wordsworth and, 238
Romantic period, 4, 45, 60, 62, 63, 75, 99, 124, 126, 137, 143, 149, 159, 170, 187, 213, 217, 218–19, 229
authentic voice in, 54
imagination in, 4, 49, 61, 77–78, 101, 117, 120, 134–35, 136, 137, 139, 140, 141, 183, 198, 199, 219–20
music and poetry in, 52
transcendentalization of perception, 54
Rousseau, Jean-Jacques, 11

Sackville, Charles, 221, 225
Sallust, 239
Scheffer, Johannes, 11, 243
Schiller, Friedrich, 11
Scott, John, 11
Scott, Sir Walter, 11
Waverley novels, 224
Seneca, 12, 172
Sensibility, Age of, 4, 7, 8, 10, 12, 14, 21, 23, 26, 27, 30, 40, 41, 46, 54, 73, 89, 90, 99, 109–10, 120, 122, 178, 190, 194, 195, 206, 213, 217, 221, 225, 227, 228, 231
imitation and echoing in, 12, 14, 26, 27, 83–110
struggle for voice in, 44–72, 90, 117
See also Akenside, Collins, Gray, Thomson, Wordsworth
Seventeenth-century literary period. See Renaissance
Shaftesbury, Anthony Ashley Cooper, Earl of (1671–1713), Characteristics, 224
Shakespeare, William, 3, 10, 12, 13, 14, 27, 56, 58, 89, 90, 91, 108, 109, 122, 123, 125, 126, 143, 147, 152, 159, 179, 189, 191, 218, 221, 225, 226, 236
A Midsummer Night's Dream, 146
As You Like It, 171, 191
Hamlet, 88, 129, 130, 166, 205, 206
Macbeth, 145, 172, 206
Measure for Measure, 87
Othello, 166
Sonnet 64, 99
Sonnet 65, 242
Sonnet 107, 125, 126
The Sonnets, 191
The Tempest, 149

The Winter's Tale, 191
Shelley, Percy Bysshe, 11, 130, 229
Shelvock, George, 11
Shenstone, William, 10
The School-Mistress, 10
Sidney, Sir Philip, 13, 78
Astrophel and Stella, 78
Skelton, John, 13
Smart, Christopher, 11, 86
Smith, Adam, 11
Smollett, Tobias, 11
Sophocles, 12
Southey, Robert, 11, 87, 178, 226
Spacks, Patricia Meyer, 51
Spenser, Edmund, 1, 3, 10, 13, 14, 25, 27, 34, 35, 88, 89, 90, 91, 108, 109, 116, 122, 126, 144, 147, 152, 159, 179, 189, 191, 218, 221, 225, 226, 230, 234
"Epithalamion," 123, 191
Muiopotmos, 191
"Prothalamion," 34, 35, 119, 230
The Faerie Queene, 24, 93, 144, 145, 191, 205
The Shepheardes Calender, 221
sublime, the, 30, 43, 44, 46, 53, 57, 61, 65, 90, 102, 127, 137, 140, 147, 148, 171, 173, 180, 218, 221, 231
Suckling, John, 225
Suetonius, 239
Surrey, Henry Howard, Earl of, 225
Swift, Jonathan, 10, 227

Tacitus, 239
Tasso, Torquato, 12, 204
Taylor, Jeremy, 13
Rule and Exercises of Holy Dying, 158
Theocritus, 12, 172–73, 193
Thomson, James, 3, 10, 14, 20, 22, 23, 25, 27, 28, 29, 30, 33, 35, 46, 51, 85, 88, 89, 90, 91, 109, 123, 137, 138, 139, 178, 200, 213, 218, 221, 227, 230, 231, 233
"Nuptial Song Intended for Sophonisba," 93
The Castle of Indolence, 123, 152, 227, 243
The Seasons, 22, 23, 84, 85, 93, 123, 124, 131, 138, 196, 200–203, 231, 240, 242, 243, 244
topographical point of view, 36, 46, 164, 187, 188, 230
tradition, English literary, vii, viii, 14, 25, 33, 86–93. See also Sensibility (Age of), Renaissance, Restoration, Wordsworth

utterance, poetic. See auditory, the, and echo

Valerius Maximus, 239
Vaughan, Henry, 13, 225
Velleius Paterculus, 239

Virgil, 10, 12, 21, 22, 37, 86, 89, 113, 152, 172, 173, 174, 178, 196, 197, 198, 206
  Aeneid, 174–75, 198, 234, 239
  Eclogues, 173, 193, 196, 197
  Georgics, 174, 196, 239, 241
Vision, Poets of, 51, 57, 74
voice, poetic. *See* allusion, the auditory, echo, imitation, Restoration, Sensibility (Age of), Wordsworth
Voltaire, 11

Waller, Edmund, 13, 221, 225
Walton, Isaac, 13
Warton, Joseph, 11, 22, 30, 61, 86, 178, 190, 196, 199, 205, 238
  "Fashion: A Satire," 192
  "Ode to Fancy," 91, 92
  "The Approach of Summer," 192
  "The Enthusiast," 58–69, 84
  "The Pleasures of Melancholy," 192
Warton, Thomas, 22, 30, 61, 84, 86, 178, 190, 196, 199, 205, 238
Webster, John, 13
Weever, John, 13
Weiskel, Thomas, 46
Wellek, René, 236
Whitaker, Thomas D., 11
Wilkie, Brian, 131
Wilkinson, Thomas, 11
Williams, Helen Maria, 11, 21
Wilson, Henry, 11
  Pelew Islands, 168
Wimsatt, W. K., 62, 86–87, 213, 221, 227
Winchilsea, Anne Finch, Countess of, 10, 21, 179, 189
  "A Nocturnal Reverie," 242
Wither, George, 13, 147, 151, 179, 225
  Fair Virtue, 189
  The Shepherd's Hunting, 151, 188
Wittreich, Joseph A., Jr., 97
Wlecke, Albert O., 140–41
Wordsworth, Christopher, 226, 231
Wordsworth, Dorothy, 43, 231
Wordsworth, John, 143, 229
Wordsworth, William
  allusion: assimilative, *see* echoing, assimilative; comparative, viii, 37, 39, 71, 93–110, 113, 119, 121, 122–41, 152, 211, 218, 236; generic, *see* echo, generic *under* Wordsworth
  art of borrowing, 113–21, 211; general aims of: Miltonic, 108–9, 110; normative, 105–8, 110; Wordsworthian, 109–10
  assertion or interruption of continuity, viii, 15, 22, 27, 29, 33, 40, 43, 44, 51, 70–71, 74–75, 76, 77, 79, 80, 81, 82, 117, 122, 126, 212–13, 219–20

ballads in, 7, 11, 21, 73, 164–65, 176–78, 239–40. *See also* ballads (main entry)
Bible in, *see* Bible (main entry)
demythologizing and remythologizing impulse, 63–64, 71, 76, 114, 155, 165, 173, 179–80, 180–204, 239. *See also* echoing *under* Wordsworth
drive to naturalize and humanize, vii, 6–8, 30, 33, 35, 36, 40, 49–50, 61, 63–64, 70, 71, 78–79, 110, 126–27, 144, 155, 156, 158, 161, 165, 168, 169, 173, 176, 180–93, 211–12, 213, 220, 242
echo: as image, 42–44, 81–82; as master metaphor, 71, 77, 81, 211–20; as screen, 213; generic echoes and allusions, 130, 131, 133, 135, 136–41, 171, 173, 192–93, 217; growth of consciousness and, 76; link with poetic genesis, 80, 81, 213; mountain echoes, 6–7, 80, 147, 148, 195, 219; poetic style and, 213–17; role in mediating nature or existence, 44–72, 79, 80, 139, 211, 213, 219–20; role in revisionary poetics, 71, 72–82, 115–16, 211, 213; thematized in poems, 4, 42–44, 66, 75–80, 214–17. *See also* allusion, borrowing, echoing, imitation, intertextuality *under* Wordsworth
echoing: assimilative, viii, 25, 31, 34, 39, 41, 71, 83–94, 105–10, 113, 114, 115, 118, 119, 121, 122, 142–209, 211, 218, 236, 240, 243, 245; assimilative classes: (1) *anthropologizing,* viii, 142, 163–78, 203–4, 239; (2) *moralizing,* viii, 142–63, *subdivided into* apocalyptic, 151–63, 203–4, epicurean, 145–51, stoic, 143–47; (3) *naturalizing,* viii, 178–204, 239, *subdivided into* demythologizing, 180–93, and remythologizing, 194–204; (4) *poeticizing,* viii, 142, 204–9, 239; composition as process of, 79–80, 93–94, 105, 117–18, 122–23, 142–43, 204, 211, 213; of past experience in the present, 71, 117, 211, 212–13; paradox of coming to consciousness and, 70–71; quasi-philosophical concept of, vii, 63–72, 75–82, 213, 218–20; role of the techniques of, vii–viii, 15, 21, 29, 39, 40, 41, 42–82, 83–110, 115–16, 203–4, 211–20. *See also* allusion, echo, imitation, intertextuality *under* Wordsworth
feeling in, 119, 120, 121, 161, 164, 213
imitation in, 87, 96, 98–105, 123, 150,

217–18, 221, 238; relation to Renaissance imitation, 83, 87, 90, 96–106, 108–10, 191. *See also* imitation (main entry)

interchange between mind and nature, viii, 15, 29–30, 35, 36, 38, 39, 44, 45, 47, 49–50, 54, 61, 63, 64, 69–72, 80, 101, 102, 103, 104, 105, 135, 139, 164, 166, 178, 183, 191, 195, 201, 202, 203, 216–17, 220, 232, 234, 243

intertextuality in, vii, 15, 21, 25, 34, 105, 109–10, 113, 121. *See also* allusion, echo, echoing, and imitation *under* Wordsworth

literary sources and taste, 9–15, 21, 108–10, 203; imagining his audience, 73–74

mediation of English poetic tradition, vii, viii, 1, 3, 9, 12, 15, 19–41, 63, 82, 87, 105, 109–10, 122, 130, 142–43, 191, 200, 204, 213

mood, 114, 116, 117, 118, 119, 120, 121, 142–63 (moralizing), 163–78 (anthropologizing), 178–204 (naturalizing), 204–9 (poeticizing)

nature, concept of, 69, 80–81, 100–102, 118, 194

offering self to not-self: 7, 8, 9, 30, 39

oral discourse, poetic utterance, speech, *see* voice *under* Wordsworth

poetic freedom in, viii, 40, 63, 127, 203, 213, 217–20

poetic influence in, 2, 21, 224, 225; struggle with precursors, 2, 96, 109, 189, 197, 218

relation to Christianity, 130, 158–63, 232, 233–34, 235

relation to Milton, vii, 10, 13, 21, 34, 35, 96–105, 108–9, 113–16, 122, 123, 126–29, 130, 139, 175, 218

revisionary poetics: "the real language of men," 73, 164; relation to books, 212, 213; remaking the heart of man, 70, 72, 74; remaking the language of poetry, 72–82, 106, 108, 204

travel books in, 164

voice: concern with authentic, viii, 1, 6, 8, 22, 27, 29, 33, 44–82 passim, 108, 109, 117, 127, 128, 178, 208, 212, 213, 218, 220; correction of and imaginative growth, 74–75, 169; internalized speech, 113, 114, 116, 118, 119; meditative internalizing through, 47, 48, 68, 70–72, 76–79, 119; nature and, 44–72 passim; oral discourse and, viii, 72–74, 218; orginary or mediating, 66–72; pro-

phetic role of, viii, 22, 53, 54, 74, 108–9, 220. *See also* auditory, the

POEMS AND ESSAYS:

"*A little onward lend thy guiding hand,*" 74–75, 126–30, 158

"A Poet's Epitaph," 238, 243

"A slumber did my spirit seal," 114

"Address to Kilchurn Castle," 116, 235

"Address to the Scholars of the Village of——," 237

Alfoxden fragment (*PW*5.342), 64–65, 76

An Evening Walk, 2, 15, 26, 158, 159, 181, 182, 187, 194, 204, 223, 226–27, 233, 235

"Beggars," 191

Benjamin, The Waggoner, 191, 205, 206

"Calais, August, 1802," 159

"Captivity.—Mary Queen of Scots," 237

cento, 90, 204, 233

Coleridge, letter to, 116

"Composed after a Journey across the Hambleton Hills," 196, 197, 198

"Composed in the Valley near Dover," 190

"Composed upon Westminster Bridge," 119

"Dear native regions," 233

Descriptive Sketches, 11, 12, 26, 158, 159, 171, 182, 187, 194, 204, 205, 226, 227, 233, 238, 243

"Dion," 238

"Elegiac Stanzas," 237

Epitaphs and Elegiac Pieces, 237

"Essay Supplementary," 73, 108

"Expostulation and Reply," 185, 241

"Fragment of a Gothic Tale," 209

"Gipsies," 185–86

"Glen Almain," 238

"Hart-Leap Well," 176, 238

Home at Grasmere, 8, 9, 106, 148, 164, 187, 229

"How sweet it is, when mother Fancy rocks," 114, 115, 116

"I travelled among unknown men," 240

Immortality (Intimations) Ode, 6, 8, 67–68, 71–72, 81, 143, 187, 189, 191, 219, 224, 242

"It is not to be thought of that the flood," 236

"It was an April morning," 116, 235

"Laodamia," 174–76

Letters of William and Dorothy Wordsworth, 229, 235, 236

"Lines, Written as a School Exercise," 169, 238

"Lines Written in Early Spring," 185, 241
"Lines Written near Richmond," 20
"Lines Written While Sailing in a Boat at Evening," 27, 29, 31, 33, 226
Lucy poems, 114, 116, 154, 181
Lyrical Ballads, 12, 19, 40, 120, 179, 204, 205, 218, 226, 235, 244
Lyrics of 1802, 13–14, 204
"Musings near Aquapendente," 207, 208, 238
"Mutability," 209
"My heart leaps up," 43–44
"Ode to Duty," 118–19
"Ode to Lycoris," 224
"On the Power of Sound," 47, 53, 67, 158, 160, 192, 193, 194, 218–20, 238
"Personal Talk," I–IV, 143, 145, 182–83, 236
Poems and Extracts, 183, 188–89, 235, 242
Poems of the Fancy, 150, 151
Poetical Works, 222, 224
Preface to *Lyrical Ballads* (1802), 72, 244
"Processions," 158
"Prospectus," 9, 47, 50, 123, 124, 125, 126, 158, 163, 183, 184, 207, 208, 245
"Remembrance of Collins," 4, 19–41, 93, 152, 229
"Resolution and Independence," 29, 186–87
Roman prose writers, 165, 171, 172, 238
"Ruth," 166, 167
"She dwelt among the untrodden ways," 154–55, 181, 240
"She was a phantom of delight," 167, 239
"Simon Lee," 177–78
"Sonnet on Seeing Miss Helen Maria Williams Weep," 204
"Stanzas Written in My Pocket Copy of Thomson's 'Castle of Indolence,'" 184–85
"Stepping Westward," 77–78
"Strange fits of passion have I known," 114, 176–77, 181
"Stray Pleasures," 118
"The Affliction of Margaret," 168
"The Barberry Tree," 224
"The Character of the Happy Warrior," 143–44, 238
"The Complaint of the Forsaken Indian Woman," 168
"The Contrast: The Parrot and the Wren," 192

"The Dog—An Idyllium," 203
The Excursion, 133, 158, 159, 160, 172, 174, 181, 236, 237, 239, 240
"The Fountain," 48
"The Glow Worm," 43
"The Old Cumberland Beggar," 159, 191, 240
"The Power of Music," 49, 149
The Prelude, 6, 8, 12, 15, 21, 42, 49–50, 53, 65, 66, 67, 69–70, 71, 72, 75, 81–82, 97, 99–105, 106, 116, 117, 119, 120, 131, 133, 135, 136, 137, 138, 139, 140, 158, 159, 160, 162, 163, 168, 169, 170, 171, 172, 173, 174, 179, 180, 181, 184, 187, 199, 200, 201, 202, 209, 212–13, 214–17, 218, 222, 224, 226, 227, 229, 230, 231–32, 233–34, 235, 238, 239, 242, 243, 245
"The Redbreast Chasing a Butterfly," 240
The Ruined Cottage, 238
"The Solitary Reaper," 78–79
"The Sparrow's Nest," 211
"The Tables Turned," 185, 188, 241
"The Thorn," 186
"The Vale of Esthwaite," 194, 229, 230, 233, 238
The White Doe of Rylstone, 144, 145, 152–53, 235, 236, 237, 239
"The world is too much with us," 225
"Tintern Abbey," 198, 244
"To a Highland Girl," 190
"To H. C. Six Years Old," 155–58
"To Joanna," 148
"To the Cuckoo," 42, 181, 231
"To the Daisy" (*PW*2.135), 150, 151, 188, 190, 242
"To the Daisy" (*PW*2.138), 190–91
"To the Small Celandine" (*PW*2.142), 191
"To the Sons of Burns," 146–47
"To the Torrent at the Devil's Bridge," 198, 199
"Upon the Same Occasion [September 1819]," 145, 206
Vaudracour and Julia, 230
"Written in London, September, 1802," 171, 238, 239
"Written in March," 160
"Yes, it was the mountain echo," 80, 147
"Yew Trees," 198
Wyatt, Sir Thomas, 13, 14, 179, 225

Young, Edward, 10, 138, 178, 180, 196, 213
Night Thoughts, 99, 123, 131, 132, 133, 134, 135, 136, 139, 237